FISTS UPON A STAR

A MEMOIR OF LOVE, THEATRE, AND ESCAPE FROM McCARTHYISM

Florence Bean James

WITH JEAN FREEMAN

U OF R PRESS

Printed and bound in Canada at Friesens. The text of this book is printed on 100% post-consumer recycled paper with earth-friendly vegetable-based inks.

COVER AND TEXT DESIGN: Duncan Campbell, University of Regina Press.
COPY EDITOR: Joan McGilvray.
PROOFREADER: Courtney Bates-Hardy

Cover photo: Florence Bean James, circa 1911 (detail). Cover photo and all photos except Photos 22, 23, and 24 are from the personal papers of Florence James, courtesy of Jean Freeman.

Library and Archives Canada Cataloguing in Publication
James, Florence Bean, 1892-1988, author
Fists upon a star : a memoir of love, theatre, and escape from McCarthyism / Florence Bean James, with Jean Freeman.

(Canadian plains studies ; 62)
Includes index.
Issued in print and electronic formats.
ISBN 978-0-88977-260-1 (bound).—ISBN 978-0-88977-407-0 (paperback).
—ISBN 978-0-88977-261-8 (pdf).—ISBN 978-0-88977-319-6 (epub)

1. James, Florence Bean, 1892-1988. 2. James, Florence Bean, 1892-1988—Exile—Saskatchewan. 3. Theatrical producers and directors—United States—Biography. 4. Theater—United States—History—20th century. 5. Anti-communist movements—United States—History—20th century. I. Freeman, Jean, 1934-, author II. Title. III. Series: Canadian plains studies ; 62

PN2287.J34A3 2013 792.02'33092 C2013-905325-5 C2013-905326-3

10 9 8 7 6 5 4 3 2 1

University of Regina Press, University of Regina
Regina, Saskatchewan, Canada, S4S 0A2
TEL: (306) 585-4758 FAX: (306) 585-4699
WEB: www.uofrpress.ca

The University of Regina Press received a grant for research and development of this publication from the Creative Enterprise Entrepreneurship Fund of the Saskatchewan Arts Board. We acknowledge the support of the Canada Council for the Arts for our publishing program. We acknowledge the financial support of the Government of Canada. / Nous reconnaissons l'appui financier du gouvernement du Canada. This publication was made possible through Creative Saskatchewan's Creative Industries Production Grant Program.

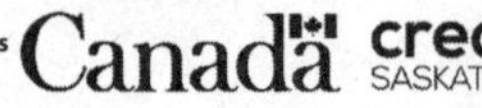

creative SASKATCHEWAN

Dedicated to Burton,
who put my hand with his upon that star,
to Marijo and Al and all the others
who lived through so much of this with us,
and to Jean, who finally gave me some joy
in the preparation of this book.

Florence Bean James
(OCTOBER 27, 1892–JANUARY 18, 1988)

About the Contributors

JEAN FREEMAN is a celebrated performer and author whose career has spanned radio, television, film, live performance, public relations, and a wide range of writing, including plays and children's books. Perhaps best known for her role on the hit TV series *Corner Gas,* her literary skills and love of drama led to a devoted friendship with Florence B. James.

MARY BLACKSTONE wrote the Introduction and is professor emerita in the Theatre Department at the University of Regina, as well as director and dramaturg for the Centre for the Study of Script Development, based in Regina, Saskatchewan.

RITA SHELTON DEVERELL wrote the Epilogue. She is a theatre artist, academic, journalist, co-founder of VisionTV, Regina resident 1971-89, and is in development for a feature film about Florence James based on her full-length play *McCarthy and the Old Woman,* first produced in 2010.

CONTENTS

PREFACE

Jean Freeman

Like many other people in Saskatchewan, I first heard of Florence James from my high school drama teacher, who was fresh from a class that Florence and her husband, Burton (better known as "Pop"), had conducted in 1951 for the Saskatchewan Arts Board's Summer School.

Burton died on November 13, 1951, and in 1952 Florence returned to teach summer classes in Saskatchewan by herself. That summer, I signed up for her two-week session in the Qu'Appelle Valley. As a bright-eyed wannabe actor, I was mightily impressed by this forceful, knowledgeable woman. I returned to take her classes for several summers after that, even after I had graduated and moved on into community theatre.

Mrs. James (we always called her "Mrs. James" in those days) was a touch formidable—you didn't fool around in her classes. But she knew her stuff. We respected her, and we learned from her.

Many years later, in her papers, I found the letter from Arts Board Secretary Norah McCullough inviting Florence to make her connection with the board a permanent one. The letter was dated September 11, 1952, and said that while Norah and Executive Director David Smith hadn't yet been able to try out the idea on Dr. William Riddell, chairman of the board, "we are afraid you will escape us, so this is to make you aware of the possibility so you won't vanish out of our ken without contacting us en route. We think we can find $4000 in the budget plus traveling expenses, up to September of 1953 anyway, with some work at Regina College, but most of it out on the flat. Let us know if we should proceed. If you want to come, we want you!"

She did want to, she came, and stayed until 1968 … mostly "out on the flat."

During that time, from her late sixties into her eighties, Florence began to write a book about her life—the girlhood years that shaped her, her experiences with Burton, their time in the theatre, building the Playhouse, their tribulations, and their successes. It was the book that Burton and Bob Johnson had planned to write. Because Florence felt she "wasn't really a writer," she took some writing classes from Saskatchewan author Ken Mitchell, who was teaching at the Summer School. She wrote and rewrote and wrote some more.

In 1962, I went to work for the Saskatchewan Arts Board as a communications officer, first part-time, then full-time. My cubby-hole was next to Florence's office in a drafty porch at Saskatchewan House in Regina, the former residence of the province's Lieutenant-Governor. As the board's drama consultant, however, she spent most of her time criss-crossing the province, in fair weather and foul, to stimulate theatre of the people, by the people, and for the people, in the province she loved so much.

Florence made no secret of the fact that she was amazed at being paid—she thought even lavishly paid compared to what she'd received during her many years at her Repertory Playhouse in Seattle—to do something she enjoyed.

On one of her stops back at home base, she told me about the book she was trying to write and asked if I could help organize some of the material. I did, and she asked if I would do some editing; then she suggested I might rewrite things here and there, and finally she asked me to write some portions of the book and pull it all together.

I was glad to help, honoured by her trust and confidence in my ability and by her growing closeness as a friend. We worked on the manuscript regularly over the following years. When Florence felt it contained what she wanted to say, and I felt that I had done all I could do to put it into finished form, the attempt to find a publisher began.

The theatre presses liked the chapters about her teaching methods and theatre experiences, but not the personal bits. The women's presses liked Florence's story, but felt there was too much emphasis on her husband. The regular publishers weren't interested because it wasn't mainstream. The University of Washington just wasn't interested. So the manuscript went into a box and gathered dust.

It was thirty years later that actress Rita Shelton Deverell, a vigorous friend of Mrs. James, and an ardent champion of her achievements and life story, tempted the Canadian Plains Research Center (now the University of Regina Press) to take a look.

As publication has become not just a dream but a reality, I am deeply indebted for the help of many friends, old and new, in checking and double-checking memories and details: sincere thanks to Rita Shelton Deverell, Joan McGilvray, Jim and Kathleen Kinzel and Debbie Scotton Kinzel, Kurt Armbruster, Anne Stewart, Terry Bleifuss, Donna Grant, Bruce Walsh, and the University of Regina Press.

For the last years of Florence's life, as her eyesight steadily deteriorated, I became a sort of personal secretary and amanuensis, writing letters, making phone calls, reading to her—mail, papers and hundreds of books, plays and poems—meeting through her the myriad wonderful people who were (and are to this day) the Friends of Florence James, and at the same time enriching my own life, and that of my family, through her example.

I spent so many hours in research, discussion and writing on the book, and in reading and re-reading it to Florence and others, that I find it difficult sometimes to realize that I didn't live through those days: I never walked home from school through the sagebrush in Pocatello, Idaho; I never marched for women's suffrage through the streets of New York City, or stood charged in a court of law for standing by my guns in opposing an unconstitutional investigation, convicted of the crime of being consistent; I never had the chance to sit in a darkened theatre and listen to Woody Guthrie play a fund-raiser for my Playhouse. But, through Florence, I did.

I hope that through her book, many others will also have the chance to follow Florence's steps, even if it's just in imagination.

The book's final form is a pastiche of memoir, biography, and autobiography. It follows a general chronology for the most part, but

Florence liked to drop in anecdotes or references when they occurred to her, or whenever they seemed appropriate. I did try on a few occasions to rearrange the text in order to straighten the flow ... but then I realized that this was the way Florence remembered the story, and told the story, so I just left it alone.

Most recently, while we've been preparing this memoir for publication, I realized that I really wanted to let you, the reader, know about some of the outcomes of Florence's story—things which didn't happen until after her passing in 1988, and therefore were not included in her own memories.

I wanted to tell you about the Playhouse, which in 1969/1970 was renovated and re-named for Glenn Hughes, who had died in 1964. In 1991/1992, his name was transferred to the University of Washington's Drama Department Penthouse Theatre, as a more appropriate location.

And what about the historic elm tree? During the 1980 renovation, much of the Playhouse's courtyard was closed in, and the elm tree ended up in what was described as a "glorified planter." Three decades later, arborists were brought in to check the elm in preparation for the 2009 renovation. They found that the tree was not healthy, and there was extensive root damage. So, the legendary elm succumbed at last. But I understand that wasn't the end of it! Urban Hardwood harvested the elm, and from its wood made benches and tables which today sit in the Playhouse lobby!

When failing eyesight put an end to Florence's work for the Arts Board, her protégé Ken Kramer provided a welcome haven for another decade as dramaturg for Regina's Globe Theatre, which she had been instrumental in founding in 1966.

Toward the end of her life, almost blind, unable to work, confined to a hospital bed, having lost her husband, only child, and many of her closest friends, Florence would rail and rage. "Why am I still here?" she'd say. "I think the good Lord is trying to teach me patience, but I'm not a very good student!"

I could never answer her question. I lamely said that there had to be some purpose, it just wasn't given us to see what it was.

Some of those who remember Florence and honour her life and achievements would say that hope is her legacy. For me, it probably *is* patience ... not patience in the sense of meek and quiet acceptance, but patience in the sense of relentless persistence: "Don't let the bastards wear you down. If we can't outmaneuver them, we'll outwit them and outlast them!"

Florence took her final curtain call on this stage on January 18, 1988, at the age of ninety-five, and promptly moved, I am sure, to Heaven's Green Room, ready for the opening of the next act.

At Florence's memorial service, I read something that I had never read to her, in all those thousands of hours together—but she would have loved it if I had, because it was jotted by the actress Ellen Terry on the flyleaf of a favourite book, and found after her death in 1928:

> No funeral gloom, my dears, when I am gone—
> corpse-gazings, tears, black raiment, graveyard grimness.
> Think of me as withdrawn into the dimness;
> yours still, you mine. Remember all the best
> of our past moments, and forget the rest.
> And so to where I wait, come gently on.
>
> —William Allingham.

INTRODUCTION

Mary Blackstone

But who shall dare
To measure loss and gain in this wise?
Defeat may be victory in disguise;
The lowest ebb is the turn of the tide.
—*from "Loss and Gain"*
by Henry Wadsworth Longfellow

The Memoir and Its Importance

As reported by Jean Freeman in her preface, this book has had a long and difficult journey towards publication, from its beginnings as a theatrical memoir by Burton James, started just before his death in 1951, to multiple incomplete or unpublished attempts by others to write the history of the Seattle Repertory Playhouse, to Florence James' unsuccessful attempts to find a publisher (see Appendix 3). The publication of *Fists Upon a Star* suggests that telling a complex and painful story takes time—and getting others to receive it as meaningful and significant takes even more time and determination.

James focuses on recollections of the Seattle Repertory Playhouse as well as the theatrical partnership and extended community of artists and supporters that made the Playhouse such a success. Despite repeated admonitions "to put more of herself" into the memoir, James remained something of an unwilling autobiographer. The memoir abounds with personal recollections and thoughtful articulations of her theatrical aesthetics and methodology as well as insights into the social and political issues of the day—particularly the contemporary pre-occupation with finding Communism in all things liberal and James' persecution at the hands of the Joint Legislative Fact-Finding Committee on Un-American Activities in the State of Washington—but readers expecting the type of personal confessions and gossip associated with many memoirs and autobiographies will not find it here. Taking her title from the book Burton James had intended to write, Florence James clearly saw herself as righting a wrong. She was writing the story of their theatre and their formidable partnership that Burton had not lived to write. Florence and Burton worked so closely together for so long that it would have been impossible for her to recount the history of the theatre exclusively from her point of view and it is frequently impossible for us as readers to ascribe agency or point of view to one or the other of the Jameses. She did not see the project as an autobiography but rather a recollection of what she was able to do in collaboration with others.

As Helen Buss has observed, this is an important characteristic of memoirs—the tendency of narrators to "speak for others and to others" by moving from "witnessing to testifying": not only speaking to "others as a witness and participant" but also speaking "'for others' who have not been able, or permitted, to speak for themselves."[1] Although others in the same group of individuals persecuted by the state Un-American Activities Committee published recollections of those events,[2] *Fists Upon a Star* is the first to provide the perspectives of the Seattle Repertory Playhouse artists. Taking the first amendment in response to the infamous question, "Are you now or have you ever been a member of the Communist Party," they insisted on their right to freedom of speech and freedom of association and refused to respond; the committee gave them no opportunity to tell their story or counter false accusations. It might have been predictable that Florence James would be the one to ultimately speak for the committee's "unfriendly witnesses," given the outburst against false accusations that led to her being physically ejected from the proceedings. It is also in keeping with her later gutsy statement to the judge about his complicity in thwarting the course of justice when her contempt case came to court. At the time, however, the three witnesses from the Seattle Repertory Playhouse were effectively silenced, first by the committee, then by the courts, and finally by the university's appropriation of their theatre. This absolute failure of justice and the ideals of the Bill of Rights could very well have led James to be cautious in whatever account she gave of the theatre and of the beliefs or values that motivated her and others—despite the apparent safety afforded by being in Canada and distanced by time—but James was powerfully motivated to testify, to tell the story as she saw it and to have its truth appreciated in a way it might not have been at an earlier point. Coming after revelations that the committee may well have had little or no evidence of any threat posed by the individuals it subjected to humiliation, the community orientation of the Seattle Repertory Playhouse and the careers of Florence and Burton James make the purported terrorist threat to the Seattle waterworks by this couple and other alleged communists seem preposterous. Given the hysteria following 9/11 and "Tea Party" extremism in the United States, James' story acquires an even broader application and a renewed urgency.

As with all life-writing, *Fists Upon a Star* lies somewhere between the non-fictional realm of history and the fictional world of constructed story but, particularly in its development of character and plot, it also owes much to the form of writing James knew best. James' life and the events she recounts here have been the subjects of more than one play[3] and, given her background in drama, it should not be surprising that a skilled theatre artist undertaking to tell an innately dramatic story would instinctively embrace some of the dramaturgical principles of good playwriting.[4] In that context it is understandable that she might eschew direct statements regarding the personal dimensions of her relationships, her individual accomplishments, and above all her emotional investment in the events she recounts, leaving us to judge from actions and subtext. Raw personal emotions do rise to the surface, but James very consciously focuses on commemorating collective and communal accomplishments rather than personal validation and catharsis. She is the kind of female subject Buss particularly associates with the genre of memoir rather than autobiography, one

> whose autonomy is compellingly intertwined with relationships, and community, a human subject that does not seek

> to disentangle herself from those compelling ties, but builds autonomy based on them. For such a subject, memoir is the much older and more appropriate form … If autobiographical practices are to produce agency for human subjects to resist conformity while performing constructive and multiple connections to the world, memoir discourse … continue[s] to be the lively art of balancing the self and the other. If women's memoirs can help show that such balancing acts are workable and performable, they will have truly repossessed a cultural world where we can be our fullest human selves.[5]

Fists Upon a Star is of interest in part as an example of women's life-writing that at times displays similarities with other examples of this genre and at other times pointedly diverges from the expectations scholars might bring to it. For instance, at times James leaves no question that she is writing out of anger and pain, something that Carolyn G. Heilbrun has identified as characteristic of autobiographical work by women starting from the 1970s. Also characteristic of more recent life-writing is the way in which she quite matter-of-factly deals with both her failures and accomplishments while at times preferring to focus on the collective success of the Playhouse company. However, Heilbrun suggests that another common characteristic of all women's life-writing is the difficulty such an author has coming to grips with the recognition that her "selfhood, the right to her own story, depends upon her 'ability to act in the public domain.'" Although she may have been selective about what she chose to include in this memoir, there is no evidence that Florence James had any qualms whatsoever about acting in the public domain whether in the theatre or in public life outside it.[6]

As moving and insightful as the memoir is, it does not tell the full story. James brought to her memoir a good dramaturgical sense of the natural climax and denouement of her story. The Canwell hearings provide the climax of her story, and the loss of the theatre and Burton James' death the denouement. However, while what she left out may not offer such dramatic material, it extends our understanding of James' accomplishments beyond loss to further illuminate the importance of her story. The demise of the Seattle Repertory Playhouse and the death of her husband constituted devastating losses to the Seattle cultural community and to Florence James personally, but Mrs. James continued to make important contributions in a new and more welcoming country. She went on to lead a full and productive life and her accomplishments led to major gains in theatre and the arts in her adopted province of Saskatchewan. And she was a remarkable role model for women who were fortunate enough to encounter her.[7] The preface, this introduction, and the epilogue frame James' life from multiple perspectives. In her preface, Jean Freeman, who has been instrumental in bringing this memoir to publication, approaches James as a personal friend and mentor. Rita Deverell's epilogue (and her one-woman play) illustrates the enormous impact James had on subsequent generations of artists, not only in Canada but also in the United States. This introduction places James' life and career historically, professionally, and socially.

Making a Life in the Modern Era

It could be said that Florence James' life story is exemplary of a generation of North Americans who witnessed and effected enormous social, cultural, and political changes in their lifetime. Between growing up as the first non-aboriginal girl born in a rural frontier community in the nineteenth-century American West and ending her days in the Queen City in the middle of the Canadian prairie, James saw the introduction of the automobile, electric lights, central heating, telephones, radio, gramophones, the commercial film industry, and air and space travel. She was a product not only of the earliest of Europeans to emigrate to the United States but also the nineteenth-century influx of Irish immigrants fleeing the potato famine. As well, she worked closely with more recent immigrant communities who swelled the slums of New York, the labour unions of the Northwest, and the ranks of ambitious young performers. She was born into a country still deeply divided by race twenty-seven years after the end of the Civil War, and she lived to not only see but also participate in the empowerment of Blacks through the elimination of segregation, improved educational and cultural opportunities, and the efforts of men like Paul Robeson and Martin Luther King. She travelled widely in North America, from Texas to Canada and coast to coast. She also travelled to Britain, Russia, and down the Ruhr through Poland, Germany, and France in 1934 at what might have been the peak of Soviet social and cultural experiments and in the midst of Hitler's rise to power. She lived through two world wars, marched for women's suffrage, narrowly escaped the devastation of the Spanish Flu epidemic, planned the building of a theatre that was nixed by the recession of 1922, opened a professional theatre on the crest of the 1929 stock market crash, managed that theatre through the Depression, led one of the most successful Negro units in the Federal Theatre Project under Roosevelt's Works Progress Administration, raised money for the Republican government in the Spanish Civil War, aligned herself closely with Seattle's strong labour unions, which had organized the first general strike in the United States, and supported the Washington Pension Union, which negotiated the first comprehensive U.S. health care program. She fought devastating persecution and personal loss in the McCarthy era, followed by emigration to Canada where she emerged as a powerful educator and advocate for the arts under the first socialist government in North America. From that vantage point she then participated in the development of national arts organizations and contributed to the growing appreciation and recognition of Canadian culture.

Florence James was recognized as a pioneer in her own day, but her personal history stands as one of thousands of stories that could have been told about the men and women who built the American West. Her life was moulded by three western frontier communities—Pocatello, Seattle and the State of Washington, and Saskatchewan. Her hunger as a young girl for the amenities of education, culture, and the arts, her leadership in Seattle and rural areas of the state in establishing quality theatre and arts education, and her tireless trips to all corners of rural Saskatchewan to ensure that even those in the smallest communities would be able to participate in the arts—these are all chapters in a much broader social and cultural history of the West. They are also chapters that reveal much about the local history of the Northwest and Saskatchewan. Particularly because of James' insistence that theatre must be rooted in its community and therefore inclusive of and responsive to the breadth of that community, the story of both the Seattle Repertory Playhouse and James' time in Saskatchewan encompasses the local cultural dynamics of ethnicity and race, the social dynamics involving unionized longshoremen and university professors, the

Farmers' Union Conference and politicians, and the political dynamics of republicans and democrats, communists, socialists and progressives. As a social document, the memoir also marks evolving changes, such as the drift to spectatorship versus participation in leisure activity, lack of attention to the needs of youth and the elderly, and the dislocation of "community" and neighbourhood that resulted from the influx of people who moved to Washington state during the war. Even the emerging challenges of urban sprawl and pollution make appearances as this story unfolds. Although it is not fully addressed in her memoir, James engaged in community affairs outside the bounds of the theatre by taking an interest in the affairs of unions and key political issues of her day to the point of running for office more than once.[8] Her vision of a life in the theatre was of a life fully engaged in the most important issues of her day and her memoir reflects that.

Unlike those thousands of pioneers who *could* have written personal histories about this era in the West, Florence James *did* so, creating a memoir in which the historical events are not simply a shorthand for marking time or a backdrop to the story but integral to a life and career profoundly engaged in and moulded by them. As Helen Buss has observed, "in historical narratives, only public events happen. In traditional fiction such public events act as a background for the personal story. In memoir, real lives happen in all their daily richness in parallel and in connection with public life. We are allowed into that richness so that we can better feel the effect when private lives are crushed by public policies."[9]

In one respect, then, the entire memoir can be read as a lead up to chapters 17 and 18, which describe how Florence and Burton James and their theatre were crushed by the steamroller of the Un-American Activities Committee chaired by Albert Canwell.[10] Their tireless work over more than twenty years to establish a meaningful, community-oriented theatre offering fully professional productions and educational opportunities to all people in the city—and to the state at large—is essential to understanding the relative merits and impact of the allegations they endured. More particularly, the Canwell hearings and the subsequent trials stand in stark contrast to the Jameses' contributions to the war effort (chapter 14) in the years immediately preceding the Un-American Activities episode. The wartime communiques[11] and

Christmas packages to members of the armed forces, along with comps for service men stationed in Seattle and more than eighty performances and special events done completely on a voluntary basis suggest patriotism rather than treason. This is particularly true if one considers the content of their spectacular show (with Bob Hope as MC) directed towards recruitment of aviation workers and the morale-boosting musical revues *Thumbs Up!* and *Here Comes Tomorrow*.

In the memoir, the effects of the Canwell Committee are all the more devastating because we approach them through the perspective of individuals who had persevered and realized their vision for a community theatre despite the obstacles presented by the Depression and war. This was a perspective that Canwell explicitly refused to consider or allow introduced into their hearings. Because they had taught at the university, worked with many liberal faculty in support of social causes and issues, and situated their playhouse in the university district, they and their colleague Al Ottenheimer were included in the persecution of University of Washington faculty in 1948. As well, because they had an especially high local profile they were particularly attractive initial targets for the promotion of fear and ostracism in the community.[12]

Numerous accounts of the effects of Un-American Activities hearings at the federal level have been written, including first-hand responses by New York and Hollywood stars whose careers languished after they were thrust into the role of "unfriendly witness."[13] The extent to which the tentacles of this persecution of innocent people reached beyond the federal level and New York and Hollywood stars is perhaps not as widely understood. Although Joseph McCarthy's Permanent Subcommittee on Investigations in the U.S. Senate did not undertake its famous televised hearings until 1954, the U.S. House of Representatives' Un-American Activities Committee (HUAC) had been established and calling witnesses for ten years when Canwell launched similar proceedings in Washington State in what has been seen as an audition for election to the U.S. Senate. Like its federal counterpart, the state committee effected a reign of terror, using stories fabricated by paid witnesses not open to cross-examination, dismissing the legal and constitutional rights of the accused, branding by suggestion and innuendo, and relying largely on the resulting social and economic effects of guilt by association and blacklisting for punishment and control of witnesses who refused to cooperate. Just as Hearst newspapers in the East fanned the flames of intolerance and exclusion ignited by the HUAC hearings, Washington's Hearst paper, the *Seattle Post-Intelligencer*, led the way, not only through slanderous headlines screaming from its front pages but by its staffs' backroom participation in drawing up the committee's terms of reference.[14] The results in Washington state were no less devastating than those at the federal level. The stock market crash, the Depression, a world war, and recurrent debt had been unable to strike a killing blow to the Seattle Repertory Playhouse and the formidable husband-and-wife partnership that had fostered twenty-three years of innovative and successful programming, but it took the Canwell committee only a month to put an end to this creative partnership and render the theatre vulnerable to an opportunistic takeover by the university. The theatre was purchased out from under them, Burton James died, and Florence James remained on the FBI's watch list until emigration to Canada allowed her to escape their surveillance.

James' perspective on these black events in American history is important for several reasons. First, it provides an important lesson in the devastation and loss that result when the individual's rights of free speech, free association, and free thought are brushed aside in favour of jingoism, confrontational nationalism, and collective paranoia.[15] Similar loss has been documented for several periods in American history, from the early witch trials to the wartime incarceration of Japanese American families to the exodus of draft dodgers opposed to the Vietnam War to the post-9/11 interrogation of Muslims and present-day political extremism.[16] Second, with James' account of this period in her life she joins a very limited list of women in the arts who wrote directly about their experiences of McCarthyism. In *Unfriendly Witnesses: Gender, Theater, and Film in the McCarthy Era,* Milly Barranger observes that "with the exception of Hallie Flanagan's *Arena: The History of the Federal Theatre,* Lillian Hellman's *Scoundrel Time*, and Margaret Webster's chapter 'Of Witch Hunting' in her memoir *Don't Put Your Daughter on the Stage,* the women published few accounts of their experiences.... The difference between the genders during McCarthyism can be found in the autobiographies written and interviews granted by congressional witnesses. For the most part, the women were *silenced* by the experience."[17] In light of the difficulties

James had getting her memoir published, it might well be asked how many other women of theatre and film who fell victim to McCarthyism also tried unsuccessfully to have their own recollections published.

With publication of her memoir, James joins a select number of women whose accounts corroborate the perceptions of men connected with Un-American Activities proceedings that women were "tough" witnesses and "more trouble than they were worth." Hallie Flanagan, director of the Federal Theatre Project, helped establish this reputation for women witnesses during HUAC's first hearings with her deft and feisty responses to the committee's questions.[18] Florence James, who had worked for Flanagan as a director for the Federal Theatre Project in Seattle, brought a similar attitude. Thanks to a stunning photo of her ejection from the proceedings after a spontaneous outburst against false accusations by a paid witness, Seattle newspapers featured the image of a smartly dressed middle-aged lady, her extended arm pointed accusingly and determinedly at the witness, being manhandled by armed guards. Despite the newspapers' bias, they could recognize good copy when they saw it and Florence James managed to project a highly performative protest to the Seattle public. The similarity between this photo and one taken of Hallie Flanagan ten years earlier during her HUAC testimony is striking.

An example of the way in which strong women from this period could "buffalo" chauvinistic males in positions of authority came later in court when James delivered a prepared speech before the judge who was to sentence her for contempt of the Un-American Activities proceedings. After indictment, complete with fingerprinting and mug shots, suppression of witnesses favourable to her, refusal to uphold demands for supposed evidence against her or even to consider the copious evidence pointing to tampering with the selection of jury panels, James delivered her own point-by-point indictment of the judge for flagrant complicity in the miscarriage of justice. The fact that it took two trials to convict her because of a male holdout in the first hung jury and that, despite her accusations, the judge gave her only a fine and a suspended sentence seem to suggest that strong women like James posed a particular challenge at the state as well as federal level and that the chauvinism of the period could work in their favour. Her male counterparts before the court were sentenced to jail, although due to the stroke Burton James suffered as a result of the whole affair he did not serve time in jail for fear it would kill him.

Nonconformity on Matters of Gender, Ethnicity, and Race

Mark Jenkins has observed that in the course of researching the proceedings of the Un-American Activities Committee in Washington state and writing his play *All Powers Necessary and Convenient*, his "main discovery" was "that all actions are, at first, *personal*," and that "all actions no matter how personal … are also *political*."[19] Such a realization has been the foundation of feminism and gender studies since the 1970s, but James clearly understood the implications of this reality at a comparatively early age. Having chosen to perform a piece by Oscar Wilde for an assignment at Emerson College she was puzzled by the scandalized rejection of her choice. Even after being given a similarly mystifying explanation that she ultimately figured out, she still could not understand why Wilde's sexual preferences should have any bearing on an otherwise brilliant piece of writing.

This cameo of James' determined response to the interpretation of personal actions in a political context is indicative of her behaviour with respect to gender expectations throughout her life. She seemed to take very little notice of hegemonic expectations and threw herself into roles and causes appropriate to her non-conformist sentiments.[20] As a woman she was atypical of her generation but, given her roots in a frontier society that celebrated the independent and self-reliant spirit, relied heavily on the work of women and afforded them greater equality, this aspect of James' remarkable career is not necessarily surprising. Breaking off an engagement to a wealthy, cultured, and highly eligible young man in Idaho, James was driven by a desire for further education and a hunger for broader cultural experiences. From the vantage point of the twenty-first century this might not sound unusual, but for an early twentieth-century girl from Idaho to transplant herself to Boston, particularly in search of a school for the arts rather than a more traditional degree-granting institution in education, for instance, was exceptional.

While James' recollections of Mrs. Pankhurst, who motivated her involvement in the successful women's suffrage campaign in New York, may be of interest with respect to early twentieth-century women's history, the less flamboyant and personal choices that receive almost matter-of-fact treatment in her story are of equal importance: her choice to work in the arts, particularly as a director, to marry someone who was similarly non-conformist in his career choice, to simultaneously and seamlessly manage a career and raise a child, and to take leadership positions in politics, education, and the arts. From these choices to James' admiration of the women she saw working side by side with men as labourers, soldiers, even crack sharpshooters in Soviet Russia, it is clear that, as on so many other issues, with respect to the roles for women, James was well beyond the American hegemony of her day.

Matters of race, ethnicity, and gender are closely intertwined in this memoir, and in the first two areas perhaps more than gender we see how James' personal actions, motivated as they were by the most fundamentally American values and beliefs, eventually led to her political persecution as "un-American." For instance, Burton and Florence James brought exceptional insight to their work with socially marginalized groups such as prostitutes, immigrants in the city's ghettoes, and Blacks at Lenox Hill Settlement House and elsewhere in New York. They recognized poverty, education, and environmental factors as responsible for a vicious cycle. They made friends within these groups and promoted the arts and culture not as mechanisms for realizing the great American melting pot but as means to help immigrants preserve their culture and dignity in the new country. James' organization of Czechoslovakian women into a cottage industry for the sale of "peasant" embroidery created successful employment that helped them sustain their families while their husbands were away during World War I, and the Jameses' theatre activities provided positive alternatives for the many problem children in these slums by "opening doors and bridging chasms" as was the case for James Cagney, who was one of the Jameses' student actors in New York. (Cagney and the Jameses maintained their connection for many years—see Photo 4 and Appendices 2 and 3.) Their early relationships with and sympathy for the working poor and ethnic slum inhabitants in New York made the Jameses' association with ethnic groups, unions, and social and political activists in Seattle understandable but, because many of these groups were automatically equated with Communism by un-American witch hunters, such associations also left them open to harassment.

Perhaps one of Florence James' most horrifying and touching vignettes is of her three-week stay in the charity ward of Roosevelt

Hospital while five months pregnant and suffering from pneumonia. Her ordeal in this dirty, understaffed, and cockroach-infested institution was tempered only by the close personal relationship she developed with another patient, a Black, middle-aged woman who cared for her like a daughter. This relationship beautifully foreshadows the personal investment apparent in her successful working relationship with the Black community in Seattle, the admiration with which she regarded the early Black activist, Paul Robeson, and her positive contributions to the careers of Black artists in both the United States and Canada. At Florence James' birth, the country was less than thirty years removed from the end of the Civil War and slavery, and liaisons like these with the Black community were politically dangerous. Yet Florence and Burton James were uncompromising in matching their actions and beliefs. It should not be surprising that after the turmoil that befell them in 1948, Burton James defiantly chose a passage from Stephen Vincent Benet's *John Brown's Body* as the title for his book and that years later Florence James saw the same passage as an equally appropriate title for her memoir:

> We give what pleases us and when we choose,
> And, having given, we do not take back.
> But once we shut our fists upon a star
> It will take portents to unloose that grip
> And even then the stuff will keep the print.
> It is a habit of living.[21]

As demonstrated repeatedly in her memoir, for James this "habit of living" and the "habit of art" alluded to in the title of Alan Bennett's play were inseparable.[22]

A Pioneer on the Frontier of Modern American Theatre

Having travelled east from her frontier community in Idaho in 1911, Florence James initially formed her approach to theatre and performance by studying elocution at Emerson College in Boston. Both here and later in New York she took full advantage of being at the perceived 'eastern centre' of American culture by seeing the work of some of the great artists of her time—for example, Sarah Bernhardt, [23] Isadora Duncan, Geraldine

Farrar, John McCormack, Charlie Chaplin, Max Reinhardt, the Moscow Art Theatre, and the Abbey Players. When after 11 years in the East she and her husband chose to take up work at the Cornish School on what was then perceived to be the edge of the American cultural frontier in Seattle, they did so consciously having turned their backs on the commercial theatre of New York and determined to devote themselves to a "theatre of the people, by the people and for the people." (5) For the next 29 years, the James partnership set about transforming the so-called frontier into an innovative centre for theatre that drew many American stars of the day into its circle and nurtured the early careers of many future stars. At Cornish School she worked with the as yet unknown artist Mark Tobey and dancer Martha Graham. She worked with the Russian musician, composer, and conductor Myron Jacobson, as director of opera, and she taught Albert Ottenheimer, who would eventually join them at the Playhouse. After they left the school to start up the Repertory Playhouse and teach at the University, their students included Marc Platt (dancer with the Ballet Russe de Monte Carlo as well as Broadway and film star); Frances Farmer (stage and screen actress); Howard Duff and Stacy Harris (both radio, television, and film actors). Pete Seeger, Earl Robinson, and Woody Guthrie all performed at various times at the Playhouse. Initially on radio and then in the musical *San Juan Story*, they had the opportunity to work with the young Martha Wright at the beginning of her career as singer and actor on Broadway, television, and radio, and they worked with Bob Hope in mounting a spectacular Seattle show to recruit workers into the aviation industry during World War II. When the Playhouse celebrated its twentieth anniversary in 1947, the center of American culture metaphorically came to Seattle as Helen Hayes offered live magnified telephone greetings to the audience from her New York dressing room on behalf of the American National Theatre and Academy:

> Many of us associate your city with the last frontier. And now we have other frontiers of a different kind. The Seattle Repertory Playhouse is pioneering among the social and cultural frontiers of the human spirit. You are held in high esteem—and greatly admired—throughout the theatrical world, commercial as well as non-commercial.... Our the-

> atre is better, finer, fuller, because for twenty years, there in the farthest western reach of the United States, the Seattle Repertory Playhouse has been striving and struggling and pioneering and building. (215)

Florence James was constantly learning and searching out new ideas and approaches. Typical of this attitude was use of proscenium, arena, and environmental staging as well as a wide range of plays in various styles and periods. However, this pioneering attitude did not evolve in isolation. From her childhood she strove to discover and experience new developments in the arts. In 1927 she did a tour of "the nerve centres of the American theatre" (66): the Cleveland Play House, the Goodman Memorial Theatre in Chicago, the Eastman School of Music, the Civic Repertory Theatre in Boston, George Pierce Baker's Yale School of Drama, and New York. On this trip she was disappointed by the "cultural desolation and apathy" she saw, but in 1934 she travelled to the Malvern and Stratford Festivals in England and to the Moscow Festival. While she was not impressed with British productions of Shakespeare, much of what she saw in Moscow related closely to the vision of theatre that she and her husband were trying to develop in Seattle. She recognized the propagandist direction of some of the drama, but she realized that they were also creating good theatre—and that it appealed to and was attended by a broad section of the population. She was impressed by the way the government was attempting to foster theatre even in rural communities, promote amateur theatre groups in collective farms and factories, and financially support professional training for amateurs. Although putting theatre under the purview of the Soviet Commissariat of Education was indicative of Russia's view of the political role of theatre, it aligned with James' conception of the broader role of theatre in education—and education in theatre. The production she saw at the Moscow Theatre for Children made a particular impression upon her and reinforced what she had learned from her work in Washington state and would take with her in helping to develop theatre for and with children in Saskatchewan. Theatre practitioners in Moscow understood children's need to participate in performances, the greater success of theatre *with* versus *for* children, and the extent to which such theatre could foster an interest that would carry into adulthood.[24]

The enthusiastic articles she wrote for the *Pacific Weekly* and lectures she gave to service organizations, women's groups, and the Unemployed Citizens' League upon her return to Seattle ultimately cost her dearly during the Un-American Activities hearings, but given what she saw in Russia and her own philosophy of theatre the enthusiasm is understandable—just as a later trip within the United States to discover new directions and practices among community and university theatres in the West was understandably disappointing, particularly her realization that most theatres were unable to articulate a philosophy on which they based their work.

Growing up in turn-of-the-century Idaho, James clearly saw books and education as precious commodities, and she credited several books as contributing to her evolving philosophy on theatre, acting, and directing: a 1936 article in *Theatre Workshop* by J. Rapoport on acting exercises used at the Moscow Art Theatre, *Problems of the Actor* by Louis Calvert, "Concerning Practice: The Connection between Cognition and Practice" by Mao Tse Tung published in *Labour Monthly*, and *Theory and Technique of Playwriting* by John Howard Lawson.[25] Yet James notes that when she began her work in the theatre there were few books that were very helpful in a practical sense for actors or directors and that she had to learn by sweeping away much of the old school approaches to acting that she had learned at Emerson and simply learn by doing. This was especially necessary for her as director, her primary role throughout most of her career in the United States. Directing was a comparatively new role in the theatre, and it had not yet engendered even the limited theoretical and methodological discussions devoted to acting.

Given that women are still in the minority when it comes to directing, James' substantial and successful career as a director in the first half of the twentieth century makes her particularly interesting. In 1933 she was praised for her "keen intelligence, rare insight and understanding, and a tremendous capacity for hard work," and hailed "as one of the outstanding stage directors of the West."[26] It is worth noting that the praise is not qualified by calling her a "woman stage director," but this may be indicative of the fairly straightforward evolution of her career and the degree of self-assurance she brought to directing. Rather than undertaking a long struggle to gain opportunities and recognition for directing, James appears to have made an early and natural transition to the director's chair that she occupied for most of her career.[27] She attributes this ease to a combination of factors—first, a willingness and ability to take leadership responsibilities and, second, the perennial overabundance of women actors that made her contribution in that area expendable. Her first directing experience while at Emerson College would seem to support this view. They needed someone to work with the young Robert Frost in the dramatization of his new play, *The Death of the Hired Man,* with Thomas Watson (who had been at the other end of Alexander Graham Bell's famous call) in the lead, and James was willing to take on the task. Whether she was directing in the theatre, organizing immigrant women as a social worker, running for political office in Seattle, speaking to labour unions and service organizations, acting as an educator for children and adults, or chairing the Washington Citizens' Bill of Rights Committee organized to resist Washington's Un-American Activities Committee,[28] she comes across as an unconventional woman for her time, a woman thoroughly comfortable in the public limelight and in leadership roles. Unlike the memoirs of many women who avoid addressing their successes and accomplishments head on or do so only to shift credit to others (often men) for their accomplishments, James almost matter-of-factly identifies her strengths and weaknesses as a director and, without coy or self-effacing modesty, proudly recounts some of the many successes achieved at the Seattle Repertory Playhouse by the theatre community she led in so many productions.

While James itemizes an impossibly lengthy and contradictory list of virtues necessary for a good director, she possessed the three essential qualities of both a good leader and a good director: she had well-thought-out insights and values, she was not afraid to speak up and articulate them publicly, and she had the capacity to organize and motivate people to support her.[29] Given the virtually unanimous response of actors who worked with her and members of her audiences regarding the strength of the acting in her productions—even with novices—theatre professionals and students will be interested in the chapters on her approaches to acting and directing. They remain surprisingly insightful and current today. Working from a definition of theatre as "a unity at the core of which is the living community finding some vital part of itself reflected in the creations of the dramatist and actor,"

(146–147) she regarded it "an opportunity and an obligation" (148) to discover, train, and open up the talents of actors who worked with her. The sense-perception exercises she adapted from Moscow Art Theatre practices will not be new to most actors, but she cites creative and useful examples of how she used sense perception and other techniques as a director in rehearsals to help actors who were blocked from realizing key dramatic moments. Some of the points on which she places most emphasis remain key issues in theatre today, but unfortunately often as aspirations rather than actualities: the importance of ensemble acting, the encouragement and production of new plays, the role of both the playwright's intentions *and* the audience in completing the meaning of a performance, and rehearsal periods sufficient to allow for the "subjective work" of full table analysis of the text and outside research by all members of the cast and design team (two weeks to ten days in the Playhouse). On rehearsal periods, she argues that only "when the actor, with script in hand, has a fairly clear idea of what he is doing, why he is doing it, and, most important, knows his relationship to other characters" could she move to objectifying the actions. To her, blocking then became a "simple matter" of actor and director working together to develop the character in relation to other characters on stage. (187)

A Model Community Theatre

Perhaps because theatre is the most social of the art forms and requires live audiences, until comparatively recently its history has tended to revolve around large centres.[30] People starting out in the theatre at the same point as Florence and Burton James still make the trek to New York, London, Paris, Toronto, or Montreal in hopes of being "discovered," becoming stars, and earning the kind of money that large and expensive commercial theatres can afford to pay. In Florence James' day another performance centre was emerging on the west coast in Hollywood, with its even greater capacity to make the most successful performers wealthy. Yet she and her husband decided early that they had a different vision of performance and theatre to which they wanted to devote their careers.

Although the Folk Theatre they proposed at the Lenox Hill Settlement was not realized, they had already begun to conceive of "a theatre of the people, which shall reach out and appeal to the tastes and pocketbooks of society," with "a director and a staff of associates who will with sympathy, understanding, training and care follow the dramatic bent of our neighborhood." (53) Their vision was of a community theatre that would reflect the cosmopolitan character of the slums in which it would be built in ways that have taken decades for theatre in most western countries to fully appreciate or achieve. They proposed "not to change the tongue or spirit of the neighbourhood's drama" because "plays produced in a foreign tongue will perpetuate age-old standards of art ... The Folk Theatre must disseminate, not exploit, must stimulate, not force ... This group should set the standard of co-operative endeavour. The Folk Theatre has no room for competitive enterprises." (53)

The couple's move from New York to Seattle demonstrates how little attraction Broadway had for them, and their new community began to contribute to their evolving vision of a people's theatre. Their time as teachers at the Cornish School and the University of Washington's School of Drama as well as their well-paid work at an early Seattle radio station, Adolph Linden's American Broadcasting Company (not related to the current ABC), all took them further towards the conception of what became the Seattle Repertory Playhouse. It gradually became clear that the Cornish School was not the place to realize their vision, but the increasingly professional and impressive productions they mounted there made a reputation for them in the community and helped develop community connections that would be important to the success of the Seattle Repertory Playhouse.

One important connection was Al Ottenheimer, a University of Washington student who had acted in their productions at the Cornish School. To Florence James' skill as a director and educator and Burton James' abilities as an actor, designer and technician Ottenheimer added his own acting and writing talents along with considerable skills in promotion. These three worked together to attract and organize a core of people who would form an ongoing company in 1928 and formally launch the theatre with their first production in 1929. Initially using rented space, they eventually moved to a new theatre in the University district in 1930. During more than 20 years they ran a theatre which served as a model of what a good theatre—regional or otherwise—should be.

With seven or more new shows a year plus a summer festival of reprised shows in repertory, the Seattle Repertory Playhouse mounted a wide variety of productions—from Seán O'Casey's *Juno and the Paycock* to Sem Benelli's *The Jest*, from Henrik Ibsen's *Peer Gynt* to W. Kerr's *Rip Van Winkle*, from G. B. Shaw's *Major Barbara* to Shakespeare's *Romeo and Juliet,* from Goethe's *Faust* to G. L. Aiken's *Uncle Tom's Cabin*. James classifies the bulk of the repertoire as "active romanticism" as defined by Maxim Gorky: plays that "strengthen man's will to live, to rouse him to rebellion against reality with all its tyrannies." (150) Sometimes this spirit of rebellion combined with a desire to include voices from all segments of the community led to plays which presented racially, economically, or politically marginalized voices. Albert Bein's *Little Ol' Boy* about the abuse of delinquents in a reformatory, Paul Peters and George Sklar's *Stevedore* about labour relations and strike-breaking in the dockyards, Paul Green's *In Abraham's Bosom* about the lynching of a rebellious Black man in 1880s North Carolina, and Eugene O'Neill's *The Hairy Ape* about the tragic dehumanizing impact on labourers of working conditions and class-based prejudices—these were all controversial plays to varying degrees, but from James' perspective they were all plays that "should be done" (149) regardless of controversy or box office receipts. She argues that "it is fatal to compromise your insights in order to acquiesce to the demands made on you," and if you do so, "you will be producing plays written about nothing for nobody." (158) She clearly lived up to that admonition even when it may not have been in her best personal interests to do so. Without question the most controversial play they produced was given only one performance and that for a private audience. However, Clifford Odets' *Waiting for Lefty* with its sympathetic treatment of strikers cost the theatre any future mention in the *Seattle Times* and situated Florence and Burton James in the middle of a storm of political controversy that would extend to the Un-American Activities hearings.

While the Playhouse was always challenged financially, James notes that the variety of plays chosen reflected their awareness that part of the attraction for theatre audiences is not just interesting plays and good acting but also spectacle. With a cast of sixty, members of the Seattle Symphony playing Grieg's incidental music, and an "ultramodern" design using a revolve for the first time in the Northwest (82-83), the

Playhouse's initial production of *Peer Gynt* proved enormously popular and established a major reputation for the company in the region, even in Vancouver where they took the play on tour. Similarly spectacular productions like *Faust* and *Uncle Tom's Cabin* continued the visual appeal, as did their forays into opera. In 1939–1940 the Lyric Theatre unit of the Playhouse produced *The Barber of Seville* with a Japanese Rosina, a modern *Die Fledermaus* with a Florence James libretto, and *La Traviata* with Ludmilla Novatna and Richard Bonelli from the Met in the leads (190). Even in 1950, during the last days of the theatre, they again worked with members of the Seattle Symphony to produce Benjamin Britten's *Let's Make an Opera* (200). For an "unofficial" listing of the Playhouse repertoire over its twenty years, see Appendix 1.

Both the scope and appeal of the Playhouse productions was made possible in part because of the theatre's strong "community" orientation. It reached out to "every ethnic group in Seattle" (210), including the Scandinavian communities with *Peer Gynt*, the German community with *Faust*, the African Methodist Church for *Uncle Tom's Cabin* and *In Abraham's Bosom,* the Chinese community for their traditional staging of *Lady Precious Stream* for China Relief, the White Russian community for the chorus in *The Living Corpse* and the musical revue *Kolokala*, and the many unions and labour organizations through plays like *Stevedore, The Hairy Ape* and *Waiting for Lefty*. It extended its community through tours to places like Tacoma and Vancouver, and it was reported to be attracting regional audiences to the theatre from California, Oregon, British Columbia, and Montana (92). The Jameses cultivated a playing company that could encompass both a society matron who arrived at the theatre in a limousine and a newspaper seller. They wanted an equally broad cross-section of the community in the audience, and kept their ticket prices at a level that would assure that mix: 25 cents for children, $1.25–$1.50 for adults, and comps for people who could not afford those prices. Using a system that was eagerly emulated by regional theatres elsewhere, they cultivated group support of the theatre by not only selling subscriptions but also making large blocks of tickets and whole houses available to everyone from businesses and service groups to women's organizations and unions.

In order to assure this kind of community support and fulfill their responsibility to the community, however, the Jameses realized that they had to go beyond offering the wide range of period and modern classics. They understood that the theatre also needed to nurture and develop local and regional playwrights and regularly produce their plays. They introduced a Sunday night series of readings of interesting plays that for whatever reason the company could not produce—as well as new plays by emerging playwrights. In conjunction with the Washington State Theatre experiment they fostered the development of playwriting programs in Seattle high schools and produced the first play to emerge from that initiative. Their first season featured *In His Image* by local playwright and English professor Garland Ethel. Ethel later figured prominently in the second hearing of Canwell's Un-American Activities Committee in July 1948 as the first of twelve University of Washington professors called to testify. He admitted to having been a communist at one point but set a strong example by quoting Polonius' "Unto thine own self be true" in refusing to name names.[31]

The Playhouse also produced several adaptations and plays by Albert Ottenheimer. He adapted Goethe's *Faust* for the company and wrote the books for two original musicals, *Calico Cargo* and *San Juan Story*, both of which addressed stories out of Washington's history. The latter musical was co-written with Walter Gyger, who had emerged out of a high-school writing program fostered by the theatre. Ottenheimer had two original plays produced, *L'Envoi* and *Funny Man*, a comedy about life in vaudeville which caught the attention of MGM for which he did some work as screenwriter. As well, James mounted three plays by the San Francisco–based playwright, Marianne King: *The Chaste Mistress; American Made;* and *Mad, Bad and Dangerous to Know.* She and Florence became friends. She not only accompanied James on her European trip in 1934 but also returned to Russia again in 1936. Over the entire period of the Playhouse they produced nineteen new plays, and this kind of encouragement of playwrights and new plays drew national attention. James proudly reports that in a review of the company's premier of *Leading Man* (a satire of Hollywood) by William Kimball, *Billboard* acknowledged that they were helping to build the future of American Theatre. (80)

Although initially the Jameses had taught in the School of Drama at the university and the school's head had been a member of the Playhouse board, the Playhouse practice of renting the theatre for use by student productions came to an end when they sensed the School of Drama was moving to mount a rival professional season in the Playhouse space. It is not uncommon for rivalry to develop between theatre schools and professional theatres, but in this case the rivalry had devastating consequences. The Playhouse perceived the school as moving to establish a potentially competitive professional, off-campus presence with unfair subsidies, and the school resented the capacity of a theatre on its doorstep to lure good students away and mount productions in facilities it could only dream about. After several skirmishes, sometimes resulting in student protests, the University of Washington bought the Playhouse from their landlord and forced the Jameses out of the theatre they had built. In doing so, they brought the curtain down on a model for community and regional theatres with such a varied mandate and visionary accomplishments that they would still be regarded as radical and unattainable for the majority of regional theatres in North America today. James' memoir of the Seattle Repertory Playhouse effectively constructs a checklist that most twenty-first-century regional theatres would find daunting. The fact that it also laid a foundation that made it possible to envision model state and federal theatres makes the Playhouse all the more impressive and important.[32]

A Model State Theatre

James saw education as an essential theatrical endeavour. From 1930 both Florence and Burton taught in the Drama Division at the University of Washington until first Burton (1934) and then Florence (1938) were let go as a result of the ongoing antagonism between the Playhouse and the university. The resulting protests over Florence's dismissal testified to her effectiveness as a teacher.[33] Their backgrounds in education, first at the Cornish School and then at the university, clearly informed their approach at the Playhouse. This was not a company afraid of encouraging thinking during rehearsals. Play selections were intended to challenge both the company and their audiences. The company undertook substantial research about its productions. It offered regular issues of "The Playhouse News" with articles about upcoming plays,[34] as well as pre-show talks and lectures on plays like *Peer Gynt* and *Faust* in order to give its audiences the background to respond to the production knowledgeably. As well, James and the company worked continually on their theatrical skills, and their School of Theatre offered an apprenticeship program as well as both a weekday school and weekend workshops for amateurs and students who wanted to acquire the skills necessary for a professional career. The weekend workshops had approximately one hundred students in 1940.[35] After the war, when GIs expressed an interest in more formal training in theatre practice, the theatre school received accreditation for that purpose.

From the beginning the Seattle Repertory Playhouse mounted shows for children, and once they moved into their new theatre in the university district they became even more committed to theatre for youth when they realized that the lack of university students in their audiences, despite their proximity, may have been the result of a lack of familiarity with the art form. Starting with *Romeo and Juliet* because it was in the curriculum, they offered matinees to an increasing number of high schools and junior high schools in Seattle and eventually to students bused in from other communities. In the depths of the Depression, they approached the State Board of Education with ideas to tour to a couple of high schools outside the city, and in 1935 they took *A Midsummer Night's Dream* on the road with a cast of fifty, including an orchestra and ballet dancers. The enthusiasm generated by this experiment was such that they quickly proceeded to apply for a three-year Rockefeller Foundation grant that launched the Washington State Theatre.[36] The importance of this venture was recognized not only by the Jameses but by state educators. In their promotional booklet, the state superintendent of public instruction hailed it as "a history-making project … unique in the annals of education and the theatre in America." He argued that "it is neither fantastic nor grandiloquent to conceive of it as ultimately achieving a powerful and beneficent influence throughout the nation for culture and education and all the great, good things of life for which we all strive."

They prepared *The Comedy of Errors* for their first tour with an eye to performing for both high school students and adults—including inmates in state and federal penitentiaries on their route. The theatre undertook surveys to learn about the needs and interests of students, provided study guides to assist both students and teachers in getting the most out of the productions, and sent advance promotional people, including Albert Ottenheimer, to address school assemblies. Eventually they teamed up with the State Librarian to foster promotional materials in libraries and radio programs, including a state-wide broadcast of a preview production of *She Stoops to Conquer* from the Playhouse.

Although they continued to produce Shakespeare, they experimented with modern dress productions, which were still strange to many audiences but were intended to make a more effective connection with the students' contemporary reality. Starting with their second tour they also began producing modern plays and looking for opportunities to engage the students more effectively—as in the case of *No More Frontier* by Talbot Jennings in which they incorporated opportunities for school musical groups to play during intervals. Yet they discovered that students still had difficulty relating to these and other plays they offered. The students really wanted plays relating to their own age group and circumstances. This led to the introduction of playwriting in the Seattle high school curriculum, and a Living Newspaper play, *Search*, which was the first product of these classes and was then produced by the Washington State Theatre as their first experiment with theatre "by youth, for youth."

Children attending State Theatre shows paid 25 cents, and even with that modest amount there were concerns because not all children could afford it. Unfortunately, adult audiences did not support the productions sufficiently to offset the costs of the tour, most likely because they had little more experience with live theatre than did their children. To further complicate matters the political winds shifted, and the ongoing financial support which the State had promised in conjunction with the Rockefeller Grant was not forthcoming. After having taken theatre to 95,000 students since 1936, the Washington State Theatre folded in January 1939, leaving the Seattle Repertory Playhouse, rather than the state, to pay off its debt. Burton James would not see his vision of a state theatre become an ongoing reality, but Florence James would move to inspire a similar theatre with a very similar mandate in another country and a more progressive time.

While the touring ceased, the Playhouse continued to mount plays for young people, and service organizations helped to make these productions available to children from outside the city. One such production was mounted in the year that the Washington State Theatre closed, and it was remembered in 1977 by a woman who had attended it:

> I was bused to the theatre at the age of seven. There was a program sponsored by the Junior League, to bring children to live theatre. I lived in a small fishing village outside of Seattle; it was a long bus ride, but it changed my life. Professional actors, who had worked together for twenty years, under the direction of Mrs. Florence Bean James … were playing *Rumpelstiltskin*. That was it. I fell in love.
>
> As soon as I was allowed to go about on my own (fourteen), I went back to that theatre and hung around and begged to clean johns and sort nuts and bolts until they took me into the company.
>
> Mrs. James and her actor husband, Burton, inspired me to write for the theatre. They always hoped a playwright would emerge from their theatre. When I joined, I was more interested in design. But watching her direct and teach acting, I got hooked on all aspects of theatre. I was fascinated by her sense-memory exercises and her classes in improvisation.[37]

This child, who was born Josephine Duffy and through her teenage years was known as Marguerite Duffy, eventually changed her name and became the internationally recognized playwright Megan Terry. Florence James became a powerful role model for her, and the actions of Canwell's Un-American Activities Committee informed her future political activism. She went on to participate in the theatre programs offered by the Jameses at the Banff School of Fine Arts, including an appearance as Hermia in their production of *A Midsummer Night's Dream* in 1950.[38] James makes no reference to Terry in her memoir, but she is just one extreme example of the way in which the Jameses' educational vision for their theatre was realized.

A Model Federal Theatre

Maintaining a fledgling theatre in the depths of the Depression proved to be a major challenge, and the opportunity to gain some financial support for core theatre staff through the Federal Theatre Project of the Works Progress Administration (WPA) was clearly a godsend.[39] The Negro Repertory Theatre proposed by Burton and Florence James has garnered more scholarly attention than any other aspect of their career. From the perspective of the twenty-first century—and even from James' perspective when she resigned from the project in 1937 because of escalating red tape and WPA censorship[40]—the success of the Negro Repertory Theatre was marked by significant limitations: a limited number of Blacks in Seattle at the time (perhaps 5,000 at most), the short span of the project (1935–39), the racial prejudices and paternalism of the predominantly White audiences and administration, and the nature of some of the plays, which forced the actors into uncomfortable stereotypes.

Although James does not mention it, her original choice for opening the Negro Repertory Theatre, *Porgy,* met with protests by the Black actors, who did not fit the stereotypical expectations behind such a play.[41] As reported by a visiting Federal Theatre Project administrator, the actors were "mostly educated Negroes, and they are actually having to teach dialect to many of the players in their opening production of *Porgy.* This makes me wonder a little if our whole White approach to the Negro theatre question isn't wrong."[42] The play was eventually withdrawn when they could not get the rights, but this early experience had already caused important reflection, and better play choices emerged as the project continued. A play like *Noah* gave the actors less stereotypical roles, if not serious acting challenges, and *Stevedore,* with its roles for dockworkers, hit somewhat closer to the actors' experiences than *In Abraham's Bosom,* which still forced the Northwest actors into North Carolina dialects and circumstances that felt strangely stereotypical. James came to understand how poorly her Black actors were served by the existing repertory of plays, so she altered her approach. According to one of the members of the company, Sara Oliver, "Mrs. James tried not to affect us with White culture, but to let us bring out our Black culture. Now she may not have realized that she was doing it that way, but that was where she was coming from."[43] She encouraged one of the strongest actors in the company, Theodore Browne, to start writing. Browne helped to put together the successful musical revue *Swing, Gates, Swing* and adapted *Lysistrata* to an Ethiopian context with allusions to the recent invasion of that country by Italy. Roosevelt was attempting at the time to maintain a neutral position for the United States in the conflict[44] and that, plus the racier bits of the original play, apparently mobilized the WPA to close the show after only one performance. Although James does not mention it, both she and Browne must have known that a year earlier the Federal Theatre Project's first Living Newspaper production, which was entitled *Ethiopia* and featured Haile Selassie, had been shut down by the government. Quite possibly James and Browne may have seen the piece as a response to this kind of censorship. Fortunately, Browne had better success with his play *Natural Man,* which concerned the legendary railroad worker John Henry and played for nearly a month in 1937.[45] After the close of the Negro Repertory Theatre, Browne went on to become the first Black American winner of a Rockefeller/Dramatist's Guild Fellowship in Playwriting and, with Langston Hughes and Theodore Ward, a founding member of the Negro Playwrights Company in Harlem. He eventually joined the American Negro Theatre, also in Harlem, which produced his play again in 1941.[46] Browne went on to earn an AB and an MEd.[47]

It is interesting how many of the actors associated with the Seattle Repertory Playhouse and the Negro Theatre unit went on to earn university degrees. Constance Pitter majored in speech at the University of Washington and was allowed to take an education degree thanks to Florence James' sponsorship of her practice teaching. At the same time, Joseph Sylvester Jackson, who played the lead in the 1933 production of *In Abraham's Bosom,* was executive secretary of the Seattle Urban League. He already had a BA but went on to earn an MA in sociology in 1939.[48]

A different issue arose around the Negro Repertory Theatre production of Sinclair Lewis and John Moffitt's *It Can't Happen Here*, which was prepared for simultaneous production in as many as twenty-two different locations on October 27, 1936.[49] All of the productions done outside Seattle had White casts, but because the Negro Repertory Theatre was regarded as by far the strongest Federal Theatre unit in the city, they were chosen to perform this play, which deals with a hypothetical fascist takeover of the United States. This "hot potato" of a play created controversy inside and outside the Federal Theatre Project, and James complains about constant tampering with the script plus escalating administrative complications throughout rehearsal, but, intriguingly, it appears to have been an early example of colour-blind casting on the basis of merit. Contrary to Barry Witham's critique of the play as consisting of parts poorly suited to Black actors,[50] it could be argued that this production gave the actors a high-profile opportunity to take on serious roles in a contemporary play that had not been written specifically for Black actors. James' attempts to localize the action in the Black neighbourhood of Seattle as well as some audience response which thought "the Negro cast unsuited to the play" suggest that people on both sides of the stage were struggling to adjust to Black actors in a "White man's play," but, like other dimensions of the Negro Repertory Theatre, it was the beginning of things that it would take decades to sort out—and of some that are still not sorted.[51]

Interestingly, the group of White actors working in Seattle under the Federal Theatre Project began to complain that the Black actors were getting better direction and training than they were, so James was requisitioned to work with the White actors as well.[52] The Living Newspaper production she directed with them, *Power*, was on a topic of considerable interest in Washington state at the time and was a spectacular show, including film, slide projections, a chorus, and an orchestra. While it proved to be an enormously successful show, "a bombshell" as Barry Witham characterizes it,[53] *Power*'s real importance, identified by James herself, was more in what happened backstage. The scale of the production required a chorus, experienced stage managers, and technicians. The White company lacked resources in these areas, but the training the Black company had received enabled them to step into the breech and thereby create an integrated production, which, according to James, sparked no backstage controversy. Ultimately, however, this integration initiative created controversy in the context of the Un-American Activities committee.[54]

In her book *Blueprints for a Black Federal Theatre, 1935–1939*, Rena Fraden notes that "surprisingly," the Negro Repertory Theatre in Seattle "put on some of the most experimental of productions of any Negro unit, partly due to its directors, Florence and Burton James." She argues that Black playwrights, actors, and musicians were allowed "to exercise direction and some autonomy." In an interview with Rita Deverell, Florence James remembered that at a later date one of the Black actors who was still involved in theatre in Seattle told her "she never felt like a person until she came to the Playhouse. She said there nobody questioned my appearance, my looks, my colour. All I was supposed to do was what I wanted to do, and I got all kinds of help and credit for it ... I just emerged."[55] By twenty-first-century standards this may seem like a small accomplishment, but Fraden observes that with respect to colour-blind casting and integrated casts and audiences we still have quite a ways to go today:

> Although non-traditional casting and color-blind casting have been tried by various companies, not a great deal of headway has been made, partly because our society is anything but color-blind, willing or able to see beyond a very narrow sense of what constitutes realism.... That color-blind casting seems problematic to producers reflects the ongoing color coding and color bias that seems perfectly natural in our society.... Operating in such a firmly entrenched color-coded environment, theatres producing ethnic work employ all those actors still locked out from the majority of productions in the United States and showcase the work of authors committed to telling their separate ethnic story. In any case, to think in terms of either erasing all distinctions or foregrounding them continues to set the narrow terms of what constitutes a proper or appropriate dramatic representation of "authenticity," "realism," or the "natural."[56]

Building New Companies

Florence James ruefully cites Norris Houghton's prediction relating to the Playhouse team at the time of the Washington State Theatre "that if the artists in the Repertory Playhouse can keep their number intact, they may have grown into a company with a forceful and incisive theatrical style." Events set in motion by the Canwell committee limited the ensemble's tenure at the Playhouse, but in some respects they also contributed to its influence and to eventual awareness of the importance of this theatrical experiment in company and community. Although its membership was specifically determined when they formally set themselves up as a union in 1936, the Playhouse company that Megan Terry so admired for having worked together for twenty years proved to be a widely extended community when the full force of Canwell's committee came down upon them. The memoir documents how people who had only worked briefly at the theatre, students of the school and their parents, audience members whom they had touched, and individuals then far removed from Seattle sent money and supportive notes.

It is in the context of this extended Playhouse community that the diaspora of the Playhouse company must be read. The building and the theatre were lost, but the artists who had gained a knowledge of theatre practice under its roof created a network of actors, writers, performers, directors, technicians, and educators who extended the influence of that company to other communities in the United States and Canada. Initially James travelled to San Francisco, where the playwright Marianne King was based. She tried working off-Broadway in New York, where Al Ottenheimer had relocated, but eventually, at the age of sixty, James headed to Canada, where she would foster the development of not one but several theatre companies and establish an enduring interest in theatre in large and small communities across the province. She was joined by her daughter, Marijo, Marijo's husband, Jack Kinzel, and their children.[58] Although Kinzel had at one time been involved with the Playhouse and in Burton James' arts initiatives for the state, he had been blacklisted for his connections with unions and their sponsorship of a concert by Paul Robeson in Seattle.[59] Like James, Kinzel came to Saskatchewan because he was offered government-related work.

Burton and Florence James began coming to Canada in 1938 to teach in the University of British Columbia summer school and from there went on to teach in the summer program at the Banff Centre for the Arts, beginning in 1945. Donald Cameron, who was head of the program, thought highly of Burton. He made a point of protecting him from investigation by the FBI while in Banff, and encouraged him to move to Alberta when the Canwell proceedings were over.[60] Apparently, however, he was not such a fan of strong women. In an interview of Esther Nelson, who was also from the Playhouse and used to teach in the Banff program, she notes that Cameron found Florence a threat because she would not "take any kind of nonsense." But Burton was hired to teach acting and directing, and direct a show, despite the fact he "was not a director." So Florence came "the last two weeks" to "sort of pull the thing together. Because he was fine at getting the thing started ... but she had a lot more experience as a director. He was primarily from an acting point of view." It was not until 1951 that Florence formally became a member of the staff.[61]

Nevertheless, Florence made a powerful impression on faculty and students later interviewed by the Banff Centre. Leona Patterson, who taught with the Jameses, remembers her as a "very outspoken" woman who "added a great deal to the School ... She was a fine, well-trained, well-organized person—he was a dreamer. She was a rod of iron."[62] Bruno Gerussi went to Banff as a student and then was offered a scholarship to the Seattle Repertory Playhouse school where he stayed for two years.[63] Like Megan Terry, he saw the Jameses, and Florence in particular, as hugely influential in his career:

> She was an incredible woman. She was one of the most dynamic, extraordinary women I've ever met in my life. There they worked as a team, the two Jameses. I mean he's the one who was on faculty but everybody talks about her. They both were phenomenal people. She was an extraordinary teacher, and just a dynamic, extraordinary person. They both were, and they were a dynamic team. They without a doubt were the first real powerful influence in my life in the way of the theatre, and probably the most important. I've worked since then with Guthrie and that's a mountain of a man, he was, and great, and Douglas Campbell and all those people, but it all started with Florence and Burton James that I met at the Banff School of Fine Arts. [64]

Before the loss of the Playhouse and Burton's death, bridges had been forged between the Playhouse and individuals from all across Canada who would contribute to new Canadian and U.S. companies, both professional and amateur. Banff Centre programs from the period attest to staff and students from the Playhouse following the Jameses to Banff, and interviews reveal that students there in turn followed the Jameses back to Seattle. Many of the Jameses' students, like George Ryga and Shirley Douglas, went on to theatre-related careers, while others, like Mary Ellen Burgess and Lyn Goldman, went back to their communities to contribute to drama in the schools and amateur drama groups.[65] Given the Jameses' impact on their students and the strong participation of people from Saskatchewan at Banff, it may not have been happenstance that Norah McCullough, executive secretary of the Saskatchewan Arts Board (1947–58), met the Jameses at a conference in Banff and invited them to move from Banff to Saskatchewan to lead drama workshops for her newly established arts agency.[66]

As Rita Deverell observes in the epilogue, after Florence James' success in the workshops, the invitation to join the Arts Board full time in 1953 was indicative of the stark contrast between the climate in Washington and that in Saskatchewan. She arrived in Saskatchewan at a turning point in the province's political, social, and cultural development. As her son-in-law observed, "in that period Saskatchewan seemed to be a sort of island of sanity in North America."[67] Tommy Douglas had set up the first socialist government in North America and its provincial health care and arts funding programs were later regarded as such important innovations that they were emulated by other provincial and national governments in programs such as the Canada Council for the Arts.[68] While Washington invested in the destructive enterprise of searching out communists, Saskatchewan invested in the socialist dream of making creative outlets available to everyone in the province. James was offered $3,600 (raised to $4,200 in 1957),[69] and she remarked with amazement that this was the first time she had received a salary for her theatre work. Thanks to Washington and the Saskatchewan Arts Board, Saskatchewan gained an experienced and impassioned artist, arts educator, arts administrator, and advocate, who would be perfectly positioned to have an immeasurable impact on the development of theatre within the province and beyond.[70]

It must have been very difficult for James to make the transition from a professional playhouse at its peak—where "everybody was used to their fullest. And you knew it. You just stretched to fill the need"—to small rural drama groups composed largely of people who had never been on a stage before, many of whom had not even seen professional theatre. It must also have been difficult to make the transition from the lush and semi-tropical Northwest to the cold and semi-arid flats of Saskatchewan.[71] However, once she had made the transition from a model theatre to a model arts agency, James tackled the demands of bringing theatre to the little towns and villages of the province with the same vision, energy, and determination that she had brought to the Playhouse. Her position, initially funded for only two years, was to assist with theatrical preparations for the province's Golden Jubilee in 1955. James travelled to large and small communities to help drama groups with choices of plays and pageants, casting, directing, and training workshops to aid in preparations for the celebrations.[72] At the same time she spoke about her theatre work and helped with issue-oriented skits for the Farmers' Union Conference in North Battleford, Wilkie, St. Walburg, Saskatoon, and Regina. Although this organization was not devoted to dramatic undertakings or long-term theatre training, in her report to the Arts Board she made a point of underscoring the importance of this connection for building audience understanding and community support for serious drama: "[this kind of work] broadens attitudes to drama and its use as something of more value than a slight play solely for entertainment."[73] At the other end of the dramatic spectrum, she directed the musical *Saskatchewan Ho!*, which was commissioned by the Arts Board and played in several communities in the province during the Jubilee year. She continued and expanded the summer drama workshops by bringing in Fred Youens, who had been part of the Seattle company in the areas of design and technical theatre. He made it possible to provide training in those areas, as well as improved technical support for resulting productions. She also directed the Fort Qu'Appelle pageant, which brought together people from the summer drama workshop, a large number of members of the community of all ages, and several families from the File Hills reserve.[74] As well, a not inconsiderable part of her duties in these early years was devoted to helping organize the Dominion Drama Festival that took place in the province in its Jubilee year.[75]

Hosting this national festival showcased the developments that were taking place in Saskatchewan, and people took notice. Because of improved theatre training in the province, Ontario's Stratford Festival auditioned in Saskatchewan and hired Walter Mills of Moose Jaw for the 1955 summer season. Word spread about the dramatic dynamo in Saskatchewan, and James was invited to speak, adjudicate, and/or provide workshops in both Manitoba and Alberta.[76] Obviously, James' expertise was welcomed inside and outside the province, but Deverell reports incidents involving Woodrow Lloyd, Saskatchewan's Minister of Education, that probably reflect the inevitable question mark left when individuals were slandered in the McCarthy era. Lloyd wanted to know if the Jameses were communists but, when given the full information about their visionary work in the arts for the state of Washington, realized that their vision was the same as the one Douglas and his government shared for the Arts Board. Florence James, Woodrow Lloyd, and David Smith, the creator of the Arts Board, all shared a belief in the inextricable link between the arts and education and the important role they had to play in a democratic society infused with socialist values. Perhaps James' remark in a report to the board regarding her observations of progress on theatre training at Balfour Technical School sums up that vision: "Work in drama can be wonderfully useful in the development of people."[77] Given the enormous interest generated in theatre during the Jubilee preparations and James' potential to carry the Arts Board's vision for theatre even further, the permanence of her position never seemed in serious question.

After the Jubilee, James' activity did not diminish but if anything increased. She continued to expand training opportunities, even developing speech courses for distance delivery over radio. In her 1957 report to the board for the winter period of December to February, she noted having worked in Regina, Wynyard, Fort Qu'Appelle, Unity, and Beechy and lists requests for further visits as coming from Weyburn, Ketchen, Unity, Venn, Sturgis, Mitchellton, Swift Current, Moose Jaw, and Beechy.[78] As demands for her time increased, there were tensions at board level over requests from groups in the larger centres of Regina and Saskatoon, which were regarded as having more access to expertise, versus those from groups in the rural centres, whose needs had been the primary motivation for her hiring.[79] Somehow she managed to maintain a vigorous presence in rural communities while also taking an active role in the Regina theatre community.[80] In 1956, for instance, she directed a well-reviewed production of the Canadian play *Ghost Writers* by Ted Allen for the Regina Little Theatre with Marijo in the cast.[81] In 1958 she directed a production of the *Diary of Anne Frank* for the Regina Section of the National Council of Jewish Women. Reviewers of these productions always note that, although many of the actors had never been on stage before, the acting was of a "remarkably high caliber and always compelling."[82]

James' support for bringing the children's theatre expert Brian Way to Regina while on his 1959 Canadian tour had both an immediate and a long-term impact. Way's talk in May and his use of arena staging was followed up in one of the two Summer Workshop productions that year. As explained in the Annual Report, it was staged "'in the round.' This is a rarely used approach to theatre in Saskatchewan and one which can be ideally suitable for groups with inadequate stage facilities and equipment, a problem faced in many small communities."[83] In the long term, Way's visit, combined with the now-extended network of the Seattle Repertory Playhouse company, generated Saskatchewan's first professional theatre company since 1927 and one of Canada's earliest companies dedicated to theatre for young audiences. Ken Kramer, a student of Bette Anderson, who had left Seattle at the demise of the Playhouse to head up the City of Edmonton's theatre programs, had trained with Way in London, and when he returned to Canada with his new bride, Sue Richmond, James managed to convince the Arts Board to give them space and a loan to start up a touring company for young people. Kramer and Richmond put together a clear philosophy and an ensemble and started touring with arena-style staging to communities of all sizes in all weather. The Washington State Theatre Company had been reborn and this time funding from the Arts Board, the Department of Education, and Canada Council gave it longevity and room to grow a phenomenal touring record stretching from 1966 until well into the 1990s. At its height it played 290 performances in 149 towns for over thirty-two weeks annually and reached an audience of nearly 90,000, 9 percent of the provincial population and one-third of its school-aged children.[84]

When James retired from the Saskatchewan Arts Board in 1968, she moved to Ottawa with her daughter's family, but soon returned to Saskatchewan, where she found the cultural environment richer and livelier. She was then appointed as the first dramaturg for the Globe Theatre, where she continued to have an influence on young artists like Rita Deverell. Sitting in on rehearsals of the Globe touring ensemble must have given her the satisfaction of knowing that, although the Jameses' vision of theatre had been cut short in Washington, a more favourable political and financial climate had allowed that vision to be realized and thrive in Saskatchewan. The Kramers' company had placed its "fists upon a star" and "the habit of art" that had become "a habit of living" for James would continue as that company introduced children like the young Joey Tremblay to the world of theatre and inspired their careers at the Globe and on today's international stages.

Honours and Recognition

As noted by Deverell, in 1957 Florence James was asked to join the executive of the Canadian Theatre Centre, which represented professional and educational theatres in Canada. This was not only an acknowledgement of her background but also recognition of her tireless advocacy for Canadian arts and theatre. Her 1956 speech to the Saskatoon Branch of the Saskatchewan Registered Teachers Association grabbed local headlines with the prediction that "Canada Will Lead the Continent in the Arts."[85] She was a strong supporter of new Canadian plays and playwrights as well as the newly formed Canadian Players, a touring branch of the Stratford Festival ensemble, and helped to promote its first appearance in Saskatchewan. Speaking to the Regina University Women's Club, she hailed the Canadian Players as "a miracle ... that could happen in no other country" and called for more opportunities for Canadian artists to work at home: "Let us make an effort to provide scope for our actors and actresses on our own Canadian stage."[86] In an article on the Saskatchewan Arts Board for publication in *Commonwealth* in 1957, she cited an observation by the Governor General, Vincent Massey—"it is the differences amongst us, the variety, which gives Canadian culture its distinctive flavour." She went on to argue that "human resources take form when people sing together, paint pictures, tell stories, make beautiful things for everyday use, act in plays and of course, enjoy such activities. The stories, songs, customs, the latent talent in our young people, the intermingling of a dozen or more different language groups—the growth and fusion of such things are the concern of the Saskatchewan Arts Board."[87]

James received numerous national as well as provincial awards, including the Queen's Silver Medal on the twenty-fifth anniversary of Elizabeth II's coronation, the Canadian Drama Award from the Dominion Drama Festival, a life membership in the Canadian Theatre Centre and the Canadian Child and Youth Drama Association, and, in 1978, the Diplome d'honneur, Canada's highest recognition for artistic achievement. As noted by Mavor Moore, at James' death in 1988,[88] the importance of her pioneering accomplishments extended well beyond Saskatchewan. It was because of this Saskatchewan pioneer and Canadian men and women like her that the central importance of the arts in all their diversity that took root on the prairies reached beyond provincial borders to inspire the recognition and encouragement of Canadian culture in the twentieth century.

However, if as Mavor Moore observed, James remained largely unknown outside Saskatchewan, it is reasonable to suggest that today she may be largely unknown even in Saskatchewan. As an American who chose to leave the United States during more external attacks on supposed communists in Vietnam, I never met her nor had I ever heard of her when I first came to Saskatchewan to take up work in the arts, theatre, and education. Even in the 1990s, when I was hired at the Globe Theatre in the position of dramaturg that she had once filled, I knew nothing of her. It took a student who had come to study at the University of Regina from one of the former Soviet Bloc countries to bring her to my attention. Following an assignment to use material in the Saskatchewan Archives in a paper on local theatre or people associated with it, she came to my office enthusiastically clutching piles of photocopies neatly assembled in binders. She thrust one of the binders in front of me, wanting to know if she could do her paper on it. I could see that it was a typescript entitled "Fists Upon a Star," so I sent her off to check if it had been published, while I promised to read it and respond to her. I started to read it that evening and didn't put it down until I came to the end; I was surprised to learn that it had not been published. After securing copies of the relevant Canwell Committee proceedings and other materials from James' papers, the student wrote a paper far in excess of the word limit comparing James' philosophy of theatre with that of young people in her own country and the experiences of her older artist friends under Soviet rule with those of James in the United States. When she returned to her home country, I feel certain that her friends came to know a great deal about this Saskatchewan pioneer, and I have come to the conclusion that this is precisely the kind of recognition that would matter most to Florence James. At her death, the compilation of the international mix of warm remembrances of her contributions to the arts and to individual lives constituted the strongest recognition of the enduring network of company and community that she forged in her lifetime.[89]

Rita Deverell remarks that Florence James seemed to have the effect on people of "an electric jolt that stayed with them." That effect continues through this book and the broad community it constructs. It richly rewards both students and professionals in the theatre and any artists for whom the "habit of art" has become a "habit of living." As well it has much to offer students and historians concerned with American and Canadian, local and cultural, women's and Black history. It will engage arts educators and literary scholars interested in women's studies and life-writing. Above all, it will appeal to anyone who admires individuals who pursue their ideals and vision with determination and challenge others to live up to that legacy.

Acknowledgments

I would like to acknowledge the efforts of my graduate student, Ian McWilliams, and my husband, Cameron Louis, both of whom made important research contributions towards this introduction through their work in the University of Washington archives and newspaper collections.

NOTES

1 Helen Buss, *Repossessing the World: Reading Memoirs by Contemporary Women* (Waterloo, Ontario: Wilfrid Laurier University Press, 2002), 133.

2 See for instance, Melvin Rader, *False Witness* (Seattle: University of Washington Press, 1979).

3 See, for instance, Mark F. Jenkins, *All Powers Necessary and Convenient: A Play of Fact and Speculation* (Seattle: University of Washington Press, 2000); Rita Deverell, *McCarthy and the Old Woman* (available from Playwrights Guild of Canada), produced in Seattle in 2010 by the University of Washington in the theatre that Florence and Burton James built.

4 It has in fact been argued that writing a memoir is a performative act, that autobiography has more in common with drama than other creative forms, and that frequently it conforms to the characteristics of tragedy described by Aristotle, particularly in the attraction of the "role model" through whom the reader experi-

ences vicarious feelings of pity and fear. See p. 209 in Evelyn J. Hinz, "Mimesis: The Dramatic Lineage of Auto/Biography" in *Essays on Life Writing: From Genre to Critical Practice*, Marlene Kadar, ed. (Toronto: University of Toronto Press, 1992), 195–212; Buss, *Repossessing the World*, 186.

5 Buss, *Repossessing the World*, 187.

6 Carolyn G. Heilbrun, *Writing a Woman's Life* (New York: W. W. Norton, 1988), 13, 16, 24.

7 For evidence of her probable effect on the women she met in rural Saskatchewan and her ongoing vision of her role and that of other women in the community as pioneers, see one of many speeches (untitled) that she gave in that province during her tenure as drama consultant of the Saskatchewan Arts Board. University of Regina Archives, Rita Deverell fonds, 90-97, Box 1, file 3.

8 When Florence ran for state senate (as a Democrat) she listed her civic activities as including membership on the Permanent Facilities Committee of King County Commissioners' Juvenile Advisory Committee, honorary membership in the Building Service Employees Union, American Federation of Labor, and the Democratic Precinct Committee. She also ran for Seattle school director in March 1944 and after her conviction in 1950 was nominated by the Progressive Party for King County Clerk. See University of Regina Archives, Rita Deverell fonds, 90-97, Box 2, File 10.

9 Buss, *Repossessing the World*, 128.

10 Full transcripts of these hearings were published by the Joint Legislative Fact-Finding Committee on Un-American Activities. *Un-American Activities in Washington State: First and Second Reports to the 31st Washington Legislature.* Olympia, 1948–49; a thorough analysis of the proceedings of the committee as well as resulting court cases is undertaken by Vern Countryman, *Un-American Activities in the State of Washington: The Work of the Canwell Committee* (Ithaca: Cornell University Press, 1951).

11 University of Washington Archives, Seattle Repertory papers, 1556-3, Box 33, Folder 2.

12 For a further discussion of the various factors that led to James' being called before the Un-American Activities Committee, see Barry Witham, "The Playhouse and the Committee," in *The Performance of Power: Theatrical Discourse and Politics*, Sue-Ellen Case and Janelle Reinelt, eds., Studies in Theatre History and Culture (Iowa City: University of Iowa Press, 1991), 151–2.

13 For example, Dalton Trumbo, *The Time of the Toad: A Study of Inquisition in America* (1949; rpt London: Journeyman Press, 1982).

14 For instance: "Mrs. James Found Guilty after Fiery Trial Ending," *Seattle Post-Intelligencer*, Friday June 24, 1949, front page; Jenkins, *All Powers Necessary and Convenient*, xxiv; for analysis of the role of the newspapers in the Canwell affair, see Countryman, *Un-American Activities*, 25–6, 394–6.

15 A report prepared by the Playhouse sales department in 1948 documents in great detail the devastating effect the Canwell hearings had on the theatre through public opinion and resulting cancellation of tickets. Comments from patrons wishing to have their names removed from the listings range from polite to rude.

University of Washington Archives, Seattle Repertory Playhouse Collection, 1156-3, Box 76, Folder 5; Bette Anderson papers, 2811, Box 19, Folder 10.

16 For more information on the ongoing strands of related extremism in American society and politics see, for instance, Richard M. Fried, *Nightmare in Red: The McCarthy Era in Perspective* (Oxford: Oxford University Press, 1990); Alice Jardine, "Flash Back, Flash Forward: The Fifties, the Nineties, and the Transformed Politics of Remote Control," in *Secret Agents: The Rosenberg Case, McCarthyism, and Fifties America*, Marjorie Garber and Rebecca L. Walkowitz, eds. (New York: Routledge, 1995), 107–23; Joseph E. Lowndes, *From the New Deal to the New Right: Race and the Southern Origins of Modern Conservatism* (New Haven: Yale University Press, 2008); John McCumber, *Time in the Ditch: American Philosophy and the McCarthy Era* (Evanston, Illinois: Northwestern University Press, 2001). Recent U.S. congressional hearings on the "extent of radicalization in the American Muslim community" have sparked groups like the American Civil Liberties Union to draw parallels with McCarthyism. "Groups Oppose U.S. Hearings," Regina *Leader-Post*, Wednesday, March 9, 2011, C8.

17 Millie S. Barranger, *Unfriendly Witnesses: Gender, Theater, and Film in the McCarthy Era* (Carbondale: Southern Illinois University Press, 2008), xv.

18 Flanagan's testimony before the House Un-American Activities Committee is included along with those of many others in *Thirty Years of Treason: Excerpts from Hearings before the House Committee on Un-American Activities, 1938-1968,* Eric Bentley, ed., 2nd printing (New York: Viking, 1972), 6–47.

19 Jenkins, *All Powers Necessary and Convenient*, xxxviii.

20 Jill Ker Conway has argued that an autobiographer reveals much about what is perceived as typical or deviant within her social and cultural context through the "subtext" of "the life plot the writer assumes is to be expected." In *Her Own Words: Women's Memoirs from Australia, New Zealand, Canada, and the United States* (New York: Vintage Books, 1999), vii. Although James is very much aware of the deviance of her politics and philosophy of theatre, she appears to be comparatively oblivious to her deviance from hegemonic gender expectations.

21 http://gutenberg.net.au/ebooks07/0700461.txt.

22 Alan Bennett, *The Habit of Art* (London: Faber and Faber, 2009), especially p. 87. In a memoir such as this it may be easy to forget the day-to-day life style implied by what is remembered but never really articulated. In an April 1951 letter by Burton James to David Stevens he remarks on the "compensations" that came with losing their theatre: "For 25 years we were constantly at the theatre, day and night. Now it's pleasant to enjoy a leisurely dinner at home with Mrs. James, without having to rush away to meet a deadline of rehearsal or performance, or to dine out together with friends, a rare experience for us. Then there are grandchildren to sit with, much reading to be done, some writing, and the garden to care for. The fact that we can choose a sunny spring day to drive out into the country gives both of us a mild feeling of guilt. Nevertheless, we do go, realizing this is an interim period and that soon we must go back to work." University of Regina Archives, Rita Deverell fonds, 90-97, Box 1, file 8.

23 James actually saw Bernhardt as a girl by travelling to Utah and then saw her later in New York. Rita Deverell interview with Florence James, University of Regina Archives, Rita Deverell fonds, 90-97, Box 2, file 11, 12.

24 James was one among many Americans in this period who travelled to Moscow and returned enthusiastic about theatre there. Norris Houghton spent six months there in 1935 and published a book on his findings: *Moscow Rehearsals: An Account of Methods of Production in the Soviet Theatre* (1936; rpt New York: Octagon Books, 1975).

25 Another book—*Making the Little Theatre Pay* by Oliver Hinsdell (New York: Samuel French, 1925)—included in the University of Regina, Archer Library collection, contains a 1965 book plate naming Florence James as donor of the book. The focus of the book on the importance of a strong connection between a theatre and its community would also appear to be closely connected with James' theatre aesthetic.

26 Caption for Florence James' picture, *Town Crier*, 28:50 (December 1933), 15. This was an arts and literary magazine published in Seattle, 1912–1937.

27 The scholarly neglect of James' directing career is puzzling. While her slight treatment in major reference texts such as the *Cambridge Guide to American Theatre*, Don B. Wilmeth, ed, 2nd ed. (Cambridge: Cambridge University Press, 2007)—where she receives only brief notice under "Seattle"—is perhaps more acceptable given the broad scope of that work, her complete omission from attention in a text like *Women in American Theatre*, Helen Krich Chinoy and Linda Walsh Jenkins, eds., revised and expanded 3rd ed. (New York: Theatre Communications Group, 2006) is less understandable. Articles on her contemporaries Hallie Flanagan and Margo Jones are included, and Dorothy Magnus' article "Matriarchs of the Regional Theatre" (203–9) credits the opening of Jones' theatre in 1947 as the birth of modern American regional theatre. However, Florence and Burton James founded the Seattle Repertory Playhouse with very similar objectives several years before this, and it is perhaps timely that Magnus' assertions be reviewed.

28 *Seattle Intelligencer*, June 23, 1949.

29 Albert Ottenheimer, who worked so closely with the Jameses for so long, clearly understood these leadership qualities as shared by both Burton and Florence: "The Jameses are essentially pioneers, creative frontiersmen. They are so from an inner compulsion … They see, I think, farther and more clearly than most people because from the vantage of a keen social viewpoint … They have a faculty, these Jameses, of inspiring in those who work with them a stubborn loyalty. Not a personal loyalty, exactly, but an imbuement of others with a steadfast belief in ideas and things that are important and right and true." Albert M. Ottenheimer, "Great Work of the Jameses," *Seattle Life*, June 1937, 24, 30.

30 See, for instance, Malcolm Goldstein, *The Political Stage: American Drama and Theater of the Great Depression* (New York: Oxford University Press, 1974), as a random example appropriate to the period of this memoir. Although purportedly about American drama, the book focuses on drama in New York and, as Florence James demonstrates in this memoir, there were other active centres of theatre in the U.S., even—or perhaps especially—during the Depression.

31 See, for instance, a virtual exhibit mounted by the Manuscripts and University Archives division of the University of Washington Libraries at www.lib.washington.edu/exhibits/allpowers/Exhibit/default.htm.

32 The final issue of the *Seattle Repertory Playhouse News* issued February 1951, estimated that the theatre had played to an audience of over half a million people with 3,000 performances of 196 productions and 140 school alumni. University of Washington Archives, Florence James papers, 2117-1, Box 5, Folder 21. For papers dealing with the ongoing conflicts between the Jameses and the university see University of Washington Archives, W. U. President, 71-34, Box 119, Folder 3; W.U. Drama School, 70-2, Box 14, Folder 2. See also Barry Witham, *The Federal Theatre Project: A Case Study* (Cambridge: Cambridge University Press, 2003), 63–4.

33 *The Argus*, April 30, 1938, 3–4.

34 These newsletters appeared in tabloid format with six to eight pages, including photographs and lengthy articles. University of Washington Archives, Seattle Repertory Playhouse papers, 1556-3, Box 33, folders 1–4.

35 Richard C. Berner, *Seattle in the 20th Century. Volume 2. Seattle 1921-1940: From Boom to Bust* (Seattle: Charles Press, 1992), 259.

36 For a full discussion of this theatre see Gloria Ann Hewitt, "A History of the Washington State Theatre 1931 to 1941." Master's thesis. University of Washington, 1964.

37 Megan Terry, "Two Pages a Day," *The Drama Review: TDR*, Playwrights and Playwriting Issue, 21, 4 (1977): 59–64 [60].

38 James Larson, *Notable Women in the American Theatre: A Biographical Dictionary* (New York: Greenwood Press, 1989), 864; David Savran, *In Their Own Words: Contemporary American Playwrights* (New York: Theatre Communications Group, 1988), 240, 242–3; *A Midsummer Night's Dream* program, August 17 and 18, 1950, Banff Centre Archives.

39 Witham, *The Federal Theatre Project*, 68, 168 n18.

40 Hallie Flanagan, *Arena* (New York: Duell, Sloan and Pearce, 1940), 306–7.

41 Witham, *The Federal. Theatre Project*, 67.

42 Gilmor Brown to Hallie Flanagan, February 20, 1936, Regional Correspondence, RG69, U.S. National Archives.

43 Esther Hall Mumford, *Seven Stars and Orion* (Seattle: Anansi Press, 1980), 72–3.

44 See Franklin Roosevelt's "Statement against Profiteering in the Italian-Ethiopian War," October 30, 1935 at John T. Woolley and Gerhard Peters, The American Presidency Project [online]. Santa Barbara, CA. Available from World Wide Web: http://www.presidency.ucsb.edu/ws/?pid=14971.

45 Flanagan, *Arena*, 393.

46 Witham, *The Federal Theatre Project*, 160, 169.

47 *Encyclopedia of North American Theater, Vol. 1: People* (Alexandria VA: Alexander Street Press, 2005). While most institutions have anglicized their degrees (for example, BA—Bachelor of Arts), Harvard has not, retaining the AB, an abbreviation of the Latin *Artium Baccalaureatus.*

48 Berner, *Seattle in the 20th Century*, 218–19; Quintard Taylor, *The Forging of a Black Community: Seattle's Central District from 1870 through the Civil Rights Era* (Seattle: University of Washington Press, 1994).

49 Florence James cites eighteen simultaneous productions, but in almost every one of the numerous citations relating to this event different figures amounting to as many as twenty-two productions are given. For instance, the *Cambridge Guide to World Theatre* (1988) cites twenty-two, and the *Cambridge Guide to American Theatre*, ed. Don Wilmeth, (2007) cites twenty.

50 Ibid., 74–5.

51 Witham, *The Federal Theatre Project*, 74–5; *Seattle Commonwealth News*, Oct 31, 1936. See also the review in the *Seattle Argus*, Oct 31, 1936: "Played by a Negro cast, the local production had a couple of strikes on it at once. They played it with no compromise to color yet it was necessary to keep reminding yourself that the scene was really the United States and not some remote village in Africa." Excerpts from interviews with Norah McCullough, executive secretary of the Saskatchewan Arts Board, and Florence James herself as cited by Rita Deverell in the epilogue suggest that James' attitude towards "colour," "physical appearance," and "accents" continued to evolve well beyond the point of most directors today.

52 Although James does not make it clear in her memoir, she was apparently at the centre of a fierce negotiation following the production of *Power* for control of the entire Federal Theatre Project in Seattle. She was championed as the new FTP director by the younger group of artists wanting more collective and local control, while the WPA administrators wanted a more conservative administrator. In the end Hallie Flanagan went with the more conservative administrator as acting director and flew in one of her close but inexperienced colleagues to assist. Florence resigned and the Negro unit did not again achieve the same success it had enjoyed under her. Witham, *The Federal Theatre Project*, 88–90.

53 Witham, *The Federal Theatre Project*, 89.

54 See the transcripts of the hearings in Countryman, *Un-American Activities in the State of Washington*.

55 Rita Deverell interview with Florence James. University of Regina Archives, Rita Deverell fonds, 90-97, Box 2, file 11.

56 Rena Fraden, *Blueprints for a Black Federal Theatre, 1935–1939* (Cambridge: Cambridge University Press, 1994), 177, 203. Barry Witham also notes that of all FTP projects across the country the Seattle Negro Repertory Theatre unit was the most "remarkable" and that under the Jameses the group "continued to excel" and create an "impressive record." *The Federal Theatre Project*, 71.

57 For the full discussion of what Houghton saw at the Playhouse, see his *Advance from Broadway: 19,000 Miles of American Theatre* (Freeport, NY: np, 1969), 64–8.

58 Marijo had grown up at the Playhouse and in 1934 at the age of fifteen played Hilda to her father's Solness in Ibsen's *The Master Builder*. In 1939/40 she went to Hollywood and had small parts in two movies, but returned to Seattle where she married Adrian Lawrence, a business representative for the Longshoremen's Union. That marriage was dissolved during the war. After coming to Canada she pursued a graduate degree in sociology and became the only woman permanently appointed to the Department of Sociology at the University of Regina. From Interviews with Jack Kinzel and Helen Taverniti, University of Regina Archives, Rita Deverell fonds, 90-97, Box 2, file 14; Box 3, file 26.

59 Jack Kinzel had started going to the Playhouse in 1930 when he was still in high school, but migrated into radio as an announcer and writer. He served in the navy during World War II and remained in the reserves after the war when he returned to work at the radio station KIRO and assist in the business of the American Federation of Television and Radio Artists. He was fired after fifteen years with the radio station and given a less than honourable discharge from the navy when he worked with People's Programs, agents for Seattle's Black community, to bring Paul Robeson to Seattle for a concert in 1952. During the war he had married and divorced a woman connected with the Playhouse, but in 1946 he married Marijo. See his personal discharge papers, clippings, etc, and Interview, University of Regina Archives, Rita Deverell fonds 90-97, Box 1, file 3; Box 2, file 14.

60 This invitation may have had much to do with the transfer of flats, curtains, and costumes to Banff when the Playhouse closed.

61 Interview with Esther Nelson by Peggy Leighton, 1981. Paul D. Fleck Library and Archives at the Banff Centre, 1990-44-47.

62 Interview with Leona Patterson by Peggy Leighton, 1981. Paul D. Fleck Library and Archives at the Banff Centre, 1990-44-46.

63 Bruno Gerussi appeared in the 1945 production of *Calico Cargo*. University of Regina Archives, Rita Deverell fonds, 90-97, Box 2, File 9.

64 Interview with Bruno Gerussi by Peggy Leighton, 1981. Paul D. Fleck Library and Archives at the Banff Centre, 1990-44-37.

65 See, for instance, the program for *A Midsummer Night's Dream*, produced in 1950, which involved a cast drawn from not only Alberta but also Ontario, Manitoba, British Columbia, Saskatchewan (five participants) and five of the United States (two from Seattle). *Comedy of Errors*, produced in 1951, drew its cast from the same provinces plus Quebec and two of the United States (three from Seattle). Burgess studied with Florence when she taught in the University of British Columbia summer school as well as at Banff. Rita Deverell interview with Florence James. University of Regina Archives, Rita Deverell fonds, 90-97, Box 2, file 11.

66 The Banff meeting between the Jameses and Norah McCullough is described by Esther Nelson in her interview with Peggy Leighton, ibid.

67 Kinzel Interview. However, according to an interview with Helen Taverniti, the whole family did not have an easy time gaining their Canadian citizenship and required help from Tommy Douglas, who had apparently met the Jameses in Banff and become a friend. Interview with Helen Taverniti by Rita Deverell. University of Regina Archives, Rita Deverell fonds, 90-97, Box 3, file 26. It should be noted that Canada as a whole may not have legislated the kind of public witch hunts undertaken in the U.S., but the RCMP was making secret lists and the "red scare" was motivating extreme behaviour in some corners. As a Baptist minister, Tommy Douglas may well have been aware of William Guy Carr's book, *The Red Fog over America*. It was published in Ontario in 1955 under the sponsorship of the National Federation of Christian Laymen, who "are convinced that an international conspiracy is in operation for the purpose of destroying our national and religious institutions in America." Addressed to Christians in Britain, Canada, and the U.S., it attempts to counter perceived propaganda advocating "One World Government." p. iii.

68 James' thoughts about life in Tommy Douglas' Saskatchewan remain relevant today: "It's this ... Medicare—it was like heaven when I got into Saskatchewan from the States. It was so different—so viable—the climate. I don't mean the weather—I mean the climate for the arts. It was rich and that's what was marvellous, marvellous coming up from the States and being here and doing the thing I wanted to do. And felt that I was really doing the thing that was worth something—valuable for people and they liked it." Rita Deverell Interview with Florence James. University of Regina Archives, Rita Deverell fonds, 90-97, Box 2, file 11.

69 Drama Committee report to the Saskatchewan Arts Board, September 9, 1957. University of Regina Archives, Rita Deverell fonds, 90-97, Box 1, file 3.

70 The process of establishing James' position with the Arts Board is laid out in W. A. Riddell, *Cornerstone for Culture: A History of the Saskatchewan Arts Board from 1948 to 1978* (Regina: Saskatchewan Arts Board, 1979), 11–12, 18.

71 See Rita Deverell's interview with Helen Taverniti, University of Regina Archives, Rita Deverell fonds, 90-97, Box 3, file 26.

72 In October and November of 1955 she worked in Regina, Moose Jaw, Marshall, Oxbow, North Battleford, Prince Albert, and Saskatoon. Drama consultant report to the Saskatchewan Arts Board for October and November 1955. University of Regina Archives, Rita Deverell fonds, 90-97, Box 1, file 3.

73 Drama consultant report to the Saskatchewan Arts Board for Jan 1-March 1955 University of Regina Archives, Rita Deverell fonds, 90-97, Box 1, file 3

74 Riddell, *Cornerstone for Culture,* 18; Report of drama consultant to Saskatchewan Arts Board June 2–August 31, 1955, University of Regina Archives, Rita Deverell fonds, 90-97, Box 1, file 3.

75 Riddell, *Cornerstone for Culture,* 18.

76 Ibid., 12.

77 Drama Consultant report to the Saskatchewan Arts Board March 3–May 26, 1956, University of Regina Archives, Rita Deverell fonds, 90-97, Box 1, file 3.

78 Drama Committee Report to Saskatchewan Arts Board, for period Dec 10–Feb 22 1957/58, University of Regina Archives, Rita Deverell fonds, 90-97, Box 1, file 3.

79 Transcript of a Saskatchewan Arts Board meeting March 3, 1956, Hotel Saskatchewan, Regina, University of Regina Archives, Rita Deverell fonds, 90-97, Box 1, file 3.

80 It should be noted that in addition to the many duties and travels described in detail James was involved in numerous briefs and presentations. She served on the Radio Committee of the board and provided input on national consultations with respect to radio and television. She also co-wrote the board's substantial brief towards the process that led to Regina's Centre of the Arts. That document would still prove useful reading for anyone planning a performing arts facility today. University of Washington, Florence James papers, 2117-1, Box 5, Folder 4.

81 Ken Fraser, "Small Attendance but Play Is Good," Regina *Leader-Post*, Friday, Feb 3, 1956. University of Regina Archives, Rita Deverell fonds, 90-97, Box 1, file 3.

82 "Jewish Play Scores Hit," Regina *Leader-Post*, Friday, Dec 12, 1955.

83 Drama section of Saskatchewan Arts Board Annual Report for 1959, 4. University of Regina Archives, Rita Deverell fonds, 90-97, Box 1, file 3.

84 For this and further information about The Globe Theatre see my article under that title in *The Encyclopedia of Saskatchewan: A Living Legacy* (Regina: Canadian Plains Research Center, 2005).

85 "Canadian Arts Progressing to Position of Prominence," Regina Leader-Post, Saturday, Jan 28, 1956, University of Regina Archives, Rita Deverell fonds, 90-97, Box 1, file 3.

86 "Drama Director Discusses Theatre," Regina *Leader-Post*, Wednesday, Jan 9, 1957. See also the drama consultant report to the Saskatchewan Arts Board for March 3–May 26, 1956. University of Regina Archives, Rita Deverell fonds, 90-97, Box 1, file 3.

87 Typescript of Florence James, "The Saskatchewan Arts Board," *Commonwealth*, November 15, 1957, University of Regina Archives, Rita Deverell fonds, 90-97, Box 1, file 8.

88 Mavor Moore, *The Globe and Mail*, Feb. 13, 1988.

89 University of Washington, Florence Bean James Collection, 2117-4, VF 1625.

Fists Upon A Star

We give what pleases us and when we choose,
And, having given, we do not take back,
But once we shut our fists upon a star
It will take portents to unloose that grip
And even then the stuff will keep the print.
It is a habit of living.

—*from* John Brown's Body *(1928)*
by Stephen Vincent Benét

PROLOGUE

IN THE TEN YEARS since I started to write this book, at the tender age of seventy-three, I have learned a number of interesting things:

- that the gestation period of a literary work is somewhat longer than that of the Indian elephant, and the birth pangs at least as severe;
- that I am no writer, but when one has a story which must be told, one does the best one can and asks for help in a loud voice;
- that pain and joy in memory may be diminished, intensified, or altered by time, but they can never be destroyed. Each of the events and attendant emotions through which I sifted and sorted to build this story has remained like a beetle or butterfly caught in amber, like beads making up the rosary of my life;
- that friends are life's one irreplaceable treasure, that help and good advice come from many sources, and that readers and editors are patient, persistent, and long-suffering people;
- and that the hardest part of telling a story is deciding where it ought to begin. I am indebted to one of the many editors who have read my manuscript for telling me that "stories, like kittens, ought to be picked up in the middle." So, with appropriate caution, that is where I will pick up mine.

Florence James, circa 1975

CHAPTER ONE

On a crisp evening in October, 1930, the Seattle Repertory Playhouse opened the doors of its permanent home to the public—the beginning of a memorable period in the development of theatre in the regions beyond Broadway and in the state of Washington in particular. But for my husband, Burton James, and me, it was the culmination of years of planning and working toward the fulfillment of a dream—the creation of a theatre that would be more than a building, more than a star-studded roster of "hits" or "classics," more than a diversion for the social set or a job for the critics.

Burton and I had been working all our adult lives, first in New York, then in Seattle, toward a theatre that would be of the people, by the people, and for the people. Our dream had finally become reality two years before, when we launched our repertory company, with its talented, dedicated nucleus of unpaid performers. We had worked in rented theatres, makeshift quarters, temporary facilities—but we had created a theatre. The next part of our dream was to have a proper home—and that, too, was about to come to fruition with the opening of the Seattle Repertory Playhouse on the corner of 41st and University Way, in the heart of Seattle's university district.

I can't remember what I was thinking as the clock moved inexorably toward 8:30, curtain time for George Bernard Shaw's *Major Barbara*, the production we had chosen to launch our third season and christen our new theatre. I might have thought back to the true beginning of the Seattle Repertory Playhouse—a Sunday in May, 1928, when a group of friends gathered in our apartment a few days after Burton and I had left our teaching posts at the Cornish School. Actors, students from the Cornish Players, theatre workers, and other local artists interested in founding a community theatre had come to cast their lot with ours in developing an acting-producing ensemble similar to the Abbey Players or Eva Le Gallienne's Civic Repertory at the old Forty-ninth Street Theatre in New York. We had nothing but our vitality and our faith in people, but we were determined to create a theatre in which the artist's integrity would stand above monetary considerations, a theatre that would truly belong to the community because it came from the community. In the two years since that Sunday, we felt that we had made a good beginning. We had an excellent nucleus of a company, constantly augmented by new people from the community who believed as we did and were willing to work to achieve it. We had produced fifteen plays, ranging from Seán O'Casey, Henrik Ibsen, and Luigi Pirandello to the works of three new home-grown playwrights, Garland Ethel, Albert Ottenheimer, and Marianne King.

We gave the public quality theatre and they responded with support, interest, and enthusiasm. However, in spite of our growing success with the public, our first two years were an accountant's nightmare and we operated with a constant deficit—a steadily decreasing deficit, it's true, but a deficit all the same. But we had hopes that in our own theatre, with a firm base of operation, we could eventually put the Playhouse in the black.

If I could have looked into the future that night, I would have seen no end to the red ink, which perhaps should not have come as a surprise, given the state of America's, and more particularly the theatre's, economy. But the eddies of financial disaster that rippled across the country from Wall Street's crash in 1929 were slow to reach the western coast and we wanted to believe that, as the politicians and the press kept telling us, prosperity lay just around the corner. We signed a ninety-nine-year lease, beginning October 1, 1930, and terminating September 30, 2029.

If I had known what lay ahead, I might have slammed the theatre doors in the faces of our arriving audience and chosen a different path. But if we hadn't gone ahead, so many good things would never have been: excellent productions of fine plays that deserved to be done well for receptive audiences; achievements, as a group and as individuals, that would be a source of lasting pride and have far-reaching consequences; joy in the development of sensitivity and responsiveness in the thousands of people who were our audiences over the years; and, most important, proof that a theatre of the people, by the people, and for the people not only *could* live and flourish but did, in the perhaps improbable setting of Seattle, Washington.

I had no time that night to think of any of those things. My mind was full of the present, and it was chaotic enough to keep me fully occupied.

Eight-thirty was upon us, and we still couldn't raise the curtain. Some kind of feud was raging among the electricians, building code authorities, and the fire department and had been for months. What one approved, the others promptly disapproved. The bedlam that this infighting engendered was still raging backstage. Electricians were installing lighting equipment, and fire inspectors were haranguing over code books. At the height of the frenzy, with the lounge and foyer crowded with patrons, spilling through the arched French windows into the flagstone courtyard around our elm tree, an electrician accidentally set fire to the building with his blowtorch!

While Burton, in costume and full makeup, battled backstage to bring order out of chaos, I mingled with our guests, apologizing for the delay, accepting their admiring praise for the wonders that our architect had wrought from an abandoned warehouse. We were all proud of the way the new Playhouse looked. Arthur Loveless, working from Burton's original sketches on a restaurant napkin, had created a building shaped like a short-barred "U," with its arms embracing our outdoor courtyard. The brick walls, natural wood trim, and dark tile and concrete floors had a simple elegance and were functional at the same time. It was an excellent place in which to work, and audiences said that it was welcoming and friendly.

I was dressed, as I always was for opening nights in our theatre, in a new evening gown, this time of blue crêpe de chine. I remember that it was very smart—and very inexpensive. I've always felt that opening nights are occasions deserving of one's very best, so I always made sure that I had elegant dresses, but that they cost as little as possible. Our budget wouldn't permit anything else. Opening nights in our theatre were always "dress up" occasions for our audiences too, especially in the early years.

The curtain finally rose, one hour late, and *Major Barbara* greeted the playgoers of Seattle. A deathly white glare illuminated the stage, for there had been no time to set lights or fix gels in the screens. We had no dimmer board. There were only two lighting levels that night: "on" and "off."

Somehow, in spite of everything, the show was a success. The *Seattle Post-Intelligencer* was out front, photographing the audience with flash bulbs, then a brand new invention, replacing the old flash powder and pan. The next day, a large picture of our patrons appeared on the front page of the morning paper, alongside a review that praised the actors and gave a short history of the group's development as well as glowing descriptions of the audience.

As we drove home that night, Burton and I were exhausted but elated. I can remember the great sense of relief that at last we were in our theatre, and that we had actually got it open. We had perhaps an inkling, but no real comprehension, of the bewildering challenges that lay ahead.

But we knew where we were going, with the brick-and-mortar fact of the building now a reality. And where we were going had been, in a very large measure, predicated by what we had come from.

CHAPTER TWO

For all of us, there are conscious and subconscious forces that prompt us to make decisions that develop into a pattern, a "habit of living." In some lives, it is fairly easy to trace the inherited or environmental pressures that create such patterns. From my vantage point in time, it is easy to identify the pressures that shaped my husband, Burton Wakeley James, and me, Mary Florence Bean James, and led to our lives taking the course they did.

Perhaps the greatest influence when I was young was my mother's attitude toward education. She craved it, revered it, and coveted it, although she never quite achieved it, and she passed her longing and loving along to me. My mother's parents, Thomas and Mary Hayney Lynch, were Irish immigrants. They settled in Cleveland in 1869 when mother was five, and my grandfather worked on the iron ore docks as a day labourer. He was completely illiterate until after he married my grandmother, who had some education, having been put in an orphanage after her parents died within a few days of each other during the potato famine in the 1840s. She taught my grandfather to read, but he never succeeded in writing more than his own name.

The family moved to Nebraska around 1878, when mother was not quite fourteen. They homesteaded a few miles from Lincoln and my mother spent her girlhood in a sod house. There was no school in their district so her education came to an abrupt end, something she regretted all her life. But she didn't give up. She was sure that there must be a way to get the education she felt was the most important thing in life. In her late teens, she decided to strike out on her own. One day, she was in Lincoln with her father, who was selling corn. They had lunch at the hotel and she heard the manager, Mr. Criley, tell my grandfather that he'd like to staff his dining room with waitresses, if he could get them, to replace his Negro waiters. When her father left, my shy mother returned and said, "Mr. Criley, I'd like to be a waitress, if I could learn how to do it."

Mr. Criley countered with, "Mary, do you think you could get some other girls to come too?" If she could recruit enough of her friends to staff his dining room, he would pay them three dollars a week, plus board and room. Delighted with the idea of making so much money, which she could save to go to school, she went back to the farm, recruited a number of her friends, and returned to Mr. Criley with the girls.

Remembering my mother's unassertive nature and strict Irish Catholic upbringing, I have never ceased to wonder at her determination and audacity. In those days well-brought-up girls left the parental roof before marriage only in cases of dire necessity. But mother's desire for an education spurred her on.

I can remember my grandfather saying, with awe in his voice, "He's an educated man," or, "If you have an education, you can talk to kings." Education was not easy to come by, and for people like my parents, it was almost an impossibility. Knowing that she was saving for an education did not, however, lessen my grandfather's displeasure at his daughter's venture into the working world. But she did it anyway.

One spring day, Mr. Criley announced that he was going to manage a hotel at a summer resort in Soda Springs, Idaho. Would the girls from the dining room like to come with him, just for the summer? The girls were delighted.

I don't know how delighted they were when they arrived, for a grimmer summer resort could hardly be imagined. The Idanha Hotel was a big old wooden building with cupolas, painted white, appropriate hotel-fashion for those days, and stuck out in the middle of the sagebrush. It did, however, have a soda spring nearby, and provided a new vista for mother and her friends, who had never been more than a few miles from home before.

Before the summer at Soda Springs was over, Mr. Criley was offered the managership of the railroad hotel in the newly formed town of Pocatello, Idaho, and asked the girls if they wanted to go with him. At that point there was nothing in Pocatello but the railroad shop, a few houses the railroad had built along its one street, and the railroad hotel.

Mother and the girls decided to take the adventure being offered them and went with Mr. Criley. Mother said the girls were so homesick after a short while in the little frontier town that when boxcars marked "Omaha" came through the station, they'd rush out on the platform and kiss them! But then my father came to town, and mother's homesickness vanished, as did her long-cherished dream of getting an education.

The man who was to become my father was the youngest son of James and Harriet Harvey Bean, English immigrants who settled in West Medford, Massachusetts, a little out of Boston. In England they had been servants on an estate—grandfather a gardener, and grandmother a meat cook. They realized that the only future their children could hope for in England would be in the servant class, so they migrated to America, seeking better opportunities for them. They prospered, and my father, the youngest, was given an education and graduated from the Massachusetts Institute of Technology.

Father had been christened Arthur Benjamin Bean—Arthur by his sisters, who had read Tennyson's "Idylls of the King," and Benjamin because he was the youngest of nine children and the only one born in the United States. He was always called Ben, or, in later years, "A.B."

Following Horace Greeley's admonition "Go west, young man, go west," father and his brother James, who was a doctor, went west as far as Pocatello, where father went to work in the railroad shop. He was also the Pocatello postmaster on a part-time basis. All he had to do was run and grab the sack of mail when the train came through, so it doesn't seem to have been too demanding a job.

Father and his brother were batching somewhere in town, but they took their meals at the hotel and before long Mary Lynch had become engaged to Ben Bean and had to go back home to Nebraska to tell her parents. They were horrified. In 1890 it was a shocking step for an Irish Catholic to marry an English Protestant—and her not even in the family way!

I never knew my English grandparents, but I knew and loved my Irish grandfather, who eventually came to accept his Protestant son-in-law. This was something of a minor miracle, because if there was one thing my Irish grandsire was anti, it was the British. He ranked George Washington with his Irish heroes Robert Emmet and Wolfe Tone because he "beat the devil out of the British." During the Boer War, grandfather Lynch raised funds to send young Irishmen to fight with the Boers against the British in South Africa. It wasn't that he was pro-Dutch because of William of Orange and the Battle of the Boyne—he was anti-British. He used to say that if the British were in trouble, he'd be for the troublemakers.

This was the somewhat formidable parent from whom my father-to-be was to request his beloved's hand, a meeting I can't imagine he looked forward to. But Fate took a hand in the proceedings. A "road agent," as they called them then, robbed the Post Office, and father had to use all his savings to make good the loss. He couldn't get to Lincoln, and Mother came back to Pocatello to marry him.

Her wedding dress, of dove-grey silk faille, was scuffed almost to the waist by the sagebrush as she walked to the church, where her marriage ceremony was performed by Father Cyril Van der Donckt, a Belgian priest. Father Van der Donckt acted as my godfather at my christening two years later, for my parents knew no other men in the area who were Catholics.

I was the eldest child in the family—the first non-Indian girl baby in Pocatello, born on October 27 in 1892 when mother was twenty-eight, named Mary because there's always at least one Mary in any Catholic family and it's usually the eldest girl. I was also named Florence because of the kindness shown to mother by Aunt Flora, the wife of father's brother Frank, who seems to have been the black sheep of the family. There I was, Mary Florence Bean. Mother used to say that I was a most unsatisfactory baby, especially for a first child, in that I didn't want to be rocked or cuddled, or, as my mother said, be a baby at all.

She had Harriet eleven months after I was born, and Grace eleven months after Harriet. Harriet Elizabeth was named after father's mother and sister, and her naming almost gave my Irish grandfather apoplexy. "Harry??" he shouted, "*And* Elizabeth???"

Later, she lost a baby boy and, when I was ten, had Ruth, who died of influenza in 1919 when she was sixteen. James, the final child in the family, arrived when I was eleven.

Mother and I were always companionable, and she was an important influence during my formative years. As a very young child, any coin I came by (and it could never have been more than a nickel) was spent for what I called a "lesson book." These were coloured ABC books: "A is for Apple, B is for Book, C is for Cat," and so on. I have a vivid memory of my pleasure in these books, and of my mother teaching me. Our companionship continued through my grade school and high school days, when I would come home to help with the household tasks and tell her what had happened during the day. Grades meant a great deal in our home, and it was a disappointment to me when I had to tell mother that I was not at the head of my class.

I went first to Pocatello Public School and then to the Academy of Idaho, now the university. The Academy had been built to provide high school classes to out-of-town students from the farms or small towns where there were no high schools. I loved going there, although it meant I had to walk a mile and a quarter through the sagebrush. After school, I would wait in the girls' washroom until my chattering classmates left so that I could walk home alone, with the pink snow in winter, the smell of the sagebrush in spring and fall. In a certain light, on the hills surrounding the town you could see the rim of the ancient inland sea, which has now shrunk to the dimension of the Great Salt Lake in Utah.

When I was a child, I remember seeing what we called the "old Indian stones." Near the Portneuf River, there were more than six acres of these lava stones, covered with pictographs. Some people said they might have predated the inland sea. As a young woman, home on a visit, I asked my father what had happened to them. He laughed. "You and Dr. Minnie Howard," he said.

Dr. Minnie Howard was a remarkable person, disadvantaged by being a woman doctor in a small town in those days, but with a vision. She cared about the "old Indian stones" and had struggled for years to preserve at least some of them and to have the land on which they lay turned into a park. When, at my father's suggestion, I went to see her, she was amazed that anyone else would remember the stones or would care about them. She pointed to two stones in the fireplace of her home. "That's what's left."

When the Pocatello Library was being built, Dr. Howard tried to get the authorities to place some of the stones in the basement of the building, so that at least a few of them would be preserved. It wasn't done and the stones were eventually smashed to make foundations for houses being built near the river. Years later, the Smithsonian Institute sent someone out to ask about the stones but all that was left for them to see were Dr. Howard's photographs and the two stones in her fireplace.

As I look back on my childhood, it seems to have been pleasant enough to be a child on the frontier in those days. We were brought up as ladies, of course, in dress, language, and behaviour. We were not allowed to ride horses, for the only horses available were broncos and riding them would not have been ladylike. Our upbringing was not permissive, but we were permitted lots of things, as long as they fit the pattern of ladylike behaviour.

An education and the "finer things" fit with my mother's plans for the proper upbringing of a young lady. One of the most wonderful of the "finer things" came in my early years, when Pocatello acquired a library! The Women's Literary Club had to raise $1,500 in order to tap the Carnegie Library Fund, and as quite a little girl I used to go to "book parties," clutching a dime and a spoon to pay for and devour ice cream and strawberries, and a children's book, which was to go on the shelves in our new library. It seemed wonderful to me that there was to be a place where you would be able to go and get books, just for the asking. The ladies raised their money and the building was built, but the shelves were mostly empty until long after I had left home to go to school in Boston.

We always had music in our home, because mother had a lovely, untrained voice and loved to sing. When she was a girl, the farmers around grandfather's farm used to remark that often, in the still of evening, they would stop and listen to Mary Lynch's clear young voice, drifting across the quiet fields. I didn't inherit my mother's voice, but I did inherit her love of music and the feeling that there were things in life worth having besides the ones that you could touch and hold.

Mother's feelings were a nice counterpoint to Father's, which were very much concerned with things that could be touched and held because he was turning himself into a successful businessman. Early in the 1890s, he and some of his friends set up a hardware store, which he managed, ultimately buying out his partners. He sold stoves and heaters, and when people began installing central heating, he set up what we called a "tin shop" to make the parts necessary for the installations.

Father also sold bicycles and had an early faith in the future of the automobile, becoming Ford's agent for that north-western area. The day father's first Ford car arrived, he took it into the carriage house of the barn and dismantled it completely, with my brothers and sisters and I permitted to stand in the doorway and watch the process. He had to know not only how the thing ran, but why.

He was perhaps sometimes too much of a perfectionist. I can remember my mother, swathed in linen duster and veil, waiting patiently on the porch while father worked at the car in the garage because it was making some sort of funny noise and he refused to drive a car that wasn't running smooth as silk. Mother would say, wistfully, "I do hope we get a ride today." Some days we did, and some we didn't.

Eventually, father built a garage in partnership with a Mr. Trist, the only garage able to service cars between Ogden, Utah, and Butte, Montana. He also dabbled in farming and bought forty acres right outside town at ten dollars an acre, hired some Chinese people to work the farm, and grew the Idaho potato, which was just being introduced then.

With all his enterprises, it was perhaps inevitable that father would get into politics. He was mayor of Pocatello for three terms: two terms when I was a child, and again when I was away at school. The 1922 crash damaged his hard-earned fortunes, and the 1929 one wiped him out. But in my teens, he was well able to afford the tuition to send his eldest daughter to the Academy of Idaho, a kindness that was to have a profound effect on the rest of my life, for it was at the Academy that I met a very special teacher, who was the single most decisive factor in turning me toward a career in the theatre.

I remember my mother one evening, reading the newspaper under the lamp. "Listen—next year they are going to have classes in public speaking and oral expression at the Academy." We knew what public speaking was, but oral expression? Never mind—it sounded educational and even ladylike.

Public speaking and oral expression were taught by Miss Alice Daly, who had her degree from the University of Minnesota and was a graduate of the Emerson College of Oratory in Boston. She must have had more than a touch of the pioneering spirit to have come to teach in this rather new institution in a frontier town. Later in life, she ran as the Farmer-Labor Party candidate for governor of the state of South Dakota and made a career for herself in public life, but during my years at the Academy, Alice Daly was a passionate and dedicated educator, who took up and carried on the moulding process begun by my mother.

We had a study room at school that was intended to be a library; the shelves were in place, but there were no books. When Miss Daly discovered this lack, she immediately sent back east for her own collection. They came in due time, packed in wooden crates, and I was allowed to help unpack them. What a thrill—books! As there was no librarian at the school, Miss Daly kept the volumes in her room and looked after them herself, but any student who was interested and responsible had unlimited access to them. Later, when I got to Boston and Emerson College, I found that my background in literature was as good as any of my classmates, all because of the influence and opportunities provided by this one teacher.

She also established a literary society. We met once a month to make speeches, read poems, and just talk. These were dress-up affairs, held in the evening. Once a year, she arranged for the best material that had come out during these sessions to be presented in a public performance for the whole school. Not satisfied with these endeavours, she organized a kind of Chautauqua, based on the adult education program popular then. She rented the local opera house and brought in play readers, male quartets, lecturers—all of a very high standard and engaged through the Ellison-White Lyceum Bureau in Boston. As there was no radio in those days and few gramophones, these programs were the only opportunity we had to hear anything other than humdrum conversation about day-to-day concerns.

Miss Daly did all this on her own. She canvassed the town, selling five programs for five dollars to pay for the performances and other expenses involved in getting them on. She was a dynamo, an inspiration, a catalyst for change in our community and in my life. When the time came for me to graduate from the Academy, my mind was made up. I was going to Miss Daly's *alma mater*, Emerson College in Boston.

Emerson College of Oratory had been founded in 1880 by Dr. Charles Wesley Emerson as a school of oral interpretation, in the belief that "communication and expression are important for the development of the individual within himself and within his role in the community."

In my day, Emerson granted no degrees, only diplomas for the completion of the two- and three-year courses. My parents raised this as an objection to my going to Emerson. They wanted me to have a degree. But my mind was made up, and even then I could talk a good case.

I spoke first to my mother. As always, in any important decision, her reply was, "You will have to talk to your father." In my mind's eye, I can still vividly see the night I decided to tackle him with my problem. He was sitting on the steps of the back porch, smoking his cigar and watching his garden grow. He seemed relaxed, so I seized what looked like a propitious moment.

"Father, I want to go to Emerson College next year. It's in Boston, so I won't be far from Aunt Lizzie." My father, a true Victorian in his attitude toward his children, was a trifle formidable. "Have you talked to your mother?"

"Yes, and she says I have to talk to you."

He went on smoking. "What do you expect to do with this education?"

"I want to be a teacher like Miss Daly. Or maybe" (this a little under my breath) "a reader of plays."

He had heard some of the readers that Miss Daly had brought out in the Lyceum programs, so he knew about play-reading. Thank goodness Emerson didn't stress actor training or theatre techniques—or any of those things. I am sure I could never have glossed over them sufficiently to overcome my father's objections. In 1911 well-brought-up young women did not go on the stage, which was considered much too hazardous an occupation. My parents were aware of some of the great actors and actresses—Richard Mansfield and Madame Modjeska had played in the opera house in Pocatello and mother and father had seen them. But Mansfield and Modjeska were a world apart from our lives, and my parents hadn't the slightest idea of how they had gotten where they were.

Finally, father said, "We'll think it over. We'll see." After the interview, my mother asked, "What did your father say?" "He didn't say no!"

As the summer drew on, it was somehow decided that I was to be allowed to go to Emerson College in Boston. One beautiful day, my father presented me with a train ticket to Boston, with the strict injunction that I was not to lose it, to telegraph as soon as I reached Boston, and "Don't talk to strangers." It was the fall of 1911, and I was almost nineteen.

Although I had worked, waited, and prayed for that ticket, I had some misgivings about leaving Pocatello for the east. I was sad to leave my family and Miss Daly, and also to bid farewell to another friend who had had a great deal to do with my awakening interest in the arts. This was a young man I had met through Alice Daly—Alex Murray, a nephew of Jim Murray, the Butte, Montana, millionaire. The senior Murray owned the Pocatello waterworks and various other public enterprises, including the Opera House, and his nephew Alex had been sent out to manage his uncle's affairs.

Alex was wholly unlike any other young man in town. He had money, he had attended the Pennsylvania Academy of Fine Arts, he had a well-stocked library, and he knew about painting, music, and drama. Seven or eight years older than me, he was fascinating and charming, and we found a great deal of pleasure in each other's company. So much so that when I was seventeen and Alex proposed, I accepted him.

For the next two years, I had a wonderful time, reading Alex's books, having long and animated discussions with Alex and Miss Daly about the arts, and, of course, attending every concert, lecture, and performance at the Opera House. As the fiancée of the manager, who was responsible for booking all the touring theatrical companies, I had access to everything that appeared. And I made the most of it.

But when the time came to make a choice between marrying this very nice, eminently eligible young man and continuing my education, I realized that I would never be satisfied until I had gone as far as I could along the road I had chosen. So I broke my engagement and boarded the train that was to take me, for the very first time, away from the familiar and the comfortable.

CHAPTER TWO

I HAVE NEVER FORGOTTEN the excitement, the thrill of my first year in Boston. Emerson College was on Massachusetts Avenue, across the street from the great Boston Public Library, with its Edwin Abbey pictures of the Holy Grail, and Puvis de Chavannes murals, and the books, the books! There were the historic sites: Old North Church, Faneuil Hall, the Boston Common, and the Symphony Hall. The opera house and the art museum were built during my stay there.

The top balcony in Symphony Hall was open to patrons, mostly students, on Saturday afternoons for twenty-five cents. You had to stand in line with the exact coin ready to be dropped into a bag when the doors were opened. When so many bags were filled, that was it—the balcony was full and the doors were closed.

The first concert I attended there was, for me, a painful, chaotic experience. I had never before heard a lot of instruments playing together, except for the Pocatello Town Band tootling on Main and Centre Streets on Saturday nights. There had not been anything remotely resembling music appreciation in my high school days, and any musical groups that had performed in the Opera House had been small. At my first symphony concert, I could hear neither the instruments nor the melody—there were so many of them, and they all played at the same time. I couldn't tell when the orchestra stopped one piece and started another.

Philip Hale of the *Boston Evening Transcript* wrote the program notes for the concerts. I studied them assiduously and discovered that symphonies and concertos had movements. The first symphony I ever really and truly heard was Beethoven's Fifth, one grand and glorious Friday afternoon. Karl Munch was the conductor of that great orchestra then, and it was as though a book had suddenly opened and I had just learned to read.

If an artist of the eminence of Geraldine Farrar, Madame Schumann-Heink, or John McCormack was performing, you had to get there early—very early, ten o'clock in the morning—to wait in line for balcony seats. "The Lord tempers the wind to the shorn lamb," an oft-quoted proverb says, and I sometimes wished He could have stood with us lambs clutching our quarters on the steps of Symphony Hall. Often, when the doors finally opened at 1:30 and we climbed to the balcony, the warmth of the hall overcame us, and we fell asleep until the music started. But it was all a valuable part of my eagerly sought education.

The courses at Emerson consisted of voice and speech training, body movement (i.e., gesture, based on the Dalcroze principles), interpretation, literature, and philosophy, largely rooted in the transcendentalism of Ralph Waldo Emerson. The courses in literature were particularly good, taught by professors from Harvard, Radcliffe, and Boston University. There was also a course in Restoration Drama, taught by a professor from Boston University. Looking back, I am amused to realize that we never actually read the plays we studied—we just read about them, the period, and the authors. The professor probably thought that the plays themselves were too salacious for us.

In our courses in interpretation, we were encouraged to find material that we thought interesting. I discovered the prose poems of Oscar Wilde. I thought they were beautiful, and I prepared and read three of them for interpretation class. I felt that I had done a good job and fully expected approval of my choice of material, and perhaps of my interpretation as well.

When I finished, I looked expectantly at my teacher. Her face was a mask. She dismissed me with a curt, "That will be all, Miss Bean." After class, she called me to her desk and informed me in hushed but firm tones that *no one* read Oscar Wilde. He had committed a terrible crime and been sent to prison for it. She gave me not the slightest inkling of what his crime might have been, though she did tell me that he had written a poem about it, "The Ballad of Reading Gaol."

I went home in complete confusion and read the poem, trying to discover what crime this marvellous writer could have committed, so terrible that it could not be mentioned, so dreadful that he had actually gone to jail for it. There was no clue in the poem, and I went to my room in tears of frustration. It wasn't until much later that the mystery of Oscar Wilde was explained to me. It didn't diminish my admiration for the man's genius or his poetry.

My education and my religion once came into conflict. I was doing my Easter duty, as a good Catholic girl, and in the confessional I happened to mention something to the priest about Balzac. His voice was scandalized. "My dear child, you can't read Balzac. It's on the Index!" I had never heard of the Index. "But Father," I tried to explain to him,

"It's my education." Education or no education, he refused to give me absolution unless I promised never to read Balzac again, and concluded by stating flatly that I was guilty of "a sin against the Holy Ghost."

I left the confessional in tears and stumbled home along Hemingway Parkway, crying all the way. That evening, we had what we called a "silver thaw." The trees were covered with icicles, and in the light wind, they rattled like bones. A sombre setting for my dilemma. I just could not believe that there were some books that were considered forbidden reading by my religion, or that the Holy Ghost would want to interfere with my education.

When I didn't go up for communion on Easter Sunday, a devout Catholic friend had to know why. She was furious with me and the priest for making an issue out of what was, to her, a perfectly simple matter. "We'll go out to the Redemptorist Fathers and see what they have to say about this," she declared.

So we travelled on a streetcar to the Mission in Roxbury. An old priest with white hair and kindly blue eyes listened, through my sobs, to the whole story. He didn't say a word about Balzac, or about my sin against the Holy Ghost. He simply said, "Kneel down, my child, and I'll give you absolution."

So, I was back in the fold. The following Sunday, my friend and I went to Holy Communion. But the golden bowl was broken, and I continued to read Balzac. I think that this must have been the first time in my life when I acted entirely on my own convictions, contrary to the authority of so formidable a body as my church.

I graduated from Emerson in 1914, and feeling well-equipped, began to look for a teaching position. I quickly found that, with worries about war everywhere, few schools were hiring teachers for public speaking and oral expression. World War I, when it started in August 1914, was considered strictly a European folly and was expected to last only a few months—"the boys will be out of the trenches by Christmas"—and, of course, we Americans would not be directly involved (or so we thought at the time).

Because of the war situation, my parents let me go back to Emerson to complete my postgraduate work. It was a very good thing that I did, for once again Fate took a hand in shaping my future's course and destiny.

There were few boys at Emerson then, but I had little time for them anyway. I was there for only one reason, and it had nothing to do with boys or teas or football weekends. One day my roommate came to me in great excitement. "Beany, you've got to do me a great favour. Please take me into Mrs. Black's class at eleven o'clock."

As an upperclassman, I was permitted to go into other people's classes to watch the teachers. But I was puzzled by my roommate's sudden enthusiasm for extra work. "Why on earth do you want to go?"

"Burton James is going to read Browning, and I simply *have* to hear him."

"Who is Burton James?"

She despaired of my vagueness about the important things in life. "Oh, Beany, he's that new boy all the teachers are talking about. They say he's so talented. And he's certainly good-looking."

So we went to Mrs. Black's class at eleven. There, for the first time, I saw Burton James and heard him read Browning's "In a Gondola." He was talented, there was no doubt about it, with a magnificent voice and a sensitive understanding of his material. And he was definitely good-looking, not tall, but slim and proudly erect, with a grace of carriage that always made him look elegant in anything he wore. His resemblance to the Barrymores made him squirm throughout his life, but I always thought, rather, that the Barrymores resembled Burton.

Sitting in that classroom, watching and listening, I knew exactly what I had to do. Shakespeare was right—Portia, Juliet, Helena, Viola, all had picked their men. I had picked mine. How far wrong can you go when Shakespeare gives direction? I set out on my new course of action with the same thorough concentration that I had been applying to the acquiring of an education.

Each Sunday, my sorority sisters at the Zeta Phi Eta house held a tea. There were refreshments in the parlour, and the young ladies' boyfriends came and brought their friends, so that the young people could meet under properly chaperoned conditions. I had never had any interest in any of it. I was bored with teas, didn't want to meet anyone, and always had a ready excuse—I had to visit my Aunt Lizzie in West Medford on Sunday afternoons.

The Sunday after the reading, I heard that one of my sorority sisters was bringing Burton James to tea. I conveniently forgot my familial obligation to Aunt Lizzie and rushed to get dressed. One of my sorority sisters popped into the room while I was getting ready, and stared at me in amazement. "*You're* coming to the tea?"

I tried to be very nonchalant. "Yes, I thought I might just put in an appearance."

She looked at me narrowly. "I'll bet you're coming to meet Burton James." So much for my skills as an actress.

We met that Sunday, which was just around Christmas, and the rest of the winter was sheer bliss. We went to the Lowell lectures and heard Alfred Noyes and Robert Frost read their poetry. Burton helped me stage the scenes and plays I was doing in my postgraduate course. We went to concerts and the theatres and sat in the gallery for fifty cents. Everything that played New York played Boston, so we had marvellous fare.

The Boston Opera House had been built by this time, and we heard Enrico Caruso in *Rigoletto*, John McCormack in *La Bohème*, Mary Garden and Vanni Marcoux in *Tosca.* We saw Nijinsky dance Debussy's *Afternoon of a Faun* and Sergei Diaghilev's production of *The Spectre of the Rose.* I don't remember what we paid for tickets for those performances, but we managed. I do remember that in those days I insisted that I pay my own way because, although Burton's father was very rich, he refused to help in his son's pursuit of "that crazy stuff." Mr. James senior "couldn't see any sense in that theatre business."

In spite of our instant affinity, and the many hopes and dreams we shared, Burton had come from a background far different from mine. He was the only son of Jennie Culver and Frederick Keller James. Frederick James, a farm boy from around Peekskill, New York, trained as a pharmacist and did very well in his profession, eventually operating a chain of twelve or fourteen drugstores in New York City and Brooklyn. Burton's mother came from a long line of Methodist ministers and bishops. Along the way a hatter from Danbury, Connecticut, and a sea captain (whose sea chest I still have) managed to get into the line, but to Burton's mother, relatives like that were specks in the clear amber of "family." They hadn't come over on the *Mayflower*, she admitted, but they had certainly arrived very shortly afterward. When Burton and I were living in New York and would go to the theatre with Mother

James, she would survey the audience with distaste and remark, much too audibly, I always thought, "There are very few of us left."

As soon as he was able to count change and carry a package, Burton became an errand boy in his father's store. As a young man, he was a clerk, after school, on weekends, and through the summer holidays. His father was training Burton to take over the business, but a less-likely prospect could scarcely be imagined. Burton told me much later of some of the business practices that appalled him, and of the tongue-lashings he got from his father for not seeing that they were necessary in order to make a profit. His father's efforts and example succeeded only in turning Burton away from the drugstore business and into other channels.

Burton's first acting experience occurred when he graduated from Public School 166 on West 89th Street in New York. He took part in a "dialogue" written by one of his teachers, a Mr. Gluck, playing the adolescent counterpart of Father Knickerbocker to another lad's equally cut-down William Penn. He said later that that was when he was really bitten by the acting bug.

With his mother's approval, and his father's accidental assistance, Burton became an avid theatregoer. Mr. James often received "comps" in return for the space he gave to playbills and posters in his stores and Burton made good use of them. He saw Joe Jefferson in *Rip Van Winkle*, Mrs. Leslie Carter in *Zaza* and practically everything else she did at Belasco's theatre, and Maude Adams in Barrie's *Peter Pan* and *The Little Minister*. But perhaps the most memorable was at Hammerstein's theatre—*A Night in an English Music Hall*, which included a young comedian with dark waves of hair surmounting a sensitive, plaintive face, who was listed on the program as Charles Chaplin.

Not all the influences on Burton's formative years were cultural and theatrical. A very important contribution was made by a Sunday School teacher named George C. Johns, who was in large measure responsible for Burton acquiring the technical skills that were to stand him in such good stead in his future life in the theatre. Mr. Johns believed that the road to personal freedom and economic security lay in the scientific and technical professions—young boys should acquire knowledge of practical technical skills at an early age, along with book learning. So he arranged for his boys to be taken on as helpers or apprentices in a variety of skilled mechanical crafts during their free time and vacations.

By this time Jennie and Frederick James had separated and Burton had stayed with his mother, so he was no longer required to work in his father's drugstore and could participate in Mr. Johns' plan during his high school days. He worked in electrical workshops, steam-fitting concerns, and hydraulic plants, acquiring a surprising amount of knowledge about some of these operations. When Mr. Johns decided that Burton had had enough education in the mechanical aspects, he decreed that science should be the next step. One of Burton's real interests at DeWitt Clinton High School was biology, so Mr. Johns got him a job at the Carnegie Institute, in its huge station for experimental evolution at Cold Spring Harbor on Long Island.

Charles Benedict Davenport was working there at the time, carrying out his monumental investigations into the laws of heredity, and Burton worked as body servant to a motley menagerie of frizzled chickens, fruit flies, ladybugs, and crickets. When you are a very small part of a vast establishment, all of whose great resources are bent toward changing a single vein in the dorsal wing of a minute fruit fly, you come face to face with the scientific attitude.

By the time Burton finished high school, his father had realized that whatever Burton was to be, he would never be a pharmacist or a businessman. His mother and grandmother had held some hopes of a life in the church, since his great-grandfather Wakeley had been presiding elder of the Methodist Newburgh Conference, but that seemed out, too. The theatre, of course, was never even mentioned, although attitudes in the family had relaxed a bit by that time and theatre was no longer referred to as "the vestibule to Hell."

What Burton really wanted, even then, was to be an actor. In his father's store at 46th and Broadway, in the heart of the theatre district, he had met all the greats and near-greats of the theatre, and his family doctor was a close relative of one of the best-known theatrical agents in New York so he would have had plenty of contacts. But family attitudes were still strong enough to preclude any possibility of even discussing such a thing. The theatre was not the place for a boy with his religious background and family position. Besides, it offered a precarious livelihood and no real economic security. Burton had an eye for colour, a knack for drawing, and loved the out-of-doors and growing things. So at eighteen, he entered Cornell University for a five-year course in landscape architecture.

In 1907, landscape architecture at Cornell had not settled into a defined area and it was unclear whether it was involved mainly with architecture or agriculture. Burton's courses included, besides architecture and architectural drawing, such varied and oddly assorted classes as cheese-making, gasoline engines, agronomy, farm mechanics, and knot-tying. He was not receiving any money from his father to pay for his education, as the senior James refused to have any part in "this foolishness," so he had to finance his own way with part-time work and vacation jobs. One of the most rewarding of these jobs was in the Pierson greenhouses at Scarborough and Briarcrest, New York. The Pierson brothers were noted horticulturalists, specializing in roses. They created the lovely Killarney variety and were the largest growers of the American Beauty in the country.

In later years, Burton's rose garden in Seattle was the envy of his neighbours, who frequently consulted him with their own gardening problems. I was his horticultural joe-boy, and he was a martinet when it came to his garden. His experience with Dr. Davenport and the Piersons would admit of no slipshod techniques. I took a dim view of roses, and still do. Like lovely, pampered beauties, they impressed me as needing, and getting, more care and attention than anything else in the garden. And if they didn't get it, they promptly went into a decline.

Landscaping was always one of Burton's interests. He loved all aspects of gardening and was always delighted to give advice or provide help to anyone who needed it. Once, one of our board members at the Playhouse in Seattle had built a house and was trying to do the landscaping himself. He was having problems, so Burton went out to give him a hand. He drew up a plan for the garden, but even then the job proved too much for the gentleman, who called in a professional landscapist to follow Burton's plan.

The professional looked at the design and said, "This is excellent. Who drew it up?"

When our friend replied, "Burton James," the landscapist said, "Burton James, the actor? My God, the things people learn in theatres!" Burton often said that he had never learned anything, except possibly cheese-making, that he could not profitably use for his own benefit and pleasure, and that of others.

His last job as a professional landscape architect was in 1913, with the widely known firm of Townsend and Fleming in Buffalo, New York. Mr. Fleming had been head of the school of landscape architecture at Cornell when Burton was there, and he set his former student to work putting in rockeries, gardens, pools, and walls. Burton, however, soon found another attraction in Buffalo that exerted a more powerful pull.

He began trying out for parts in the productions of the Studio Club, later called the Buffalo Studio Theatre, directed by Jane Keeler. Many of these, such as Percy Mackaye's *Sanctuary: A Bird Masque*, involved works by local authors, but Burton also did an assortment of readings and dramatizations of Robert Browning. His partner in one of the latter, a he/she rendition of "In a Gondola," was the teenage daughter of the manager of a small Buffalo movie theatre, the Majestic. She was making her first appearance on any stage, but she obviously knew even then what she wanted to do. Her name was Katharine Cornell.

This was a time when great new things were beginning to happen in the theatre. Amateurs were standing in the wings, doing things, changing things. Little theatre, community theatre, theatre for the people, theatre in out-of-the-way places, theatre for the actor, theatre for the scene designer with no actors (puppets only), theatre for the playwright—all of these theatres, generally very self-conscious and artistic, were pushing forward, putting down roots, and getting attention. They were usually held in great contempt by the commercial theatre, but they persevered, survived, and were the forerunners of today's experimental and regional theatres.

It was an exciting time to become involved with non-commercial theatre in America, and Burton heard about, or experienced firsthand, many of the new developments and met many of the people who were making them happen.

Maurice Browne and his wife, Ellen Van Volkenburg, were directing the Chicago Little Theatre, which was in the front ranks of the new movement. The Provincetown Playhouse on McDougal Street in New York gave a young playwright named Eugene O'Neill his first opportunity. When one of his later plays, *The Hairy Ape,* proved to be outstanding, it was moved to Broadway and became a commercial hit, establishing O'Neill as a playwright.

These burgeoning theatres were greatly influenced by the work of scene designer Gordon Craig, son of the famous actress Ellen Terry. Terry was Sir Henry Irving's leading lady for many years, but her son rejected the heavy, authentic sets that Irving demanded. If Sir Henry wanted the Rialto for *The Merchant of Venice*, scenery that duplicated the Rialto in Venice as nearly as possible had to be produced. Craig pushed all this aside. His dictum was no scenery, just curtains. This idea was a great boon to the rising little theatres, which had limited money and few skills in designing and constructing sets. Another of Craig's ideas was not embraced with quite as much widespread enthusiasm—he rejected actors as well as scenery. Actors got sick and were sometimes temperamental (and expensive). He wanted just marionettes. Marionettes you could control.

Before long, Burton was so thoroughly involved with the Studio Theatre that he was probably giving more of his time and attention to it than he was to his job in Townsend and Fleming's office. Mr. Fleming, a perceptive man, said to him, "Burton, landscape architecture is like theatre in a way. You have to love it a lot to like it at all. I think your real love is the theatre."

Burton came to Emerson College to get the training he felt he needed to pursue his goal. But why Emerson? Why not one of the few schools then that, unlike Emerson, taught actor training or stage techniques? While Burton might have preferred to follow Eugene O'Neill as a student in Workshop 47 at Harvard, getting into Harvard was one thing and paying the tuition costs another.

Burton had begun to save his money when he decided that theatre was to be his future, and a lady who saw his work with the Buffalo Studio Theatre gave him some scholarship money. But it was still far short of what he would need to attend Harvard. On the other hand, entrance to Emerson was quite simple and the tuition wasn't high—seventy-five dollars a term. And although Emerson didn't emphasize actor training and stage technique, it had classes in voice and speech training, body movement, and interpretation.

I wasn't the only one who was glad that Burton chose Emerson. He was an eager and enthusiastic student, the delight of teachers and classmates alike. He was imaginative and very skilful in constructing something interesting out of nothing. His brilliance—and his love—made my remaining months at Emerson joyous ones.

I graduated from my postgraduate course in May of 1915. The week of graduation, when I was to play Imogen in Shakespeare's *Cymbeline*, I was stricken with acute appendicitis and rushed to the hospital late one night for an operation. Immediately after the operation, I developed a frightening diabetic condition. Diabetes in that day, especially in the young, was inevitably terminal. Little was known about the condition, and Dr. Banting had not yet discovered insulin. My cousin Grace, Aunt Lizzie's daughter, was a diabetic and had died at twenty-two, shortly after her graduation. The parallel frightened my parents, and my father came east to be with me. It was decided that I was to stay in or near Boston to be close to the specialist in diabetes at Peter Bent Brigham Hospital.

For years, Burton had spent his summers as a counsellor to a boys' camp in Denmark, Maine. Camps for children were a new development, and this was one of the first, managed by Mr. and Mrs. C. E. Cobb. They had begun with boys' camps, and then added three camps for girls. The camps were rather primitive, though they catered to children from very upper-class homes—some of the children had nannies or companions who lived nearby in more conventional quarters, while their little charges slept in tents, went to bed with candle lanterns, and took baths in the lake. The Cobbs believed that part of the pleasure of camping was experiencing its rigours. I persuaded my father to let me go to Maine. I could get a summer position at the inn at one end of the lake, I would be close enough to Boston to keep in touch with the doctor, and the Maine air would be good for me. Father agreed and I was overjoyed when I got a job at the Inn, arranging the flowers and table appointments. Coincidentally, Burton was spending the summer at the boys' camp nine miles away at the other end of the lake.

By the time summer ended, my diabetic condition had disappeared. The doctor called it "phantom diabetes," and the only time it has flared up since then has been when I've had to stay in the hospital for some reason. Fortunately, those stays have been infrequent to say the least—four times in eighty-three years!

After our summer in Maine (during which we managed to spend a fair amount of time together, to our mutual delight), we returned to Boston, Burton to finish his year at Emerson and I to a part-time teaching job at a convent school in the Boston suburbs. We began to make plans for a future for ourselves, together, in the theatre.

To begin, we cut and arranged scenes for man-woman characters from the plays we had studied, with short introductions for background. Mrs. Whitney, one of our teachers at Emerson, was enthusiastic about the idea and, as one of the most popular readers with the Ellison-White Bureau (the same bureau that had provided my introduction to play-reading back in Pocatello), was able to introduce us to the manager. We gave an audition and he agreed that our selections would do admirably for church groups and women's clubs. The bureau produced lovely brochures for a set of such performances, which we had titled *Passers-by*, and we believed that we were really starting our careers.

We were married May 16, 1916, in Boston. Albert Lovejoy, a friend of ours from Emerson, was our best man. Burton's sister Josephine was my bridesmaid. His parents did not attend. My mother was to come east for the wedding, as Burton and I couldn't afford the trip to Pocatello, but my young brother was stricken with strep throat, so she didn't make it. My wedding, so far from my family, followed the precedent established by my mother so many years before. And I, too, had married a Protestant.

Burton and I left for Maine, to be camp superintendents at one of the girls' camps. When we returned to Boston, we found that, even with the charming brochures, our program for Ellison-White had not sold very well. They proposed that we do something with more popular appeal than *Passers-by* and suggested a cut-down version of an old melodrama, *The Old Homestead*. They wanted to include a male quartet to liven up the proceedings, and Burton and I were to act in it, while Burton did the stage-managing. The proposal looked cheap, shoddy, and commercial. We always knew what we did not want, so we decided against the venture, badly as we needed the money.

Burton was designing sets for Henry Jewett, who had taken over a new little theatre called the Toy Theatre, in Boston. Mr. Jewett now wanted Burton to design something tasteful in the way of three permanent sets for his theatre: a "woods set" that would do for all outdoor scenes, a "kitchen set" to serve for cottage scenes or homely interiors, and a "palace set" for drawing rooms, parlours, or any scene needing something elegant. This work could have led to many similar commissions, for such sets were common practice, and in that day most theatres had them. We decided, however, that a move had to be made, and that now was the time to make it, before we got too deeply committed to compromises. We agreed that our next step should be to New York, the big city, centre of all theatrical activity in the United States.

CHAPTER THREE

In September 1916 I left for New York to try my luck with acting and see what the Fates might hold. Thousands before me had done it, and thousands are still doing it. Thousands undoubtedly had the same results I had, and perhaps came to the same conclusion—that it was not for me.

After making the rounds of the theatrical agents' offices, I wrote a letter to Burton, still in Boston:

> I wish you could see the people lined up in these offices. I wish you could. They would make you shiver, such derelicts—awful! That's not what we want … The theatre is dreadful and these poor people looking for jobs in them—dreadful.
>
> Listen, today I read this sentence: "There is a time in every man's life and education when he arrives at the conviction that envy is ignorance, that imitation is suicide, that he must take himself for better or worse as his portion. Who would be a man must be a nonconformist."

This letter was in a way prophetic, for it became for us a "habit of living." Burton never sat in an agent's office. He had realized years earlier, while clerking in his father's drugstore, what I saw then in New York City's casting mills.

But we had to find some sort of work to keep us alive. Was there nothing, anywhere in New York, that we could do? Burton's sister Josephine was working as a secretary in the Lenox Hill Settlement House, then on East 69th and Avenue A. The settlements, as they were called, had grown out of an undertaking by Canon Barnett and his wife, who had set up similar institutions in a depressed slum area in London, England. They had seen the ignorance and the depression of the people of the neighbourhood and hoped to ameliorate it by providing education, a few cultural advantages, and a place where people could meet. The settlements were financed completely by donations from the well-to-do, who sat on committees or boards and directed the activities of the institution. They were sometimes called Neighborhood Houses or Community Centres, but all were established for the same purposes and operated under the same conditions.

I immediately saw them as a possibility for the use of our talents. I was so enthusiastic that I wrote to Burton immediately:

> This Lenox Hill Settlement is a perfect gold mine of opportunity for a neighborhood theatre. The people who come here are wonderful. The house is considered the very finest in the city in equipment. If you could only see what wealth is here.
>
> The house is heavily endowed, is loaded with equipment, and has absolutely nothing distinctly educational. Think what could be done if we could only get something to keep us alive, some work, perhaps our opportunity lies right here. The paid positions in the house are of course filled, but we could make a place for ourselves in a year.

So Burton joined me in New York. He brought with him all our worldly wealth: sixteen dollars and twenty-odd cents, all that was left after paying for his transportation out of the twenty-five dollars that he had raised by pawning (on my instructions) the twin-diamond engagement ring that had been my mother's and was now mine.

The first job we got was for an agency organized by a man and his wife for the relief of the starving Albanians. They had printed up brochures with pictures of the miserable plight of the Albanian people and were asking for contributions. It was our job to stuff the brochures in envelopes and send them out. The husband was away, carting wheat to the Albanians, and management of the office had been left to the wife, who, unfortunately, was prone to temper tantrums, screaming, pulling her hair, frothing at the mouth. Burton and I would come out of the office at night so shaken that we could scarcely eat.

When it seemed that both of us were bound to have nervous breakdowns, I found another job—as a file clerk and part-time switchboard operator in a brokerage office at 49 Wall Street. I'm sure I couldn't have realized what I was doing, taking a job as a Wall Street switchboard operator when the mechanics of operating a simple pencil sharpener can throw me. I discovered that the frenzy of the woman at Albanian Relief was a spring breeze compared to what happens when the market starts going up or coming down. It was an experience, as I learned to say, that I shouldn't have picked and wouldn't have missed. I witnessed the lunacy of speculators at first hand, an education for anyone.

My salary was twelve dollars a week, and at Christmas they gave me a bonus of twenty-five dollars, a real kindness since I'd only been there for a few weeks. With this blessed yuletide windfall, I went merrily out and bought a wicker chair, some pots and pans, some extra sheets, and put the remainder of the money, twelve dollars, in a safe hiding place under the shelf paper in the kitchen cupboard of our tenement apartment.

Unfortunately, in an excess of housewifely zeal while getting ready for the holidays, I cleaned the cupboards only a few days later and threw out the shelf paper, twelve dollars and all! Perhaps I knew even then that "easy come, easy go" on a field of empty pockets would be an appropriate heraldic emblem for the James family.

Our apartment was in a so-called "model" tenement in the Yorkville section, on 76th Street between Avenue A and John Jay Park, erected by the man for whom the park was named, the philanthropist grandson of the first chief justice of the United States. Mr. Jay had built it for people with tuberculosis, but when a Vanderbilt put up a better TB residence across the street, the Jay building was opened to everyone.

Our main, and largest, room was the kitchen, a comparatively spacious twelve by fifteen feet, containing sink, washtub, gas stove, kitchen cabinet, tiny closet, and our trunk with a poncho over it. There was, of course, no refrigeration (it hadn't been invented yet, or at least it hadn't reached 76th Street), but we did have a bathroom—a converted clothes closet.

The bedroom was larger than the bathroom, but smaller than the kitchen. In fact, when our friends at Settlement House kindly found us a bed we discovered that the bedroom door couldn't be shut once the bed was moved in. Burton's drawing board, balanced on the radiator, was our dressing table, and that, along with an odd chair or two and a couple of pieces of carpet, completed the furnishing of our new home.

Its main charm was the price—I believe it was three dollars a week, plus quarters for the gas meter. The cockroaches were a free bonus, and if there had been a bounty on them, we would soon have been rich. Burton puttied all the cracks he could find, and we used all manner of baits and poisons, but nothing discouraged them. When we went out in the evening, Burton would leave his slippers behind the hall door. When we came home, we would slip in quietly, grab a slipper apiece, then snap on the light and swat as many roaches as we could reach before they had time to scurry away to their hiding places. We were never very successful as pest controllers, I'm afraid.

Looking back on that particular period in our lives, it all sounds very grim and depressing, but I don't remember it being that way. We were young, healthy, optimistic, and very much in love. And we were sure that we could cope with anything.

Well, just about anything. Though I was managing to keep up with the filing at my brokerage office, the switchboard was growing more and more malevolent. Even when it was quiet, it frightened me, but when it lit up like a Christmas tree, I was a quivering mass. I could see somebody's millions going down the drain because I pulled the wrong plug. So my chief emotion was one of overwhelming relief when I was finally fired. "Let go," I believe the euphemism is. And no captive was ever happier to be let go than I was.

Soon after that, my life took another unpredictable turn. We were having dinner at the Settlement one evening and a suffragette had been invited to be one of the guests. Votes for women had become an issue in England and the United States during World War I, following not-very-quickly the introduction of the idea by John Stuart Mill in a speech at Westminster on March 30, 1867 in one of the early debates on the Reform Bill. Mill suggested that the time was ripe to give women the right to vote. The suggestion was greeted with loud guffaws from the British male, and *Punch* made good use of it in cartoons. British women—even the educated ones—quietly acquiesced to this male judgment of their inadequacies and incapacities, comforting themselves with the aphorism that "the hand that rocks the cradle rules the world." Then Emmeline Pankhurst and her daughters entered the scene.

As a student in Boston, I had heard Mrs. Pankhurst speak about women's problems in England. She was a gently spoken lady, dressed in a grey chiffon gown, carrying a bouquet of pink roses. She defended the extreme measures taken by the women of Britain in their struggle and said, "You American women can never understand the thick-headed, stubborn stupidity of the British male."

Yet in 1917, all over the North American continent, women were rising, demanding the right to vote. It didn't seem a large or unreasonable request.

I had first recognized gaining the vote for women as an issue when I was attending Emerson, and it came as a surprise to me. Women in Idaho had had the vote for years. I can't ever remember my mother not going with my father to the polls to cast her ballot. Politics were frequently discussed in our home by friends and relatives of both sexes and all ages. But in Boston, for the first time, I heard women's suffrage described as if it would be a calamitous happening for women to get the vote, or even to become involved in the suffrage movement. They would begin to frequent "grog shops," their children would land in the gutters, and home and motherhood would disappear.

I knew from my own experience that this just wasn't so. My mother was not only a good mother and a good wife, she was a responsible citizen who cherished highly and took seriously her right and obligation to steer and shape our democratic nation.

My first real bit of political education had come from her, when I was about six years old. William McKinley had defeated William Jennings Bryan to become president of the United States. We, being Westerners, had been for Bryan and against the famous "cross of gold." (Burton told me that, as a child, he had worn a "gold bug" button to indicate his family's loyalties.)

In those days, the only "hot" news we ever got in Pocatello was from the trainmen, so it was from a trainman, calling to a neighbour, that I heard, "McKinley's been shot in Buffalo, New York!" I was delighted that our "enemy" had been dispatched, and ran to tell my mother.

To my amazement, mother burst into tears. "But Mama, we didn't like him, did we?" She answered, through her tears, "Mr. McKinley is the president. We didn't want him for president, but the people elected him, and all the people have to support him. That's democracy."

I didn't know then exactly what democracy was, but I never forgot. Twenty years later, the lady at the Settlement House dinner talked of the struggle that women all across our democratic country were waging to get the right to vote. I was impressed. In New York State, they had to collect a million signatures to get suffrage on the ballot in the coming election. They were looking for people to ring doorbells and talk to women and collect signatures.

She asked if I was interested. I certainly was, and when I heard that they paid twelve dollars a week, which was what I'd been getting on Wall Street, I said "yes" right away and set out rapping on doors for the cause of women's suffrage.

We got our million signatures and had a parade from 59th Street and Fifth Avenue to Washington Square. Many men marched with us in that parade, Burton among them. Suffrage was on the ballot and won. On November 6, 1917, the women of New York State got the right to vote.

Women today, in all parts of the country, are too often careless about exercising that right. They forget, if they ever knew, the struggle that was waged to get it. Women not only marched in parades and rapped on doors, they picketed the White House, they heckled speakers, they spoke from pulpits, they got themselves arrested, and at least one was killed. When they were thrown into jail, the suffragettes were generally put in the worst section, with the most hardened of the women prisoners. They made friends of these prisoners, and when the jailers in Washington discovered that their charges were not suffering enough, they opened a rat-infested jail that had not been in use since the Civil War and put them into that. Women who had gone to jail had the privilege of wearing a little iron pin shaped like a jail gate. The fact that many of these women were socialites from the first families made little difference. When they began demanding rights that the "establishment" of the day thought they did not need and should not ask for, masculine opinion was that they had to be taught a lesson. Mrs. Pankhurst had flattered the American male.

When the franchise was granted, the first presidential candidate we voted for, in 1920, was Eugene V. Debs, who was serving a term in Atlanta Penitentiary for "obstructing" World War I. He had said that it was actually a power struggle for markets and that none of President Wilson's fourteen points, including the ideas that it was "the war to make the world safe for democracy" and "a war to end all wars," would ever be realized. The Versailles Treaty had been signed, and we could discern the scaffolding that was to support World War II.

THROUGH THE SUMMER OF 1917, which was horribly hot in New York City—so hot that the Humane Society couldn't get around fast enough to pick up all the animals that dropped in the streets, and a dead horse lay on Park Avenue in the heat until it exploded—I was employed as a sort of social worker.

Mrs. James F. Curtis, a woman of wealth and good heart, had set up a project for those prostitutes, amateur and professional, who were picked up in raids on dance halls and bawdy houses and sent for treatment for venereal diseases to City Hospital, an adjunct of Blackwell's (now Welfare) Island Prison. The "girls" ranged in age from twelve to seventy and it was my job to supervise their training in how to run a sewing machine, bring them magazines, take them for walks, and try to prepare the way at home for their reception when they were released. Although I was twenty-four and married, I was still the quite-innocent product of a sheltered Catholic home and it was a heart-wringing experience, a lot like trying to empty the ocean with a fork. The basic environmental situation could not be altered in any substantial way, the method was unorganized and unscientific, and the project never succeeded in becoming anything more than the good-will gesture of a generous woman. However, some of the "girls" I met became my friends and used to drop in at our flat from time to time, even after I had moved on to other employment.

That fall I went to work, first for the State and then the Federal Food Board, as an inspector, at the unbelievably generous salary of one hundred dollars a month. (It took me from 1928 to 1946 to get my salary at the Playhouse up that high!) Since Burton had finally been put on staff at Lenox Hill as a playground and camp supervisor, at a salary of fifty dollars a month, we felt we were finally going to be able to make ends meet.

The Federal Food Board was an agency that had been set up by the government to control profiteering in food during the war. Every morning, food prices were listed in the paper. Grocers were supposed to sell food at the prices quoted, but of course in some instances they didn't. They also resorted to dubious practices, like forcing customers to buy a large order of groceries before they could get anything that was in short supply, such as sugar. Customers would send their complaints, enclosing their bills as proof, to the Federal Food Board, and we as inspectors would go out to investigate the complaints and later testify if charges were laid. Anyone who violated the price regulations could be summonsed and fined, and many were, which seemed to exercise sufficient control to keep prices in line.

Three women and a couple of men actually did the work, but the staff also included a collection of terrible old crocks, political appointees who had been wangled into their jobs by some ward-heeler and spent most of their time sitting in the office playing cards. Our superior, a young and dedicated lawyer, depended on the five of us to get the work done. Sometimes he'd sigh, "I hate to send you women out on this complaint. It could be a rough one." (He worried more than a little about me in particular because by this time I was pregnant, making my rounds in a terribly smart maternity wardrobe loaned to me by one of the society women on the board at Lenox Hill. No one, however, ever suggested that I should remove myself from the work force or from public view because of my "condition.") He would then look around the office and say in a loud voice, tinged with resignation-blunted hope, "One of these men should do it." None of them ever did, at least not while I was there.

As a result of my war effort, I developed pneumonia and an ear infection, and was trundled off to New York's Roosevelt Hospital on 59th Street, five months pregnant, flaming with fever, and in considerable pain because my ear had been operated on at the Settlement House that afternoon. It was wartime, hospitals were understaffed, there were shortages of linens, facilities, medicines. I would like to think that they were doing the best that they could to cope, but my three weeks in

Roosevelt Hospital were exquisite torture that would require the pen of a Theodore Dreiser to describe adequately.

I was a paying patient—fourteen dollars a week, I believe—but the only bed available to me was in the huge charity ward. I didn't care. I was too sick to worry about where I was. I only wanted to get better and to keep any part of my illness from affecting my baby. The night I arrived at the hospital, a student nurse took me into an icy bathroom, where she washed my long, black hair, but neglected to dry it. Back in bed, my fever mounted, and I asked for water, which I wasn't supposed to have. Someone gave it to me, and a short while later I threw it up, all over my covers, my pillow, my bed jacket. The overworked attendants hastily wiped up the mess, but no one came to change my clothes or the bed linen. I lay that way all that night and through the next day. But when on the second night I awoke momentarily from my fevered dreams, my pillow was fresh and clean again. Someone had taken my bed jacket, washed and dried it, and spread it on the pillow in place of the soiled case. When I asked who had done this, someone said, "Mary."

I lost track of time while I slipped in and out of the delirium of fever. I was occasionally aware of people touching me, moving me, and later realized that these were the student nurses, with varying degrees of expertise. Once a day, a white-capped, stern-visaged nurse would sweep through to check the ward. I always thought she must have been kept under glass between rounds, because she was more concerned with her position as a nurse, and the appearance of the ward, than the condition of the patients.

But none of these women, whose professional responsibility it was to oversee and speed my recovery, was named Mary. It took a night straight out of Dostoevsky for me to finally meet my benefactress. I had regained enough strength to sit up a little and to totter to the bathroom and back by easy stages. This night, I had just dropped off to sleep when a hand on my shoulder shook me awake. There was thunder, the sound of rain on the windows, and pitch blackness all around me. In the momentary flash as a bolt of lightning illuminated the scene, I saw the figure of a nurse beside my bed, holding out a bathrobe.

"Go sit in the diet kitchen. Quickly."

Dizzy and still half asleep, I wondered what was happening, where the lights were, and what the keening and screaming were from the other end of the ward. But my mind began to clear as I moved slowly and gingerly down the ward, using the ends of the beds for support in the darkness, to the little diet kitchen. I realized that the spring thunderstorm must have caused a power failure and that at least one of the patients in the ward was dying, for part of the noise was the tearful intoning of the litany by two women holding flickering candles near an unscreened bed, and part was an old Jewish woman at the other end of the ward, loudly reciting the Hebrew prayers for the dead.

After what seemed like a very long time, I made it to the diet kitchen and collapsed shakily into a rickety old kitchen chair, clutching the hospital bathrobe around me. The eerie uproar in the ward had increased, as an elderly Irish woman left her bed to screech and shout at the Jewish woman, in an effort to stop her noise. I gritted my teeth and tried not to think of anything except that everything would soon be over, the noise, my illness, the night, the storm, and soon I would get well and leave this awful place and have my baby. They had told me, quite casually, when I was admitted, that pneumonia in pregnancy was usually fatal to the woman, or to her child—or both. I refused to think about that.

"I've come this far," I said to myself, "I'm not going to give in now. I'm going to keep this baby."

The diet kitchen was a small, dingy room, stale with the odours of thousands of meals, millions of dirty dishes. A single guttering candle, placed on the counter, cast a fitful light over the yellowed woodwork, the chipped cabinets, the patterned walls—and then I realized for the first time that the pattern on the walls was moving. It was a pattern of cockroaches, hundreds and hundreds and hundreds of them, almost obscuring the pale plaster. And on the open shelves that ringed the pantry, I could see in the candlelight larger shapes, mice, scurrying back and forth, back and forth.

I didn't dare scream or cry out. I would have gone completely to pieces if I had. And it's unlikely that anyone would have heard me anyway. I sat very still and drew my feet up off the floor, as best I could given my cumbersome bulk. I prayed to God that no mouse would drop on me. Cockroaches I was familiar with, but mice terrified me, and I was afraid that if one touched me in the dark, my heart would stop with fright.

At last, I decided that being in bed in the ward, surrounded by the noise and confusion, could be no worse than sitting here in frozen shock, surrounded by bugs and rodents. Somehow, I managed to get out of the chair and stumble to the door, but I couldn't get any further. I made it beyond the sill, into the dark hallway, then my legs crumpled and I slid down the wall to sit on the floor, like a rag doll without its sawdust.

After a long moment, someone was beside me in the darkness. Someone picked me up as though I were a child, cradled me to an ample bosom, and carried me easily back to my bed. I was tucked in and covered up, with my back to the dying girl, whose bed had now been screened, and then my someone sat beside me, patting my shoulder reassuringly, singing comforting old songs in a rich, loving voice, until I fell asleep.

When I awoke in the morning, I had a blinding headache that lasted for twenty-four hours, and then I fell asleep for three days and nights without a break. When I finally woke again, I told myself that the worst was now over, that I was ready to get well, and that I had to find my mysterious friend.

It was Mary—Mary White—a patient in Roosevelt Hospital too but able to be up and around. She was Black, about fifty, large-boned, ample-breasted, with a boundless capacity for compassion and love. Mary was the one who had cleaned me up, as best she could, the night I had been so sick. And she was the one who picked me up and comforted me, the frightening night of the thunderstorm. Mary helped everyone she could, in every way she could, and her love and humanity made a tremendous impression on me.

She continued to care for me as my own mother might have, watching over me, helping to feed me, giving me pieces of ice to suck, for she knew that drinking water made me sick. Mary didn't talk about herself, and I was too ill to ask many questions. When I finally left the hospital, our paths never again crossed. But the memory of that wonderful woman has stayed with me for nearly sixty years, and I bless her for the way she helped me survive and grow in courage during that terrible time.

Because I did survive. Once a week, a doctor with a flock of students would gather round my bed and the doctor would expound about me and my case in the third person, explaining why this and that condition would make the patient's recovery highly unlikely, if not impossible. Then they would shake their heads sadly at the thought of me, so young, so pregnant, etc. etc., and pass on by.

I thought to myself, as I lay there like some dummy on display, "You old dodo! I'll show you. I'm going to walk out of this place, and take my unborn baby safely with me!"

The day came when doctor and students made their regular trek to my bedside, to find me sitting up, hair neatly brushed, face set in a determined smile. The learned gentleman's jaw fell. "You're still here?" he sputtered. I laughed out loud at his amazement. "Still here. Alive. And getting well, I hope. *My* determination was better than your prognosis, Doctor. I had resources."

He harrumphed a bit, then said, "I think I can discharge you today." I was out of there on wings. I had made up my mind that no child of mine would be born in a New York hospital. I had survived, but could a baby? So I went home to Pocatello, carefully, on the train, with a list of doctors and hospitals along the way, just in case.

But my trip was uneventful, and our daughter, Mary Josephine or Marijo, was born on September 23, 1918.

CHAPTER FOUR

Now that our baby had arrived safely, I was anxious to get back to New York, to Burton, and to work. But we expected Burton to be called in the draft at any time, he had not been able to find larger living quarters suitable for us and a baby, and the dread influenza epidemic had struck New York.

As a settlement worker, Burton knew where the flu cases were in the Lenox Hill district, so he was riding the ambulances as a volunteer. He wrote that one trip had taken him out to a cemetery where he watched mass graves being dug with a steam shovel in order to accommodate the stacked and ticketed coffins that had piled up too fast to be handled in the usual fashion. After taking a hard look at the situation, Burton advised me to stay in Pocatello with Marijo for a while.

I did, but the flu soon struck there, too. Just two weeks after I left the hospital, the "Spanish" influenza swept through it. Either the mother or the baby, and often both, of every maternity case there at the time died of the flu. As well, two of the Catholic Sisters of Mercy who had cared for me and my baby succumbed to the disease.

In the meantime, the war had ended in Europe. Burton would not be drafted. He was able to find us a place to live, an apartment in the two upper floors of a well-kept old brownstone at 318 East 69th Street, not far from Lenox Hill. We were to live there happily for three years.

A month to the day after the armistice, I left Pocatello with Marijo, on a train that seemed to be crowded with servicemen. They took a great interest in the baby, who was travelling in a basket, and helped us most considerately on the long journey.

I was back home, and ready to take up our struggle toward our eventual goals. Though our primary purpose in going into the settlement was to eventually build a theatre, we were forced to take a circuitous route. In one of my early letters to Burton, I had said, "If we could only get something—anything—to enable us to live for a year, there would be an opening at Lenox Hill." Miss Manning, the director, was interested in us and was trying to prepare a place for us on her staff. But it took time.

So at first we volunteered our services. I taught classes in "English for Foreigners." My classes consisted mostly of men who had applied for citizenship. On the day that they were to acquire that citizenship, I went with them as a kind of bodyguard, to lead them past an old she-dragon, a Mrs. Quin, who checked their applications and administered the oath. There was no dignity or graciousness in these proceedings, but the men seemed grateful and I don't suppose Mrs. Quin's attitude was new to them. Given stories I'd heard from friends who worked as interpreters at Ellis Island, my students had probably experienced much the same treatment from their first moment of landing in "The Land of the Free."

Burton volunteered for work in the Lenox Hill gym, coaching basketball and other activities for the young boys. He also managed the Saturday night dances, for which there was a ten-cent admission charge. And we formed a drama group. Sports and the weekly dances attracted a great many young people to the Settlement Houses, but some of the more serious youngsters were drawn by drama groups, and young people came from all over the city.

These young people, many of them American-born, growing up in slum neighbourhoods, going to overcrowded, unsanitary public schools with the street corners and back alleys as playgrounds, were exposed to only the worst in American life, and many of them became real problems. Their charming, dignified Old World parents would come to us at the settlement about their children's problems, and when we questioned them, they would say, "Our children pay no attention to us. They say we are greenhorns. This is America."

Those parents recognized the evil that seemed to be engulfing their children's lives and most of them were willing to try to understand and correct it. Burton and I hoped that perhaps a theatre at the settlement could bring some much-needed positive results. At first, our theatre work at the settlement was extracurricular. We used a flat-floored recreation hall that was a combination gymnasium-auditorium and many times the space had to be surrendered to Hungarian wrestling matches and other similar events.

All lighting equipment, sets, and costumes had to be improvised, but we managed to produce many of the one-act plays of Lady Gregory, J. M. Barrie, George Bernard Shaw, and Lord Dunsany, one or two original plays, some pantomime—and, of all things, Ibsen's *Enemy of the People*, my first Ibsen, and Shakespeare's *Twelfth Night*.

As there were always more women than men in this drama group, the job of directing fell to me. It was an excellent experience, as the group met two or three times a week. It was exhausting, often frustrating, and frequently rewarding, especially when some progress could be made or some spark of talent fanned. One such spark was in a young Irish lad, just past his middle teens, stockily built, with a boxer's shoulders and dancer's legs, and the typically Hibernian red hair, blue eyes, and lavish freckles. His father was a bartender in Yorkville, his mother a wonderfully indomitable woman whose spirit seemed more than a match for poverty. The boy was one of a clamouring and nonconforming clan of five brothers and one sister who shared the honest Irish patronymic of Cagney. His name was James … Jimmy.

He was working in the Yorkville Branch of the New York Public Library at 78th Street and Avenue A, putting books back on the shelves, when he first learned about us and our activities at Lenox Hill. I used to spend a good deal of time at the library, and he apparently watched with interest as I followed my usual practice of dealing with several volumes at the same time. He often said that I was the only woman he'd ever seen who could read three books at once, and in later years he enjoyed pantomiming my bibliophilic gymnastics.

Jimmy's brother Harry, later a physician in New York, arrived at Lenox Hill first and soon brought his brother along. Jimmy did his first acting under our direction and attacked it with the earnest dedication with which he tackled everything. From time to time he would disappear from our acting group, and then we would know that he was working. Mrs. Cagney was dogged and inventive in her desperate determination to see that her brood got an education. The little girl, Jean, was still a baby, but the four boys had to have schooling. So they would take turns: two would go to school while the other two worked. Then, after a time, they would trade places. When it was Jimmy's turn to work, he usually jerked sodas at a place over on West End Avenue.

But he played with us in a number of things, including a kind of *commedia dell'arte* written by Jasper Cusamano, one of the Sicilian boys from the neighbourhood. Jimmy struggled valiantly to give his characterization of Pierrot the meaning he and we wanted it to have. At dress rehearsal, his frustrations overflowed, and the tough, pugnacious seventeen-year-old sat down on the edge of the stage and wept, tears running through his clown-white makeup.

Then he wiped his face, got up, and did the show, wrapping it up with his remarkably graceful and agile dancing, which was to stand him in such good stead in later years.

Jimmy was a fine and dedicated performer, and also a handy fellow to have around the theatre in other capacities as well. The hard-fisted physical prowess that he so often displayed in his movies was never a mere cinematic invention. As a kid in Yorkville, you had to know how to take care of yourself, particularly if you cared much about living long enough to grow up.

One May night in 1921, we were doing a performance of Ibsen's *An Enemy of the People*. Some neighbourhood rowdies who didn't go for this "art" stuff began throwing rocks through the gym-auditorium windows and started to make an organized sortie into the building's backstage and dressing rooms by way of the fire escape. Jimmy wasn't in the cast but he was around, and when Burton, dressed for the character of Morten Kiil, started after the intruders with his cane, Jimmy appeared, whispering hoarsely, "It's all right, Mr. James. Go back to your acting. We'll take care of them."

Young Cagney recruited a friend, ready-fisted John Kohler, and swiftly organized a punitive expedition. John came up the alley to the fire escape and Jimmy executed a flanking movement across the playground to cut the invaders off. For the next few moments, Henrik Ibsen's excoriation of private and municipal corruption was performed against an unrehearsed counterpoint of muffled cries that drifted in from the alley. *Smack!* "Ow!" *Smack! Smack!* "Aw right! We'll pay!" *Smack!* "We'll pay! We'll pay!" And pay they did, with coin as well as with blood, black eyes, and tears.

Jimmy's elegant muscular equipment served him well in less warlike pursuits as well. He was a first-rate ball player and an excellent boxer. He was interested in drawing. But most of all, he was a dancer and when, toward the end of our stay in New York, he decided to take the plunge and go into show business, he became first a chorus boy and then a "hoofer." He used to bring his partner, a pretty little girl named Billie, back to the settlement for a place to rehearse their dance routines. We weren't surprised when they got married soon after, nor when Jimmy's career went steadily uphill to the very top in the entertainment field.

Although the adult years of Jimmy's life were considerably different from those of his childhood pals, his early environment, financial situation, and educational opportunities were much the same. And it was for all the young people like Jimmy that we persisted in our dream of providing theatre that would open doors and bridge chasms. As well as artistic considerations, our early plays grew out of social necessity. We did plays at Lenox Hill to help centre the interests of disintegrating families on things they had in common. Our work grew out of trying to preserve family units that were falling apart in the New World. We urged the Czechs and Hungarians and Italians to put on festivals and pageants representative of their homelands, to conserve the art they had brought with them to America. They were being laughed at and looked down upon and their children needed exposure to something they could take pride in in their past, as well as to something better in their future.

Finally, Miss Manning and her Board of Trustees began to look with approval on the work of our drama group. Burton, who had been put on staff full-time at a salary of $125 a month, was given an extra $100 a month for the theatre work he was doing in the evenings and on weekends. In effect, the board received "two for the price of one," as my work with the Lenox Hill Players remained on a volunteer basis for as long as we were there. However, in February of 1919, I finally achieved my goal of joining the staff at Lenox Hill—though certainly not in any way I might have imagined.

Lenox Hill House was situated in a Polish, German, Hungarian, Czech, and Italian neighbourhood. The men in many of these families were highly skilled workers, craftsmen in factories making surgical instruments or pianos, or employed as cigar-makers. Their salaries were not lavish but they were adequate in most cases, and they were generally steady. Then World War I intervened. Drafted men were paid only thirty dollars a month, so families whose breadwinners had been called to fight for Uncle Sam faced hardships. Many of the women who had been left to eke out a living for their families were skilled embroiderers and it occurred to someone that their peasant embroidery might find a market. So the Mothers' Club of the Settlement, composed mostly of Czechoslovakian women, organized a sort of cottage industry for the manufacture and sale of this colourful needlework.

I was working with the Mothers' Club as a volunteer at the time and the embroidery project interested me. I watched, asked questions, and trotted down to the library to read all I could about this art/craft and the Moravian communities in which it originated. The infant project caught on. It was the beginning of the popularity of "peasant" fashion decoration, which has waxed and waned but never entirely disappeared. The ladies decided that the project should be expanded and to that end sent me on behalf of the Mothers' Club to the Lenox Hill Board of Trustees to request a modest amount of money so a designer and trained salesperson could be hired. To my surprise, and delight, the board not only voted the money for the project but hired me on the spot to head it up.

At first, I was laughed at when I tried to interest dress designers and garment manufacturers in our output. "No American woman would ever wear that stuff," they said, although I was wearing it and I liked it. Gradually, however, we gained a market, though it never reached the proportions it would achieve in later years. Our efforts, however, led to an even more important development.

I still remember the committee meeting of the Lenox Hill Board of Directors, attended by Mrs. Marshall Field, wife of the Chicago millionaire. She was building a home, which she was furnishing with fabulous antiques, imported from abroad. The furniture came into the country duty-free, because it was more than a hundred years old, but the duty on imported coverings to re-upholster it came to nearly one hundred percent. At the meeting Mrs. Field said, "I am not interested in peasant embroidery, but if you can do crewel embroidery to recreate the traditional materials I need, I will loan you $6,000 to get started." She turned to me. "Do you think you can do it?"

I had never heard of crewel embroidery, but I said, "I think we could try." As soon as we left the meeting, I rushed to the library to find out what kind of embroidery could be "crewel"—at that point, I didn't even know how to spell it. I found that it is one of the most ancient forms of embroidery, dating back to the fifth century A.D. in Egypt, and takes its name from the use of a special "crewel" yarn, a fine wool yarn with a slight sheen that usually comes in two plies twisted into a single strand. Crewel work is durable, perfect for household and personal accessories.

When we began our new project, we were really starting from scratch—we had to import the wools, the backgrounds, and just about everything we needed. I hired a skilled embroideress who taught the less-skilled, stitch by stitch, and I haunted the museums, using a magnifying glass to study the fabrics, yarns, and stitches of centuries-old originals.

Burton, along with his duties in the drama group and supervising the gym and the dances, became our designer. It was not long before we had satisfied Mrs. Field and the committee. As soon as the project became known, we began to get orders from decorators all over the city. The whole scheme was a great success. The women were gainfully employed and delighted to use their skills in this new effort, and I became knowledgeable enough in the craft to keep things going.

With Burton and I both on the staff of Lenox Hill, our monthly income had risen to a total of $225, so we had no worries about food, clothing, and a roof over our heads. We felt hopeful about the future and, though busy as the proverbial beavers, we were able to keep all our activities moving along successfully.

Thinking back, I am sure that one of the reasons I, in particular, was able to do so much at that time was that Marijo turned out to be an extremely accommodating and self-sufficient baby. I would rise early (a habit I've never been able to break), breast-feed our daughter, then get dressed and make breakfast. That done, I'd walk the block and a half to the settlement to get the day's work started in the embroidery shop.

After an hour or so, I'd go back to the apartment, bathe Marijo, give her her 10:00 feeding, open the windows, wrap her up, put her down for her nap, and go back to work. I usually ate lunch at the settlement, but at 2:00 I'd go home again to give the baby hers. The rest of the day was spent in the shop, which closed at 4:30 so I could be back home in time to feed Marijo again and put her to bed. Between my visits, she was left to her own devices, at first in her crib and later in a playpen. The people in the apartment downstairs were there, of course, and looked in on her from time to time, but really she was on her own.

Always, though, she was a part of us and what we were doing. At night, I'd take her to rehearsals, and she'd sleep or wake up and play around, never causing a fuss, never getting in the way. Then, our methods of child-rearing seemed natural. I don't think I'd do it that way now.

One of the side benefits of the embroidery project was that Burton and I came in contact with the ethnic groups in the neighbourhood and their interest in music, dance, and even opera. These new Americans produced plays that they had known in the countries from which they'd emigrated. I remember seeing a charming production of Bedřich Smetana's *Bartered Bride* staged in a Czech community hall, not far from Lenox Hill. These neighbourhood halls were most inadequate, and the people worked in frustratingly difficult situations. We offered our services and the facilities of the settlement, but those had great limitations too.

The ethnic groups welcomed our suggestion that perhaps something could be done to provide more adequate surroundings for this type of activity. Burton proposed a folk theatre, and we approached the settlement director, Miss Manning, with the idea. She was most enthusiastic. She, too, wanted the settlement to become an enlarged centre for cultural activities and took the matter up with her board. There was a vacant lot next to the Settlement House, which seemed ideal for expansion. The board agreed, and Burton designed his first theatre, a forty thousand dollar structure, and came up with ways and means of financing it.

I am sure that many members of the board recognized our idea as a positive step in the process of Americanization for our neighbourhood's minorities. Burton had outlined our hopes for such a development in an article that he wrote for a little fortnightly New York publication called *The Little Theatre Review*:

> A theatre of the people, which shall reach out and appeal to the tastes and pocketbooks of society remains an unrealized ideal. But the Folk Theatre seems to offer a practical beginning to meet these demands … Its elements are alive and growing in our midst today. It proposes not to change the tongue or spirit of the neighborhood's drama. It takes the position that plays produced in a foreign tongue will perpetuate age-old standards of art.
>
> … Our neighborhood is most cosmopolitan. Though plain, it has a taste for better things. Broadway holds no appeal for us.
>
> … The Folk Theatre's only reason for existence is that it offers to the neighborhood plays a wider field of activity. It proposes to be so equipped that our neighbors may, with right and dignity, request their best artists to work with them and for them.
>
> Above all, the Folk Theatre proposes a director and a staff of associates who will with sympathy, understanding, training and care follow the dramatic bent of our neighborhood. The Folk Theatre must disseminate, not exploit, must stimulate, not force … This group should set the standard of co-operative endeavour. The Folk Theatre has no room for competitive enterprises.

We made our plans, hoped, prepared, and waited. From time to time, some encouraging things did happen. Hunter College celebrated its fiftieth anniversary in 1920 and asked for our help in preparing a production of the old melodrama *The Two Orphans* as part of the celebration. They offered to donate the proceeds from the play to the building fund for the folk theatre.

But though the people of the community, the staff of the Settlement House, and Burton and I were enthused and ready to get to work, there seemed to be no particular haste on the part of the Lenox Hill Board to proceed with things. When we submitted our plan for the final approval of the full board, it was tabled and another proposal was brought forward—forty thousand dollars would enlarge the gym and build a swimming pool. The recession of 1922, a mere preamble to the crash of 1929, had frightened possible investors in culture and Americanization. A tennis court eventually sprouted on the site that Burton had selected for a folk theatre, and we began to feel that perhaps the board-dominated Settlement House milieu was destined to remain fallow ground as far as our dreams for a people's theatre were concerned.

CHAPTER FIVE

We were more than a little downhearted as we left that summer for our old jobs in the children's camp in Maine. Ironically, the enlarged gymnasium and the swimming pool were never built, for the whole area was eventually bought as a site for a hospital. A new building was built for Lenox Hill at 331 East 70th Street and the new Settlement House had a small, fairly well-equipped theatre, so some seeds planted by our efforts came to fruition.

That summer, we received a telegram from Nellie Cornish of the Cornish School in Seattle, Washington, offering us positions on her staff. We were familiar with the theatre work of the Cornish School through Maurice Browne and his wife Ellen Van Volkenburg, who had established a successful little theatre in Chicago and then gone to Seattle to take charge of the drama department at Cornish. At the time Miss Cornish contacted us, during a staff-recruiting mission to New York, the Brownes had left the Cornish for London, England, where Mr. Browne produced Robert Sherriff's *Journey's End* with a group of amateurs. It was a very successful production, which later played in a theatre in London's West End. He made quite a bit of money and established his reputation as a producer.

When Miss Cornish began to look for staff to replace the Brownes, our old friend from Emerson, Albert Lovejoy, who was then teaching in the drama department of the University of Washington, recommended us. We considered Miss Cornish's offer very carefully. If we accepted, it would mean leaving Burton's hometown and giving up the advantages of the big city—which were greater then, I think, than now. We had put down roots at Lenox Hill. We liked much of the work we were doing there, and we loved the people in the neighbourhood where we lived.

We decided that I should go from Maine to New York for the interview, with the possibility of accepting the offer of jobs, while Burton would remain in Maine to finish the work we were doing there. When I met Miss Cornish in New York, I was somewhat surprised by her appearance. She was short in stature and inclined to corpulence, and in no way resembled a dreamer of dreams or the director of an art school. She had gone to the pioneer town of Seattle from the border community of Blaine, Washington, rented a small studio in the downtown area, and begun giving piano lessons. While this work provided a modest living, she began to think about founding a school of art that would encompass all the arts, providing opportunities for study and creating a cultural centre in the last of America's geographical frontiers. She established the Cornish School in 1914.

We liked each other immediately, but she was disappointed that Burton had not come with me. As she told me, with her characteristic forthrightness, she was more interested in him than in me. She had already engaged someone to direct plays and teach the acting courses. What she really needed now was a person to teach stage design, stage construction, and lighting, and to act as a producer. There was an opening for me if I could teach speech and "elocution."

In those days parents sent their offspring to teachers of elocution for private training in "speaking pieces," a process that involved voice and speech training as well as some kind of personal development. My education at Emerson had given me the skills to do this work, but I took a very dim view of its value. I could see little point in teaching young people to "speak pieces" for the gratification of their parents and the boredom of everyone else who had to listen to them.

I told Miss Cornish that I would be able to teach speech and elocution but explained my reluctance to do so. First, the fifty-minute period allocated for individual instruction allowed very little time for speech or voice training. As well, I believed that speech presented special problems and needed special instruction. I had heard that Columbia University had created a speech department, directed by Professor William Tilly. His approach to this subject was through something called "phonetics," quite new and different from the methods I had been taught at Emerson. Miss Cornish, always interested in anything that would improve teaching methods in her school, approached Professor Tilly and on his recommendation hired Miss Margaret Crawford to teach classes in speech.

Later, at Cornish, I attended Miss Crawford's classes with the drama students, for whom it was a required subject, and learned the phonetic symbols that made it possible to use Daniel Jones' phonetic dictionary as a guide to the correct sounds of speech in the English language. Miss Crawford told us that something called an "Oxford accent" was a necessary acquisition for beautiful speech. For many months we struggled, learning the symbols for correct sounds and then trying to apply both sounds and English inflections to achieve "Oxford speech," or what we would call today "phony English accents." The drama department became a source of amusement for other students. Miss Crawford even attended rehearsals to correct the speech and inflections of the actors as they rehearsed, which created an impossible situation. An actor cannot develop a character in a play if, at the same time, he or she has to worry about speech problems. So we stopped assuming that our actors' speech was a problem and accepted the fact of our American accents. With voice training and good articulation, we acquired what is now called "mid-Atlantic speech," more than adequate for actors whose problem is essentially to communicate with each other and with an audience.

When Burton finally arrived in New York for his interview, Miss Cornish was pleased with him, as well she should have been. He was personable, talented, energetic, ambitious, and had the techniques and skills to teach the backstage work that she needed in her theatre department. She offered us contracts, which we accepted, and we prepared to pull up our stakes in New York and go west. I was to go immediately to prepare classes in the subject I was to teach (my adaptation of the disputed "elocution") and to find living quarters for Burton and four-year-old Marijo, who would follow me later. Burton remained in New York to tie up the strands of our work there and to wait until Miss Manning could find replacements for our jobs at the settlement.

So one September evening in 1922, we stood in the rotunda of Penn Station in New York, waiting for my train and looking up at the great map of the United States on the east wall. The dot that marked Seattle seemed a long way off. For me, it was a little like going home, since I had crossed the continent before, coming from Pocatello to Boston for school and going back and forth when Marijo was born. For Burton, it would be an adventure. He had never been west of Buffalo.

It was raining the morning I arrived in Seattle. The porter who helped me off the train at first expressed concern that I had neither raincoat nor umbrella. Then he reassured me that it really didn't matter, as "Seattle rain doesn't get you wet."

No one met me so I asked the conductor for the name of a hotel. He suggested one and added, "It's a small hotel, but lots of Alaska folks stay there." It seemed like a nice enough spot, so I checked in. The hotel had no dining room, and I asked the desk clerk where I could get breakfast. He suggested a restaurant across the street. As soon as I sat down at the table, the waiter brought me a bowl of oatmeal porridge, a platter of pancakes, fried eggs, sausages, and coffee. Perhaps I looked surprised at all this, for he explained, "It's family style, lady." When I paid my bill, it was fifteen cents!

This was Seattle, and I liked it. I was to spend the next twenty-nine years of my life there. Seattle is a beautiful small city, with the Olympics and Cascade mountains, Puget Sound and the lakes. A new, fresh wind seemed to be blowing. Energy and imagination were in the air.

Something must be said here about the State of Washington, which was probably the last of the frontiers of the continental United States to be settled, as what we were able to accomplish there was, to a great extent, influenced by the history and development of the state and its people. In the 1880s and 1890s, hordes of the dispossessed from the eastern United States and Europe crossed the continent to Washington, fleeing railroad blacklists, wheat famines, and the wage slavery of the mines and mills to seek freedom and security in this faraway corner of the country. Many came in groups, bought land, and established colonies where they could freely profess their beliefs in cooperation, religion, or socialism. There was much talk of the "New Day," the "New Era," the "Dawn." The dedication, energy, and struggles of these colonists to hold on to their beliefs now seem incredible. Many thought that if they could establish the sort of society Eugene Debs described, one that could "dethrone Gold and elevate humanity," in one corner of this vast country, the rest of the country would follow and "transform the days to come into a virtual paradise." Those whom the colonists saw as their oppressors also thought this might be a possibility and feared it.

In the years that followed, many of the hopeful migrants failed to find the paradise they had come for and became instead migratory labourers in the forests, in the mills, and on the docks. Their frustrations eventually drove them to organize a militant union called the International Workers of the World, thoroughly hated by lumber and waterfront employers. The stage for battle, sometimes bloody, always bitter, was set.

Reading today of the violence and vehemence of these struggles, the simplicity of the causes is amazing: unionism, the eight-hour day, free speech, an uncensored press, freedom from poverty in old age, unemployment and health programs. And for many of them, accepted in principle but not in practice, the struggle is far from over.

A history of the United States records many "firsts" for Washington, initiated by the early "social dissidents" and the energetic, like-minded citizens who followed them. Their visions, hopes, and struggles created a climate where imagination and hard work could flourish. Miss Cornish could not have chosen a better place to start her school of the arts.

I was enchanted with my first glimpse of the Cornish School. It was situated on the corner of a tree-lined street in a residential area. The architecture was something called Spanish Baroque, different from anything else in the city, and was covered with peach-coloured stucco, trimmed in sage green, with touches of dogwood as the decorative motif. It was unmistakably a school of the arts.

The school had been carefully planned to provide adequate facilities for all the arts, with a ballet studio, space for painting classes, and studios for all the music faculties. Best of all was a lovely small theatre seating around three hundred. The place hummed with activity, so much so that residents in the neighbourhood once took out an injunction against the school—they claimed it was too noisy and had to go because property values were going down. The case was taken to court. The judge's decision was that the city was growing and the school was an asset. Those who complained should move to a quieter area.

Miss Cornish wanted only the best instructors for her school, and she had a genius for attracting such people. Eminent artists, when they visited the school and saw its program and activities, frequently returned as members of the faculty to teach summer school and sometimes became permanent members of the staff. Among these were Adolph Bolm, formerly of Diaghilev's Ballets Russes and later ballet master for the Chicago Civic Opera; Walter Reese, well-known commercial artist; Peter Meremblum, violinist, who had graduated from the Petrograd Imperial Conservatory; Kolia Levienne, cellist; Jacques Jou-Jerville, formerly tenor with the Paris Opera; Myron Jacobson, a graduate of the Petrograd Imperial Conservatory and, after he fled the Russian Revolution, accompanist for Feodor Chaliapin; Berthe Poncy Jacobson, graduate of the Schola Cantorum in Paris, who taught Dalcroze eurhythmics and was a fine pianist; and many others of equal distinction.

The yet-unrecognized Mark Tobey, later called "the painter of the epoch" by European critics, taught painting. And Martha Graham said that Miss Cornish permitted her, as an unknown, to give a performance one Sunday evening "on pure speculation."

Dancer Merce Cunningham and composer John Cage were students at the school. One Sunday evening, Cage was to give a lecture-recital on modern music. He was not much of a lecturer, and said so himself, adding, "I think I'd better show you." He ran his hands over the piano keys, sometimes using his fists and elbows, then ran around the piano and played the strings. His lecture and his performance were equally mystifying to the audience. He was years ahead of his time with his achievements in "implementing Music into space."

It was an exciting, challenging place to be. Burton arrived with Marijo, having seen the vast expanses of the prairies and the soaring majesty of the Rocky Mountains, and immediately fell in love with Seattle, Puget Sound, the trees and flowers—and the charming small theatre at the Cornish School. We set to work enthusiastically to build a life for ourselves in this exciting environment.

Burton was to teach stage design and technical skills, and he began in his tactful but effective way to mould his classes and courses into shape. There were a few problems to begin with, since there were those at the school who were reluctant to change anything which had been done by his predecessor, Maurice Browne. For a time, whenever Burton made a suggestion, the inevitable reply was, "Well, Maurice did it *this* way." Burton persevered and overcame, however.

I had problems of my own in the speech department due to the existing tradition of "florid" elocution. I still remember one of my first students rendering Vachel Lindsay's "The Congo" while hammering on a table with two sticks. Another typical "piece" was presented by a young girl who had selected a hundred lines from Shakespeare for recitation. She had picked the hundred lines that she thought were "most beautiful" and mixed them into a literary hash that even Shakespeare himself would probably not have recognized.

However, we knew what we wanted to achieve and slowly but steadily worked toward it with rewarding results. The person Miss Cornish had hired to teach acting and to direct plays was an apple farmer from eastern Washington. He had done some work with amateur theatre groups in his own community and had come recommended by someone whose judgment Miss Cornish trusted. We were not impressed by the gentleman, or by his theatrical abilities.

One incident that confirmed our initial impressions occurred during our preparation for a Nativity play at our first Christmas at Cornish. Burton had managed, with much effort, to secure a perfectly smooth cyclorama as a background for the production. The department head cut a hole in one end of the cloth for the pianist to peer through, creating a network of wrinkles that completely destroyed the effect. Burton, normally a mild-mannered man, blew his top.

Miss Cornish had also become disenchanted and one morning, shortly after the first of the year in 1924, she sent for Burton and me, to say: "I want you to take over the theatre department and preparations for the Spring Festival. The theatre department has always presented an exciting performance for our Spring Festival of the Arts but Mr. A. thinks that he can do no better than scenes from Shakespeare, given the limited registration in drama."

The registration in drama had dropped to five students, all girls. Nothing daunted, we took over the department. I taught the acting course and directed the plays, and Burton continued his classes in stage design and construction but now with an objective in mind. We received a combined salary of $400 a month, which would rise to

$440 after about two years. Miss Cornish was never hesitant about displaying her faith in her staff in practical terms.

For our maiden effort as department heads, Burton and I planned the production of three one-acts, George Bernard Shaw's *Man of Destiny*, Frederick Fenn's *'Op-O'-Me-Thumb*, and Laurence Housman's *The Queen, God Bless Her.* We needed men, so we persuaded our old friend from Emerson, Albert Lovejoy, and a student of his, Albert Ottenheimer, to slip over from the university after their classes to take part in these plays. We had seen Ottenheimer in a university production of Leonid Andreyev's *He Who Gets Slapped*, playing the small part of the bandmaster, and were impressed with his ability.

Al Ottenheimer would be associated with us for many years. Remembering, I can scarcely imagine how we could have done without him. He was so enthusiastic about theatre that he arranged his schedules at the university so he could continue his work with us at Cornish. Despite this extra work, he graduated *magna cum laude* from the university, becoming Phi Beta Kappa in his junior year. He developed into an excellent actor, a good playwright and teacher, and, many years later when he was with us in the Seattle Repertory Playhouse, a phenomenal promotion man.

Burton played the lieutenant in *Man of Destiny*, 'Orace in *'Op-O'-Me-Thumb*, and Disraeli in *The Queen, God Bless Her.* Mark Tobey, always keen for adventure, played John Brown in *The Queen*, because, as he said, he "would like to try acting to see what it was like." Burton staged and lit the productions, which were very well received. Miss Cornish was pleased with the drama department's exciting contribution to the Spring Festival of the Arts. One newspaper, reviewing the program, even commented that there was no lack of excellent male actors at Cornish!

Though the school's drama department had begun, for the first time in a long while, to pay its own way, money for costumes, staging, and all the other things we needed had to come from the general budget, and there was never enough. In our third year at the School, Burton suggested a series of programs by the music, dance, drama, and opera departments, for the coming 1926–27 season. It would serve as a "showcase" for the school, and contribute to Seattle's cultural life. And subscription sales of tickets could be created to provide money for production costs. The plan was accepted and there were enthusiastic audiences in full houses.

In the 1927–28 season, however, the other departments began to feel pressured by the deadlines involved. As Burton had initiated the whole showcase idea, the drama department was blamed for the pressure, and the claim was made that the school was becoming "too professional." Fortunately, as the schedule had been set and tickets sold, we managed to get through the year's program.

When Myron Jacobson came to the school as opera coach, I began my work as a director of opera. Jacobson was a martinet when it came to his work but a delight to know and to work with. He had the appearance and manners of an old-world gentleman, always elegantly groomed, with his spats, cane, and perfume. Since I had no qualification in music, my forays into opera caused qualms in some quarters, but Mr. Jacobson always defended me vigorously in his limited English. "Mrs. James does not know music from de nuts, but she is musician," he would proclaim. Whether you pronounce it "nuts" or "notes," he was absolutely correct. Miss Cornish once said of Jacobson that he could get more mileage out of eight English words than anybody she knew.

He was unexcelled as an opera coach. Many concert artists, including Mary Lewis, John McCormack, and Roland Hayes, arranged their concert schedules so they could have time in Seattle to build their programs with Myron Jacobson. He had worked with the Moscow Art Theatre, where he composed the incidental music for their production of *Cricket on the Hearth* and others. He arranged *Romeo and Juliet* and Charles-François Gounod's *Faust* and music dramas for our showcases at Cornish. Burton staged the productions and played Valentine in *Faust* and Tybalt in *Romeo and Juliet*. I did the dramatic direction for both, a marvellous experience.

My experience with Myron Jacobson taught me how a dramatic director approaches opera. The opera cast had to be absolutely knowledgeable about the music. He would tolerate no fumbling about with scores or trying to remember music or words in the drama rehearsals. I sat in on his classes to become familiar with the score, and could then plan action so that the singers could always see the conductor without falling into the rigid stances sometimes associated with opera. He and I wanted them to act as well as sing.

When our students did John Gay's *Polly*, the sequel to *The Beggar's Opera*, Mr. Jacobson helped us with the music and played the musical accompaniment for the songs. When we left the school, we continued to work with Myron on operas he produced, and at the time of his death in 1934 were at work with him on Mozart's *Cosi fan tutte*.

The productions presented in the showcases showed that the quality as well as quantity of drama productions at Cornish had increased. We had gathered a nucleus of actors, theatre workers, and students, and with the help of Harold Johnsrud, a young actor whom Miss Cornish had brought to Seattle from the Provincetown Players to do publicity for the school, we began to systematically raise the level of public taste through a well-rounded repertoire.

In the early years, we presented such varied productions as John Galsworthy's *Joy*, Charles Dickens' *Cricket on the Hearth*, Arthur Wing Pinero's *Enchanted Cottage*, Shaw's *Man and Superman* and *How He Lied to Her Husband*, Githa Sowerby's *Rutherford and Son*, J. M. Barrie's *The Will*, Harold Chapin's *Autocrat of the Coffee Stall*, Theodore Dreiser's *Laughing Gas*, and *The Rider of Dreams* by Ridgely Torrence. There was nothing startling about any of these plays, but they were well-produced in a serious and dedicated fashion and were a success from the standpoint of the students, the audiences, and the school.

Others began to notice, and make use of, the talent at the Cornish School. We were part of a production of Ermanno Wolf-Ferrari's *Secret of Suzanne* and Erich Wolfgang Korngold's *Snowman*, directed by Karl Krueger, then resident conductor of the Seattle Symphony. Singers from Cornish and other musical studios in the city as well as musicians from the Seattle Symphony worked on these productions, which were staged in the ballroom of the Olympic Hotel.

In August of 1927, Burton was engaged as technical director by the Wayfarer Pageant Society to stage a mammoth production of Giuseppe Verdi's *Aida* in the University of Washington Stadium. The society had produced a number of religious pageants in the huge stadium and had decided to undertake something even more ambitious. Five prominent singers from the Metropolitan Opera—Frances Peralta, Marion Telva, Paul Althouse, Fred Patton, and William Gustafson—were imported to perform the leading roles under Karl Krueger's direction. Jacques Jou-Jerville of the Cornish School vocal department was retained as chorus master, and Mary Ann Wells as choreographer. The production was not connected with the school, but a number of the faculty and students were involved.

Ruth Kreps, one of Burton's students at Cornish, and Burton designed an Egyptian temple more than 150 feet across and 50 feet deep. A huge 70-foot sounding board, one of the walls of the temple at the rear of the stage, created a shell for the musicians and the singers. Beneath towering Egyptian columns, circular stairways on each side led from one level of the stage to another. Dressing rooms for cast and chorus were built behind and beneath the enormous structure.

When the Wayfarer Committee saw the designs for the sets, they felt that they were beyond the capabilities of the local stage technicians and planned to have them built in San Francisco or shipped out from the east. Their production was on a scale with what was being done in Los Angeles, St. Louis, and other major cities in the country and because of its magnitude, the attendant publicity, and the stature of its guest artists, the committee felt that the technical details were too important to be left in the hands of "locals."

Burton convinced them that the sets could be built, efficiently and much more economically, by the local stagehands' union. The sets were excellent, the committee was delighted, and the Seattle members of the International Association of Theatrical and Stage Employees (IATSE) were so grateful to Burton that they later presented him with a lifetime gold card membership in the union. It was an honour that smoothed many difficulties for us in the future with stagehands, musicians, and any other union help we needed in our own theatre. Whenever and wherever we worked, at Cornish and later, we always attempted to put local professional craftsmen to work.

The production was tremendously successful and gave Burton outstanding qualifications for working on other spectacle productions. He said later that it was the first time in his life he'd ever had enough lights to work with. Even nature gave an added fillip to the stage effects—on opening night, the moon rose behind the set, as if on cue, to a round of admiring applause.

We felt that our success in such activities, as well as the appreciation of our productions at Cornish, which frequently played to standing-room-only audiences, redounded to the credit of the school. We began to see, however, that it caused professional envy in part of the Cornish School. There were some who feared that Burton might expand beyond the orbit of the little school and resented it.

The situation at Cornish was frustrating, so in November of 1927 I took a trip back east to see what was going on in the "real" theatrical world. I visited the Cleveland Play House, the Kenneth Sawyer Goodman Memorial Theatre in Chicago, the Eastman School of Music's Drama Department, the Civic Repertory Theatre in Boston, and Professor George Pierce Baker's new school of theatre at Yale. Then I spent three weeks in New York, seeing a total of thirty-three plays, mostly bad. The only ones that impressed me favourably were Max Reinhardt's productions of *Everyman*, Shakespeare's *A Midsummer Night's Dream*, and George Büchner's *Danton's Death*, perhaps a natural reaction after I had just seen the cultural desolation and apathy at the nerve centres of the American theatre.

When I returned, thankfully, to Seattle, I gave lectures on the debility and sterility of American drama. I spoke at teas, women's clubs, and drama leagues and was interviewed by the press. My rejection of what I had seen went much deeper than a superficial scoffing at commercialism, as I indicated in a statement to the *Campus Crier* of the Washington State Normal School: "Our whole theatrical stream has been frozen by our Puritan ancestor, and it will probably take a thousand years to thaw it out." When I said that, I had no idea that very soon that same Puritanism would rear its head to breathe frostily over our own shoulders.

We were in dress rehearsal for Luigi Pirandello's *Six Characters in Search of an Author*, when Miss Cornish called us to her office. Some member of the board had heard (though Miss Cornish admitted than none of the board members had actually read the play) that *Six Characters* was immoral and would do the school inestimable damage if produced on the Cornish stage. It must be withdrawn at once. The board then issued an edict that all future Cornish plays must be submitted to them for prior approval. This directive would have created an untenable situation for any artistic director. The director alone must be responsible for play choice, as only he or she knows the casting and staging problems and what is planned for the material.

The only reason given for the dictum was the arbitrary one of immorality, which we found hard to accept, as did the students working on the production and anyone to whom we spoke who had actually read the script. The most likely motive for killing the play seemed to be the unspoken but tacit fear that we were trying to turn the Cornish School into a theatre.

There were fervent protests from the students and faculty over the board's censorship, but, for the first and only time in our lives, we cancelled a date and produced something else to fill the commitment. We chose George Kelly's *The Torch-Bearers*, an amusing farce about the struggle of amateurs to produce a play, which was something we could cast and prepare in a hurry.

Six Characters was not withdrawn without a struggle, and some of the cordial relations we had previously enjoyed went with it. From the first, we had recognized that we were in a school situation and that much of the work would be done by students. We had exercised discretion and sufficient good taste that the propriety of anything we had done had never before been called in question. As well as the regular seasons' productions, we had done a variety of presentations for the two years of showcases—*Caste* by Tom Robertson, Shakespeare's *Twelfth Night* and *Winter's Tale*, John Gay's *Polly*, Leo Tolstoy's *Living Corpse*, an original musical revue, *Cornish Capers*, and Henrik Ibsen's *The Wild Duck*.

We felt that we had done what we could and done it well, but obviously we had failed to accomplish all that we had hoped for. In various ways, we were made to feel that "School was School" and that perhaps our aspirations were too ambitious. Finally, in the spring of 1928, we decided to resign and establish a theatre that would be free to do the adult and professional things we were most interested in. So we left, with some of the more mature young people who had been our students and co-workers. We hoped to become co-workers in the establishment of a living theatre.

Our years at Cornish were happy, fruitful ones, in spite of internal politics and the usual frustrations and frictions involved in any job. In the years that followed, our love for Miss Cornish and a vast respect for her accomplishments never wavered. The people we met at the school, either as students or teachers, such as Bonnie Bird Gundlach, Merce

Cunningham, John Cage, Myron Jacobson, Berthe Poncy Jacobson, Mark Tobey, and a great many others, remained fast friends and gave us lasting memories of a happy, stimulating association.

CHAPTER SIX

On a Sunday afternoon in May 1928, a few days after our departure from the Cornish School, a group of friends gathered in our apartment to talk about establishing a theatre. We all agreed that Seattle needed a non-commercial theatre where artists could work as a group, refining their skills and accumulating experience so that they could become a competent acting and producing company. We wanted a theatre in which community involvement was central, so that any defeat or triumph for the theatre would be one for the community as well. We planned to uncover and awaken the common bond of creative responsibility that welds the artist to the people.

Most of the people in the group were no longer students in the school sense but adults, entering that greater classroom, the world, where the questions posed are not hypothetical but all-important ones that would challenge and possibly change the whole flow of their lives. Could they earn a living? What about getting married, having children, acquiring a home and security? Would they be able to "make it" or would they become artistic drifters always pursuing phantom careers and always on the fringe of poverty? Could they meet the future?

The questions applied to Burton and myself as well, of course. We had had a fairly strong taste of reality already. We had a daughter. We had responsibilities. But we also had faith, and a dream, and on those tenuous rocks we were determined to build our future.

We were confident that our theatre could succeed, because it would rise *from* the community, rather than being imposed *on* it from outside. Seattle was our community. Our theatre would belong to our community and would become the possession of every neighbour who entered its doors. The theatre and the community would become inseparable members of the same social family. It was the only way to triumph over the commercial competition of movies and road shows. And it was the only way in which we, as artists, could survive under a system of industrialized culture.

We adjourned late on that May afternoon, having agreed to meet again in September to begin rehearsals and launch a theatre. Our decision was publicized on July 10, 1928, in *The Christian Science Monitor*:

> The Pacific Coast is to have another important provincial theatre. The Seattle Repertory Playhouse, which has announced its first season opening in October, is the enterprise. Neither a little theatre, a community theatre, nor an "art" theatre, the Seattle Repertory Playhouse hopes to maintain a permanent professional acting company capable of building and keeping a repertory of good plays.

Despite the *Christian Science Monitor*'s disclaimer, "community theatre" best describes what our theatre ultimately became. All segments of Seattle society were involved: ethnic groups, artists, intellectuals, labour, and young people.

The previous fall, when I had made my trip to New York, I had called in to see Harold Johnsrud, whom we had met at Cornish and who was now on his way to a fairly successful career as an actor. "Cornish will always resist the taint of professionalism you are bringing into it," he had said to me. "You should start your own theatre—all you need is about fifty thousand dollars." As it turned out, we started with a good deal less than that—Burton's and my final paycheques from Cornish. We told Johnsrud of our plans, and he agreed to come to Seattle to help us get started, leaving a successful play in New York to do so. During the summer, Harold worked hard at building up publicity contacts and laying a foundation for public relations with the local press, radio, and magazines.

Burton and I scoured the city of Seattle looking for some building or part of a building that would serve our purposes—lofts, old churches, lodge halls, stables; we looked at anything and everything that could conceivably be converted into a theatre. We found nothing. Either rents were too high or buildings too dilapidated, requiring large expenditures to improve them so they could pass building and fire laws. We finally rented a vacant hole-in-the-wall building on University Way to serve while we continued looking. It had the advantage of office space, a large room where we could rehearse and build scenery, and another back room for storage. We bought a few furnishings—table, desk, chairs—for, as I remember, twenty-seven dollars, installed a telephone, and began a promotional campaign for our plays, which would open in October.

An anonymous donor sent us an unsolicited cheque for five hundred dollars to get the campaign going. The angels smiled. We were operating on a season ticket basis, six plays for five dollars, which would give us our working capital. The theatre-going public knew us from our work at Cornish and that first season we sold 997 tickets before a single play had been produced.

Burton was firmly convinced that the theatre should be self-sustaining and felt subsidies limit freedom of operation. Today, I suppose this would be considered quixotic, as it is generally recognized that all performing art must be subsidized in order to exist.

Though we had had experiences at Lenox Hill and Cornish that made us leery of boards and board dictatorship, we still felt that our theatre needed a board to provide backing, prestige, a socially stabilizing force, and a link to our community. We intended to limit the board's powers when it came to such things as play choice and casting, and we did not want a board committed to personal financial support for the theatre, an arrangement we were certain would become ingrown and constricting, both socially and artistically.

We had made many good friends during our years at the Cornish School. Among them was Arthur Goodwin, who had developed the Pike Street Farmers' Market, subsequently made famous by Mark Tobey in his painting "The Market." Mr. Goodwin had a national reputation for his originality and was frequently called upon as a consultant in other cities in the country. He agreed to act as president of our first

Board of Directors. He understood Burton's reluctance to have a board that had a financial responsibility for the project, so our first board was composed of some of Seattle's first citizens, well-known men and women who came together to act as sponsors and advisors, lending their names for prestige only. One of these was Glenn Hughes, head of the University of Washington's School of Drama.

Many of our friends, solicitous of our future and that of our theatre, suggested that Seattle might not be the best place to start. Why not Portland, or San Francisco? There was a curious humility in the city about its place in culture and the arts. People thought that artists who chose to come to, or to stay in, Seattle could not be very good—if they were, they would be in New York or San Francisco or anywhere else. I can still remember Myron Jacobson bristling with indignation when asked why he had selected Seattle as his home and base of operations. "I liked it," he said. "It looks like Sebastopol." We filed articles of incorporation that set the theatre up as a non-profit corporation, without stockholders and with surpluses, if any, to be ploughed back into the institution. I may say that the problem of surpluses never caused us much trouble.

Several years later, our articles of incorporation were amended to give the theatre the status of an educational institution, thereby exempting it from at least the corporation tax. At one time we were paying five different taxes and the State Legislature, when it amended its tax bill, included "repertory theatre" by name, so we could not escape. The articles allowed us to operate theatres of every description, to organize schools, to present all manner of performances, to organize touring companies, to sell memberships, and to buy and sell real and personal property. In short, we were to be allowed to grow into a full-fledged theatre.

To excite interest in our new undertaking, and to promote sales of our season tickets, we publicized the program the theatre would undertake: a children's play series, a one-act play contest, dance programs, opera *intime*, productions of plays by local authors, a state-wide play festival, and tours of successful productions. Eventually, most of this program came to fruition.

With sales and promotion under way and money coming in from subscriptions, Burton, always careful with public funds though vague about his own, cast about for an accountant. One of the girls in our group interested her accountant husband in our project and he set up the books. Many a time I saw Mr. Bower look up with a pained expression from the pile of bills and say, "I don't see how we can go on. You know, we're broke." But go on we did, for twenty-three years, and in the end it took more than financial problems to shut us down.

Anyone excited about "free enterprise" should have worked with us over the years. We were as enterprising as all get out, and as free as the birds to go hungry if necessary. No one was getting a salary, though expense money for food and a roof was provided when necessary. We never had financial incentives, tax relief, or subsidies, but we managed somehow.

Everything seemed to be going well. We were working toward the opening of our first season, rehearsing Seán O'Casey's *Juno and the Paycock* and Ferenc Molnár's *The Guardsman*, building scenery, making costumes, and wondering where in the world we could play the shows. As time was getting short and the dates were set, we finally settled on the Metropolitan Theatre in downtown Seattle. It had an enormous overhead for our limited resources, but there were some advantages: it was Seattle's most highly regarded road show theatre and the public would associate us with all the professional troupes that had played there. We felt we needed to impress on the average theatregoer that we were no longer a student group but a company of theatre artists.

We had announced that our first plays would be *The Guardsman*, *Juno and the Paycock*, and Sem Benelli's *The Jest*. The first was a comedy, the second a realistic tragedy, and the third a pageant-like melodrama. All three had been recent Broadway successes and had never been seen in Seattle.

The decision to open with *The Guardsman* had been arrived at on the urging of Harold Johnsrud, who knew Cheryl Crawford of the Theatre Guild in New York, which held the rights to the Molnár play. Ten days before our announced opening, the Theatre Guild wired that *The Guardsman* was not available for Seattle. Publicity, sets, costumes, and rehearsals all had to be scrapped at the eleventh hour, and *Juno and the Paycock* (which luckily had been in rehearsal at the same time) was moved up to fill the number-one spot.

We had not wanted to open with such a starkly realistic tragedy, but there was no alternative. *Juno and the Paycock* is a great play—one of the greatest. It is also the sort of play some playgoers label "depressing," so it made a difficult pacesetter for our first season. But it was a great thrill for all of us when O'Casey sent a handwritten letter giving us permission to produce the play in Seattle at five pounds a performance.

The Seattle Repertory Playhouse began in October 1928 with four performances of *Juno*. We played to fair audiences and had good reviews. Our total costs for the production came to $1,200. We earned $1,100. On the surface, it looked as though we had lost only $100, but that didn't take into account such things as office rental, sales costs, staff expenses (minimal though they were), publicity, and general overhead. Don Bower attempted to make order out of the chaos of the theatre's economics—an overflowing desk basket of unposted bills and statements. While he wrestled with the accounts, the rest of us launched into production for Benelli's *The Jest*.

The Jest, a melodrama laid in Renaissance Italy, presents a number of technical problems to a successful production and we hoped to use it to establish the technical competence of our young company. We threw caution to the winds, economically, and engaged a young artist, Norman Kelly, to design three lavish sets. We engaged the Scenic and Lighting Studio to construct fireplaces, huge doors and windows, pillars, and handmade furniture.

We needed eighteen-foot sets for the production. Hugo Alde, our stage technician, told us that he knew of some flats, stored in an old warehouse, that could be purchased cheaply. We went to have a look at them and found that they were covered in linen. Mr. Alde told us that linen had been used as ballast on Russian ships coming to Seattle ports, then dumped on the docks when cargo was loaded and could be taken away for little or nothing. We purchased the flats for around four hundred dollars.

Catherine Stetsky, who had been a costumier in pre-revolutionary Russia and had worked for us at Cornish, was turned loose among bolts of silk, brocades, and taffetas, bundles of fur, and hanks of lace to create an eye-filling display of stage dresses and uniforms. Wigs were made, tights knitted to order, shoes, weapons, and jewellery purchased.

An elegant spectacle was in the making, a calculated investment in our future.

The play was praised by both audiences and critics for the skill, beauty, and lavishness with which it was presented. We had acquired a good deal of material that could be (and was!) used over and over, and our theatre's reputation for production was indelibly etched in the public's mind. We had spent more than five hundred dollars on scenery, four hundred dollars on costumes, nearly six hundred dollars on advertising, plus properties, royalties, rental for the Metropolitan Theatre, and the cost of hiring some stagehands. The total cost of mounting the production, fantastic as it seems now considering the costs of plays today, came to nearly three thousand dollars. Mr. Bower, with an aggrieved air, said that some kind of dementia must have affected us, since we took in less than half that amount.

When we were informed that our first four months of operation had cost over one thousand dollars a month, we realized that some drastic curtailment was necessary. The Metropolitan Theatre was definitely out; other arrangements had to be made.

We finally rented the auditorium at the Women's Century Club. However inadequate the stage and backstage facilities, we had to make do, for we had four more plays to produce to fulfill our obligations to our subscribers. The auditorium was attractive, with seating capacity for between 350 and 400, and we occupied it for the rest of that playing season and for our second year. We also decided to eliminate all paid advertising and to rely on the free space provided by local newspapers for our press releases. And no salaries whatever would be paid.

We finished our first season with G. Martinez Sierra's *The Romantic Young Lady* in March, Henrik Ibsen's *The Wild Duck* in April, *In His Image*, an original script by local playwright Garland Ethel in May, and Tom Taylor's *The Ticket-of-Leave Man* in June. At Christmas time, we produced *Rip Van Winkle* by W. Kerr and G. H. Leverton for our younger audience.

We wound up our first year in operation with an income of $9,771.60, and expenditures of $11,129.73—a deficit of $1,358.13. But we had gained invaluable stature in the esteem of our audiences and potential audiences, had stockpiled a good deal of material for reuse, and had begun to achieve the things we had set out to do—the production of original plays by local playwrights, for example.

Garland Ethel was a University of Washington professor. *In His Image* was set in Okanagan County, Washington, and dealt with a religious family corroded by a restrictive fanaticism that centred on preparing for the end of the world. It had a reasonable run, though some censoring had been threatened by both church and moralistic groups because of its subject and a Freudian dream fantasy scene that, at that time, seemed very daring.

We had also begun to develop the wonderful camaraderie that was one of the strongest pillars of the Playhouse throughout its existence. One of the events which contributed to this was our first Christmas dinner on stage, a dinner cooked by the wife of the custodian at the Women's Century Club. Only the cast and crew of the current Christmas play attended that first dinner, but it became an annual Playhouse event, frequently attended by as many as 150 guests, with special invitations going to the members of our board, the mayor, and other local or visiting notables.

Our second season, 1929–30, opened with Molnár's *The Guardsman*, which the Theatre Guild had finally released to us. This was followed by another original script, *The Chaste Mistress* by Marianne King, a young playwright from San Francisco. Louisa M. Alcott's *Little Women* was our Christmas production. We also toured to Everett, Washington, playing *The Guardsman*, Ibsen's *Master Builder,* and Gregorio Martinez Sierra's *Romantic Young Lady.*

Another original script in this season was *L'Envoi* by Albert M. Ottenheimer, now an actor with our group. The author's name was withheld before the run, so that the play would be given fair and impartial criticism. It was well received, as were all of the original plays that we did. We concluded the season with Luigi Pirandello's *Six Characters in Search of an Author*, the play that had seemed so controversial at the Cornish School. It now played without adverse comment or censorship of any kind.

In two years of operation, we had produced twelve plays for subscription audiences, three of which were original scripts. Two plays, not included in subscriptions, were for young audiences. And we had gone on tour—to one city, it was true, but it was a beginning. We seemed to be realizing some of the objectives that we had set for ourselves in our early press releases—and we finished our second season without a staggering deficit, something unheard of in the annals of regional theatres.

While we were playing at the Women's Century Club, we realized that as long as we were in rented quarters, our development and expansion, both artistically and financially, would be held back. For instance, without control over our playing space, it was impossible for us to extend runs. We had to have a home of our own. After our fruitless search for premises, we decided to build, preferably in the university district, with its convenient location. In 1928, our prospects looked hopeful. A complex of shops was to be built in the district and, similar to the shopping malls being constructed today, was to have a theatre—our theatre, we hoped.

One Sunday evening we were having supper with friends, and our hostess was reading our fortunes in tea leaves. In proper tea-leaf etiquette, one must make a wish before the reading begins, and of course my husband's wish was for the theatre in the shopping complex.

Our hostess said, "No, Burton, I don't see the complex. But I do see a theatre. And I see a tree. Most definitely, a tree!"

We laughed about it on the way home. A tree? The one thing we really didn't think we needed at that moment was a tree.

I remember vividly the day Burton came into our little office and said, "I've been looking at that old building on the corner of 41st and University Way. With the vacant lot that's right next to it, it might really make a fine theatre." Then he laughed. "And you know, there's a big old elm tree on the vacant lot!"

He called Arthur Loveless, one of Seattle's leading architects, and they went up the street to look at the property. Mr. Loveless saw possibilities in the location. They went to a restaurant for coffee and sketched out the plans on paper napkins. Their plans remained unaltered in the final building.

The existing building had been built by the Denny Renton Tile Company and had been used as a stable and for storage. The lot with the building and the vacant lot next door were owned by two different people. But now that we had set our hearts on this location, we set about finding some way to get it, beginning with raising the money to finance our dream. We had no experience and little talent for that kind of activity, but we had to learn, and learn we did, by doing. We approached banks for loans and were told that what we wanted was money for a "specialty" building and that that kind of money was difficult, almost impossible, to borrow. We were somewhat less daunted when we were informed that hospitals, churches, country clubs, libraries, and many others, were "specialty" buildings.

Our accountant said, "I know a man who specializes in specialty buildings." Specialist Wendell Pike seemed not at all perplexed by the problem and within what seemed a remarkably short time obtained the loan from the Prudential Savings and Loan Company. Pike was one of those rare informed and helpful persons who take the problems of the theatre to heart. He worked out the purchase of the property from its owner, Sam Fitz, a Bremerton tailor. He persuaded Mr. Fitz to buy the lot with the tree, which adjoined his property, with the assurance that we intended not only to lease the lots and his building but to remodel the latter at our own expense. A ninety-nine-year lease was drawn up and duly executed around these plans, with a multitude of legal stipulations attached to the venture.

The lease was to begin October 1, 1930, and terminate on the 30th day of September, 2029, "at the agreed rental of $175.00 per month for the first five years … $200.00 for the next five … $225.00 for the next five," and so on, on a rising scale up to $300 per month for the last eighty-five years of the lease. A year's rent, $2,100, was paid in advance.

In order to purchase the adjoining lot, Mr. Fitz had to pay off a $3,000 mortgage. This mortgage was taken out jointly by Mr. Fitz and the Repertory group.

A loan of $22,000 was obtained from the Barron Corporation, a local loan company at which the Prudential Savings and Loan Company placed the loan, on August 21, 1930. Monthly payments of $210 were to be made until the loan was paid in full. This was separate from the ground lease payments to Mr. Fitz.

When I reread the complicated arrangements and think of the rabbit-like costs that multiplied seemingly overnight, I am appalled at our temerity. We did all this with the consent and approval of our Board of Directors, who were good businessmen. But none of us realized that not prosperity but the worst depression that the United States or the world had known was just around the corner.

With the major financing accomplished, we had to find money for installations and the various other unexpected and surprising expenses that came up as the building progressed. Once, Burton and Al Ottenheimer went up and down the avenue to raise $1,100 that was urgently required to keep the contractor happy and the bricklayers laying bricks. They sold life memberships for one hundred dollars apiece and debenture notes of fifty or one hundred dollars. By the end of the afternoon, they had raised the needed funds. This was what our board called "junior financing." As I remember, it never amounted to much, but every little bit helped. We were still operating a subscription series, and that season we had sold two thousand subscriptions and were hoping for an eventual list of five thousand.

With all our "junior financing" and our fiscal wheeling and dealing, we still hadn't come close to approaching the fifty thousand dollars that Harold Johnsrud felt we needed to launch our enterprise. Discouraged, and finding the rigours of building this kind of theatre frustrating, he returned to Broadway and the New York stage. Al Ottenheimer, along with acting and writing plays, now became our promotion man, and he was a gem. He had newspaper experience and had a wonderful way of making friends and meeting people, as well as what seemed an inexhaustible fund of ideas for promotion.

With a good deal of help from our friends, and what seemed like endless hours of toil, the Repertory Playhouse gradually took shape. The old building on Mr. Fitz's lot was substantial, and its walls were extended upward to make the auditorium and the top of the stage house. Wings were added at each end of the building, with offices on one side of the horseshoe-shaped plan and workshops and dressing rooms on the other side. This created a rectangular walled courtyard surrounding the elm tree, which had been carefully preserved in the building process. Arched French windows in the theatre foyer opened onto the flagstone courtyard and garden. My father had given us the money to have this garden landscaped as a memorial to my mother, who had died the year before. There was a fountain and some nice planting, and the whole area made a charming addition to a theatre on a busy street.

And so, our theatre, just as it had been sketched by Arthur Loveless and Burton on restaurant napkins, became a reality. It opened on October 30, 1930, the third season of the Seattle Repertory Playhouse.

Major Barbara, our opening play, went well in spite of the problems we had in getting it on. The reviews were good, tickets were selling, and we were optimistic. We knew where we had come from and where we were going. We had at last accomplished one big purpose: we had a home of our own, although bewildering challenges lay ahead.

We had produced Seán O'Casey, Henrik Ibsen, and George Bernard Shaw in the same season. As one columnist observed, "John Public has right-about-faced. You see him standing in line to buy tickets to Shaw, Ibsen, and Shakespeare, and you see him coming out after the performance with that certainly-got-my-money's-worth expression." We did not do slight comedies to attract the unsophisticated theatregoer, as most new producers think they must. Great drama attracted audiences, and they paid their way.

The second play in our third season was another original script, *Leading Man*, a satiric comedy on Hollywood by William Kimball. *Billboard* carried a review of the play with a picture of the Playhouse and commented on the importance the production of new playwrights by theatres such as ours had on the development of theatre, plays, and playwrights for the country at large.

In the spring of 1930, we made a decision that was to have a significant impact on our theatre and its development. Since our student days, we had been interested in Ibsen's *Peer Gynt*. Most actors dream of plays and parts they would *like* to play, and my husband, I am sure, had for a very long time dreamed of the day when he would play "Peer." It was a fascinating play, a challenging play, a prestigious play, a good play. So, we decided that one of the first productions in our new theatre would be *Peer Gynt*. Our Board of Directors was understandably concerned about such a production, with its large cast, an orchestra to play the Grieg music, and an abundance of production costs. I suppose it didn't seem like the wisest choice, faced as we were at the time with mountains of bills. But, as Al Ottenheimer later described it, "Starry-eyed with the idealism which characterized some of our decisions, as frequently wrong as right, we went ahead."

CHAPTER SEVEN

Our production of *Peer Gynt* was to be the fifth presentation of the play in the United States. Richard Mansfield had produced it and acted the leading role in Chicago in 1905. Later, Louis James (no relation) produced and played "Peer." It was done by the Theatre Guild in 1923 and at Santa Barbara Community Theatre in California a few years after that.

Ibsen had written the play as a poem in five acts and thirty-eight scenes. It is said that once, as a birthday celebration, the total play was produced in two evening performances and Ibsen fell asleep in the middle of it! We obviously had to adapt it, so we arranged it in three parts and fifteen scenes, with Al Ottenheimer and myself largely responsible for the adaptation. We are absolved from any charges of literary vandalism by Ibsen himself, who had said, "Of course it's impossible to stage *Peer* except in an abbreviated form. I shall be satisfied as long as the piece is reduced to a proper length. Not to do this would spoil everything."

Ibsen frequently complained that people who considered *Peer Gynt* an angry social document were reading into the play meanings that were not there. "Why can they not read the book as a poem? For as such I wrote it." He insisted that *Peer Gynt* was a poetic fantasy. But, as Chekhov once said of one of his plays, "Read the play—it's all there."

In order to make the arrangement for production, we had five different play scripts, one of them from the National Theatre in Oslo, Norway, with Ibsen's cutting of the play and his own ideas for the interpretation of Edvard Grieg's music. Al's program notes for our first production anticipate some audience confusion over the play's essential meaning: "Just what is the meaning of the whole message is still a mooted question, although reams have been written in its interpretation." But for an acting version, we had to make decisions about the material. Some of the scripts we studied left out scenes that we felt were necessary. These included the scene with the Boyg that enunciates Peer's philosophy, "Go round about," and the madhouse scene where he is crowned emperor with a wreath of straw by the madhouse keeper, who overhears Peer's answer to the riddle of the sphinx, "Of course he is himself." Ibsen once said, "Only an insane man can be completely himself."

The first announcement of the production of the play was in the *Town Crier* in September 1930. For weeks, the press publicized the proposed production of *Peer Gynt* by a local group. "The theatrical event of the decade in Seattle," wrote the *Jewish Transcript*. "It will be, in every respect, a production unparallelled in the dramatic annals of Seattle," said the *Seattle Times*. To give the public a better understanding of the play's position as literature and drama, we arranged for a series of lectures for our subscribing members, with professors from the university discussing Ibsen's masterpiece on Sunday afternoons preceding the opening. This proved to be a wise move, for the subsequent long run was no doubt partly due to this scholarly popularization of the piece.

The cast of sixty included those in sectors of the cultural life of Seattle that had never before been engaged in a cooperative effort of this magnitude. Mary Ann Wells Studio of the Dance furnished the corps de ballet, and Myron Jacobson arranged Grieg's famous incidental music, which was played by members of the Seattle Symphony. The city's Scandinavian community entered enthusiastically into our preparations. One man called to ask if I would like him to paint the barn as the Norwegians would have painted it!

Scenery for the play was designed by Robert Mahaffy, who had taken careful note of the fifteen scenes in the play. The production, in playing time alone, took three hours, so long scene changes were obviously out. Bob designed a set that was ultramodern in approach and execution, allowing the entire drama to be played on a series of levels against a seemingly limitless expanse of blue sky. A revolving scenic base, the first time such a thing had been used in the Northwest, allowed many combinations and a variety of settings.

The first productions of *Peer* in Europe and the United States had been staged with realistic scenery. Whatever may be said for or against scenery of this kind, it must have lengthened the playing time. Our settings were presentational, as opposed to representational, and ideally suited to a production of this type. Scenes were changed in an average of one minute, the longest change taking only three minutes. A rickety fence, a little hut, a sphinx projected in the sky, an exotic palm tree, bed coverings that cascaded over the stage for Ase's death scene—these were some of the devices used to create the illusion of realism. Lighting was emphasized, and many people, including the reviewers, felt it the finest that had been seen in the Northwest. The settings were exceptionally effective for the wedding dance, the troll maidens' dance, and Anitra's dance with her Arabian maids. Masks, made by our costume department, were used for the trolls and some of the characters in the madhouse scene.

Owing to advance publicity, demand for reservations began to show very early. Inquiries and reservations poured in from individuals and groups up and down the coast. On February 6, 1931, the play opened. In the newspapers, it was as though a dam of newsprint had suddenly burst, gushing forth space and printers' ink. Pictures, interviews, features, rave reviews that reflected amazement at the magnitude of the undertaking—all of this gave our company an emotional lift beyond anything we could have imagined.

After the first performance, when we returned home tired, satisfied, and flushed with victory, Burton said, "Well, how did it go?"

"It could have been a hell of a mess," I replied—and fell into bed. Burton had achieved a long-awaited ambition. He had played Peer Gynt, and it was a success.

This was our fifteenth production. We added playing nights and extended the run months beyond the original dates. "Crowds Force Extension of *Peer Gynt*," said the headlines. "*Peer Gynt* Run Record Breaker Extended Again." We were playing to standing room only, night after night, and the admission prices were $1.25 and $1.50, based on another of Burton's convictions—that people should be able to afford theatre. The production ran from February 6 to the last week in April, and we played to 13,000 people in our 342-seat house.

The *Christian Science Monitor*, hard-pressed to understand the unprecedented popularity of this "highbrow" play, said: "Neither the Norwegian population of Seattle nor the Grieg music could have sustained audience interest unless Ibsen had been made into a good show. This was the work of the Repertory Players ... Not until *Peer Gynt* was it realized how great the need is in Seattle for more good spoken drama." The paper seemed quite surprised that the play had "turned out to be one of the most popular hits of any movie or play in the city in years."

The *Seattle Times* drama critic wrote: "Watching the finished production at the premiere last night—the beautiful lighting and staging of the piece, the flawless performance of certain actors and the so near perfect performance of others—a capacity first-night audience realized fully the magnitude of such an undertaking and were just a bit in awe. That I consider the greatest of compliments."

Audiences filling the theatre were not only from the intelligentsia or the social set. During the run of the play, a man fixing streetcar tracks in front of the theatre came to the box office for tickets. "I want my kids to see this," he explained. People in all walks of life and in all parts of the state felt the same way. Twenty years later, on the night my husband died, our daughter was being driven to the hospital in a cab. She said, "My father, Burton James, died tonight." "Burton James?" repeated the taxi driver. "I saw him in *Peer Gynt*."

While we kept extending the run of *Peer* to accommodate the audience for it, we were preparing our next production, *Our American Cousin*, by Tom Taylor. This is an American classic, best known for having been playing at Ford's Theatre the night President Lincoln was assassinated. When this production was ready, the only way we could get it on the boards was to run it on alternate playing nights with *Peer* until the end of the latter's run.

In June and July, not traditionally good months for "serious" or "heavy" drama, we produced *The Living Corpse* by Leo Tolstoy, a play we had done successfully at Cornish some years before. This was our first summer show, which was originally scheduled to run in June only.

However, it received such popular support that we extended the run through July as well.

Living Corpse required settings quite different from those used in *Peer Gynt.* Instead of the all-exterior scenes against which the Ibsen drama was played, the Tolstoy required only interiors. Instead of setting each scene in a fully closed interior, we showed only a corner of the room, sufficient to suggest the whole.

In the Moscow of Tolstoy's day there was a restaurant called the Yar, which was frequented by men of the same class as Fedya, the hero of *The Living Corpse.* It was famed for its excellent gypsy chorus, which had an attraction for the patrons that amounted almost to addiction, and large sums of money were spent there. For the restaurant scene in *The Living Corpse*, therefore, we needed a gypsy chorus. We were fortunate in having the services of Myron Jacobson, who owned the arrangements that had been used by the Moscow Art Theatre in their production of the play. Mr. Jacobson directed the chorus, most of whom were Russian émigrés like himself, and, with its guitar accompaniment, our gypsy music was a great success. This contact with the White Russian colony of Seattle was invaluable later on when, in our 1933–34 season, their assistance enabled us to produce *Kolokala*, a musical revue.

For the 1930 Christmas season, we engaged the Williams Marionettes for Saturday matinee performances. That rounded off our first season in our new home, and our third year as a company.

The experts were loudly proclaiming that this had been the worst year in theatrical history, but for us it had been by far the best. We had increased our subscriber list to nearly three thousand and extended our season by nearly three months. In the face of the deepening depression, the financial success of this season, which had enabled us to pay off the most pressing debts accumulated in the process of acquiring our building and installations, led us to expect future financial security—however ill-founded that expectation may have appeared in later years.

Now that we had our own theatre, we were able to extend runs to accommodate the demand created by one of the most compelling forms of advertising—word of mouth. "Don't miss it. It's a good show," filled many houses for us. We did thirty-nine performances of our 1931 *Peer Gynt*, as compared with only four of *Juno and the Paycock* in the rented Metropolitan Theatre.

In our first season, we had an income of nearly $10,000 and a deficit of $1,338.15; in our third season, our income was over $33,000, with a deficit of $955.96. As all the money we earned went into the cost of interest on building loans and other debts, I suppose it's logical for people to wonder what the actors and producers did for money. No one was on the payroll except the stage technician, the office manager, and the janitor. The rest of us had "day jobs," or made enough to live on as best we could.

I'm sure that many of the repertory regulars might not have been able to carry on, if it hadn't been for a happy stroke of luck during that first season. A local banker, Adolph Linden, bought a radio station. He was a gentleman who was years ahead of his time in his belief in what a radio station should do and be in a community. This belief included live, well-produced performances, and that's where our people came in. Mr. Linden hired Burton as a reader and actor for his station. I came on staff as continuity editor and director of plays. Part of my job was to read and pass on all scripts. Such scrutiny may be common practice now—it wasn't then. Mr. Linden would accept only the best for his station. Certain commercials were absolutely taboo, and even the best of them were run only at certain times so that they wouldn't interfere with the programming.

Opera—yes, live opera, with a good orchestra, chorus, and cast—was presented. Fine plays were done, dramatizations of good stories and the classics. For instance, at Christmas time we presented a dramatization of Charles Dickens' *A Christmas Carol*, years before Lionel Barrymore's version became a holiday tradition.

Mr. Linden's belief in Seattle and in its artists, and his willingness to pay those artists an adequate salary, deserves to be recorded. Radio personnel were woefully underpaid at that time and Mr. Linden established a precedent. He hired the best musicians, writers who "had names" or were making names for themselves, and excellent announcers. His operation was successful but perhaps overextended, for his station failed in the Great Depression. In the years that followed, however, I never knew anyone who had been associated with him and his American Broadcasting Company (not to be confused with the later ABC Network) who did not remember him with love and deep appreciation.

This work in radio, which provided substantial salaries for Burton, myself, and other Playhouse people as well, tided us over the difficult months of that first year. Ultimately, we accepted austerity and tightened belts, for we enjoyed tremendous rewards. Having the opportunity to do great plays in the way we wanted to do them was compensation enough, and money never really seemed to matter too much. Our daughter once said, "You know, some of those years must have been rough, but I can't remember. We always had so much to do, and so much excitement doing it." By the time we mounted our fourth production of *Peer Gynt*, for our 1940–41 season, a friend pointed out, "Mr. James has played ninety-two productions of *Peer Gynt*, and never received a twenty-five-cent piece for doing it."

We had "day jobs" to support ourselves and Marijo as well. In the fall of 1930, my husband and I were appointed to the Drama Division of the English Department at the University of Washington. We taught two-hour laboratory courses four days a week. Mine were in actor training and Burton's in scene design and construction. We also produced all the university plays. Any student on campus who wanted to take part in these plays came for try-outs and could be cast. The fact that we were working for the most part with untrained actors did not restrict us to doing plays of little importance. It was our belief that plays of merit, plays that raise important ideas, make demands on young actors that cannot be experienced in plays of no consequence. We also thought that teaching and producing in a school of drama at a university entailed some responsibility to maintain standards in dramatic literature. So, in our years there, we produced such substantial works as the Greek classics *Medea* and *Oedipus Rex,* and Hugo von Hofmannsthal's *Jedermann*, a poetic arrangement of *Everyman*. We also did Oscar Wilde's *Lady Windermere's Fan*, Karel Čapek's *R.U.R.* (*Rossum's Universal Robots*), and other plays of that standard of dramatic excellence. The interest that these plays generated among the students and the public was surprising. Sadly, in later years, after we had left the university, the new director chose to do plays "of popular appeal"—*Charley's Aunt, The Bride the Sun Shines On*, and the like.

During our time at the university, plays were produced four times a year, one in each quarter. At first, we worked in Meany Hall, long since torn down. It was said that when it was first built a member of the Board of Regents had commented with satisfaction that "no damn plays will go on there." Certainly it made it next to impossible to stage anything successfully, as it was cursed with a large hall with an enormous stage and awful acoustics. When the problems of trying to produce plays in such an unpromising place became too great, we rented the Playhouse to the university for a nominal sum.

In 1931, we opened our fourth season at the Playhouse. The depression was deepening throughout the country and actors were vying with producers for places in bread lines. Actors no longer winced when telling friends, "I'm at liberty," or "I'm waiting for a part." Everybody was "waiting for a part" in some production that would bring economic life back to the nation.

It took time for us to fully realize the situation. The west coast had not been hit as quickly as the east: the slow tremor of economic disaster had not reached Seattle in 1931–32. It was not until 1933 and the bank moratorium that we fully understood what we were facing.

We opened our fourth season with Frederick Lonsdale's *Aren't We All?*, a charming modern comedy with taste and style. As it was played in a Mayfair drawing room, we designed a very good Adams-period set that served us for many years, with set pieces added when needed. Once when Maurice Evans was touring Seattle, we entertained him and some of his company on the Playhouse stage, where the Adams set was in use for the evening's performance. Mr. Evans said, with some awe, "Think of finding a set like this in a regional theatre in Seattle!"

While playing *Aren't We All?* we were in rehearsal for *Romeo and Juliet*, which we were able to produce at very little cost. We still had the sets and dress materials, wigs, tights, and shoes that had seemed fantastic extravagances when we purchased them for *The Jest*, the second play in our first season. Now, they enabled us to produce a beautiful Shakespeare, the first in our new theatre, for next to nothing.

The vital duel routines were worked out by Paul Cope, the duelling instructor at the Washington Athletic Club. He later went to Hollywood to direct the duel scenes in MGM's production of *Romeo and Juliet* with Norma Shearer and Leslie Howard, using many of the dagger and rapier routines he had developed in our production.

Our next major production was Goethe's *Faust*, which was in rehearsal during the run of *Romeo and Juliet*. Frederick J. Patterson, who had been in our classes at Cornish, and Helga Lund were playing in *Romeo and Juliet* and were cast as Faust and Marguerite. Burton was to play Mephistopheles. We had planned the production of *Faust* as a centennial commemoration of Goethe's death and were enthusiastically supported in this by Seattle's entire German community, including the German consul, Walter Reinhardt.

This production presented many of the same practical difficulties we had wrestled with in *Peer Gynt*. For one thing, the play was too long, and had to be cut. We were fortunate that Al Ottenheimer was available to help with this, but we lacked an acting version of the play to work with. Acting versions are helpful, as they give a key to what other producers have thought about themes and the scenes chosen to develop them, as well as to what was omitted. *Faust* had none of the technical theatrical history of Shakespeare or Ibsen. Finally, using an early translation by Bayard Taylor and a later translation by Alice Raphael, we were able to reduce our too-long script to eighteen scenes.

We again had scenic backgrounds that had to be changed in the shortest time possible. Our scene designer, Dorothy Woempner Hichen, designed two pairs of Gothic arches, one sixteen feet high and the other eighteen, with steps, ramps, and platforms. They were mounted on trucks and could be moved very quickly from the Prologue in Heaven to Marguerite's cell at the end of the play. The arches were backed by a blue cyclorama and with effective lighting did a fine job of projecting the meaning and mood of the play.

Al spent many months on the arrangement of the play script and all of us delved into the historical background—the period, the author, the play itself. *Faust* has been described as a "play with a biography," meaning that it had been written during the long flow of Goethe's life. Christopher Marlowe's *Doctor Faustus* had toured Germany as a puppet show when Goethe was a youth, and it is said that it inspired him to write his masterpiece. He began the play in 1775, at the age of twenty-four, and finished it on his eighty-second birthday, August 28, 1832, a few months before his death. The play script was in two parts. For our production, we made the playing script from Part I, which Goethe finished when he was fifty-nine.

Briefly, the story of *Faust* is that of an old man who sells his soul to the devil to regain his youth, his love affair with the village maiden Marguerite, whom he deserts, her murder of her baby and her madness, execution, and redemption. Goethe, like Ibsen, was living through the social disorientation of his age, faced with the destructive reality of an industrial society. As with *Peer Gynt*, we arranged for Sunday lectures to be given by professors from the Germanic Department of the University of Washington. They dealt with *Faust* as literature and drama, as well as Goethe's philosophic approach in writing it.

Music for our production—Berlioz's *Damnation of Faust*—was arranged by Franco Mariggiali, a gifted and highly trained musician, and a member of the Seattle Symphony. Mary Ann Wells Studio of the Dance prepared the ballet for the Walpurgis Night scene.

We had a cast of sixty and were soon up to our necks in the extraordinary amount of work that goes into mounting a production of this kind. One Sunday morning at ten o'clock, we started arranging and lighting the sets for the eighteen scenes. At four o'clock the next morning we were still at it, when a policeman, having seen suspicious signs of activity, entered the building waving his flashlight and demanding, "All right, what goes on here?"

"We're working."

"Working? At this hour?" he responded. "My God, you've a worse job than I have." And he took himself off, shaking his head in amazement.

We opened in March to excellent reviews. On opening night, we received a cablegram of congratulation from the National Theatre in Berlin and, at a special Goethe centennial celebration held by Seattle's German community, Consul Walter Reinhardt received congratulations on the production from the Goethe-Gesellschaft and the Foreign Office in Berlin.

We did not have the substantial advance box office that we had for *Peer* and were a little apprehensive. However, through news, reviews, and word of mouth, the audiences began to build, and by the second week we knew we were set for a longer run than the usual six weeks.

Faust ran from March to the middle of May. During the run, we played in Tacoma to a standing-room-only house and also in Vancouver, British Columbia. A young Seattle businessman, not a member of our board, considered *Faust* so important that he felt it should be seen in Vancouver. Touring to Tacoma, which was only thirty miles away, was quite different from transporting the entire production to Vancouver, and our budget was in no condition to permit a gamble. But the young man assured us that if we had a deficit (and we did—$1,600 worth) he would meet it. And he did.

We went to Vancouver in May. It was a bad time of year. Spring was upon us and audiences were not thinking of theatre. Or perhaps they wondered why they should be interested in a Seattle troupe playing *Faust*. Robert Cromie, then editor of the *Vancouver Sun,* came on the second night because, as he said, "I have never seen *Faust*, and probably will have no other chance to see it again, and no matter how bad it may be, it's worth the effort." During the intermission he came backstage to Burton's dressing room and exclaimed, "This is tremendous! I have seen many fine things in this old house, but nothing better than this. This house should be filled. What can I do?"

He needed no suggestions from us. Next day we appeared in five different places in his paper, with a front page story, an editorial, a review, and pictures, and he jumped our ad from a two-by-four-inch size to a quarter of a page. He became a firm friend, frequently coming from Vancouver to see something that interested him at the Playhouse.

One night when he came, we had a tremendous downpour of rain. We took him back to our apartment after the performance for tea and a snack; the rain was pouring in, but we set out pans and buckets and had a good time around the fire. Later, making a speech at a dinner which we had for some occasion or other, he said, "I've swilled champagne and plovers' eggs in some dandy Mayfair drawing rooms, but one of the best times I've ever had was at the James' apartment, sitting around the fire, with the rain pouring through the roof."

During *Faust*'s Vancouver run, I came up on a bus and arrived late at the theatre. The play was already on as I entered the balcony, and I thought to myself, "It's really beautiful!" That feeling is one of the compensations for a difficult task.

A young German artist living in Vancouver came to the box office on the last night of *Faust*'s run there, with a request. "I've come every night to see this, and I've no more money. Do you suppose I could have a ticket for this last night?" Of course he could. We were not reluctant to give tickets to see our plays. He said, "There will be many beautiful productions of *Faust* in Germany this year, but nothing better than this. You are all so young and beautiful."

Back home in Seattle, we tallied up statistics on the production. People had come from thirty towns and cities in the four western states, and young people had been brought in by bus from all around

Washington. Over ten thousand people saw the twenty-five performances of the play. *Faust* did not earn the money that *Peer Gynt* did, but it garnered us a great deal of prestige. At a time when Broadway was bankrupt, *Billboard* wrote in March 1932: "The Seattle Repertory Theatre is attracting audiences from many surrounding cities in the Pacific Northwest—Oregon, California, British Columbia, and from as far away as Montana. Seattle is fortunate in having this Repertory Playhouse where this theatre finds its home. The players of this theatre are to be lauded for the really artistic work they are doing at the present time."

Reviewers praised Burton as an actor and my abilities as a director. My husband was not only an excellent actor but a man who thought of and contributed to the life and people of his community and country. I haven't mentioned these reviews, for we were building a theatre, not ourselves. We fit only into whatever the theatre achieved. I used to read reviews in those days not to see what they said about us but to see the space and position they gave the theatre in the paper. It wasn't just Burton and I who thought this way—our co-workers did as well. The success of the theatre was what counted for us. We were an oasis in a desert of cutthroat competition.

We finished our season with Anton Chekhov's *Cherry Orchard*, which we loved doing. It received favourable reviews, but did not do good business. Unlike the Norwegian support for Ibsen and the German support for Goethe, there was no large Russian population in Seattle to support Chekhov. The public seemed to expect that the play would be an exercise in Russian gloom, rather than the charming, easily understandable comedy that it is.

That summer we inaugurated our first summer drama festival, with a revival of *Peer Gynt*, *The Wild Duck*, and *A Doll's House*. During this all-Ibsen festival we alternated performances on every day except Sundays and Mondays from June 11 through July 9. It was our first attempt at performances in repertory.

The theatre had been in existence for four years, two of them in our own building. We had survived and had paid many of the pressing debts incurred in the building process. With the productions of *Peer Gynt, Romeo and Juliet*, and *Faust*, we had achieved the shadow, if not the substance, of victory.

CHAPTER EIGHT

The Seattle *Jewish Transcript* of October 7, 1932, predicted in its columns that "The Repertory Playhouse's fifth season opening next Wednesday will draw aside curtains on the most flourishing of Repertory years." It did, but it also ushered in the shattering years of the Depression.

It had been our custom from the first years to mail season tickets to our subscribers. In 1932 the tickets were being returned with letters saying "We can't afford season tickets this year." We began to realize that the Depression was upon us, its talons sinking into our flesh.

The wounds opened and blood began to flow when we had to quitclaim our building to the owner in 1934, giving up our rights to it. We had been paying $175 a month to the owner and had hoped to be able to buy it. We did manage to lease it back under new conditions, since the landlord was stuck too—it was a "specialty" building, and we seemed to be the only people who could make use of it. The new lease arrangement was 15 percent of the gross on everything we earned. One of our board members said, "Not too bad an arrangement. I wish I could be assured of 15 percent of the gross on the property I own."

At the time we were building the theatre, we had borrowed $4,000 from the bank, guaranteed by us and some members of our board. Over the years, we had managed to reduce it to $1,500. Then came a quarter when we could pay only the interest, then another quarter when we couldn't even meet the interest. We were threatened with the note being called.

We were out of oil and the electricity had been cut off for non-payment of bills. We coped with the oil problem by burning odd scraps of wood in the furnace and mollified the power company by going around to collect sub-rental debts that other local artists owed us for use of the theatre for concerts and recitals. We went on rehearsing, paying something here and something there. If we hadn't, everyone would have lost. Somehow, we managed. We survived until another, more disastrous, cloud loomed.

Burton and I were employed in the Drama Department on the university campus and had been renting the Playhouse to the university for student productions. Then Glenn Hughes, head of the Drama Department, began using off-campus people for his plays, and it came to a showdown when he proposed a production of Ibsen's *Ghosts* with a retired professional actress in the leading role. We realized that an Ibsen production with a non-student cast would be professional competition to our company and cause no end of confusion, especially in the mind of the ticket-buying public, so we refused the rental. Burton was dismissed from his university post for "non-cooperation," but I stayed on. We needed the money. I continued teaching acting classes at the university and directing Associated Students of the University of Washington (ASUW) plays until 1938.

The threatening cloud of disaster began to develop shape and substance. Glenn Hughes, who was vice-president of our Board of Directors and thoroughly familiar with the financial crisis we faced, went to the board and said that he would pay off the bank note if they would turn the theatre over to him. They refused. Hughes then resigned, stating that he disagreed with its policies.

Then it was rumoured that the Board of Regents of the university had been approached to buy or lease our building for the Drama Department. When we heard this rumour, I went to see Dr. Leslie Ayers, dean of the Law School and legal advisor to the Board of Regents, who was reported to be investigating the situation and the possible purchase. Dr. Ayers was a friend of ours and an interested patron of the Playhouse. He told me that Hughes had informed the Regents that financial difficulties would soon force us out of business and that our building would be coming up for sale. Hughes had approached the owner, who understandably would have been very willing to free himself, for hard cash, of this "specialty" building.

While I was in Dr. Ayers' office, he called a prominent member of the Board of Regents and said, "I have had some clarification on this business of the Playhouse and Hughes. I would advise that the Board of Regents not be involved." The disastrous cloud was diminished, if not dispersed, at least for the time being. This episode gave us our first indication of the lopsided competition that would develop between the state-subsidized university student theatres and the private enterprise of the Repertory Playhouse, with its adult professionals.

That fifth season we opened with Ferenc Molnár's *Liliom* and followed it with Marianne King's *Mad, Bad and Dangerous to Know*, an original script based on the life and loves of Lord Byron. The title was taken from an entry in Lady Caroline Lamb's diary the night she met Byron: "Mad, bad and dangerous to know, but that beautiful pale face is my fate."

For our children's play at Christmas, we did *Prunella*, by Laurence Housman and Granville Barker. It was done in collaboration with the Junior League, which was responsible for promotion and ticket sales while we took care of the production. This most satisfactory relationship went on for the next few years. Our second Shakespeare at the Playhouse was *Comedy of Errors*, done with the active cooperation of the high schools of Seattle. We had expanded our playing nights and were now playing Wednesday, Thursday, Friday, and Saturday, trying to perform in repertory, part of our original plan and captured in the theatre's full name.

We produced another original play that season, *Funny Man* by Al Ottenheimer. It was an amusing comedy about vaudeville and life in that kind of theatre, and the audiences enjoyed it. A local society matron played one of the leads and it must have been with at least a touch of irony that Al noted in the log of our almost bankrupt theatre, "She comes to rehearsals in a limousine with a chauffeur who calls at the end of rehearsals for her."

Bert Hoog, one of our actors who played in *Funny Man*, took the script to Hollywood, where he met Ginger Rogers' mother, Lela, who wanted to try her hand at directing a play. When we knew that Al's play was to be produced in Hollywood, we took up a collection to send him down for the opening. Burton called Al to the stage and presented him with $30.20, collected in nickels, dimes, and pennies from the group, from the children up.

Al hadn't been in Hollywood for more than forty-eight hours before he was being interviewed by Harry Rapf of MGM, who offered him a job as a writer. Al agreed to work for ten days on *The March of Time*, a musical, and was assigned a private office with his name on the door. But he explained that he couldn't stay in Hollywood very long, as he was the promotion man for the Playhouse in Seattle.

Mr. Rapf, assuming that salary must what was interfering with his negotiations, asked Al how much he was paid at the Playhouse. "Ten dollars a week—when I get it."

Rapf stared in utter disbelief and said, "You like it, huh?"

After his ten-day stint on the Metro-Goldwyn-Mayer lot, Al returned to Seattle and the Playhouse, and rejoined the rest of us in the struggle of trying to keep our theatre afloat.

In 1931, with the Depression advancing on us, we had decided to produce *Uncle Tom's Cabin*. At that time, it was considered a quaint American classic. Everybody knew of it, but few had seen it, so we decided a production was in order. Because eyebrows are raised today at the mention of such a "racist" play ever having been produced in our theatre, I did some research on the history of the play and the book from which it was taken. Carl Sandburg, in his biography of Lincoln, *The Prairie Years*, devotes a whole chapter to *Uncle Tom's Cabin* and its author. He writes: "As Lincoln walked the streets of Springfield and as he rode the circuit of twelve counties, living in hotels and court-houses, he met people shaken and stirred by slavery; they had read a book, the book had set their hearts on fire with hate ... It was a hate that made them hate their own country, its laws, its flag; they believed that their own country was guilty of a crime worse than the crimes of any other country in any other time; they had read a book."

The book was Harriet Beecher Stowe's *Uncle Tom's Cabin, or Life among the Lowly*, published in 1852. Her book aroused anti-slavery sentiment not only in the United States but throughout the world and acted as a catalyst, unifying all the anti-slavery forces in the United States and leading to the nomination of Abraham Lincoln for president. Shortly after the novel was published, it was made into a play and played in many places for many years.

When we produced it, *Uncle Tom's Cabin*, the book that had contributed so much to the abolition of slavery, was anathema to "Black Power" and other forces fighting for the rights of Black people. The names of Uncle Tom, Simon Legree, and Topsy are still used as stereotypes: Uncle Tom for a Negro collaborator, Simon Legree as a harsh, slave-driving boss, and Topsy, a child knowing neither father nor mother, who "just growed." I knew of no Black actor who had ever played the role of Uncle Tom—it was always played in blackface and this is how Al Ottenheimer played it in our production.

We got a script of the play from Samuel French, written by G. L. Aiken. Aiken was no playwright. The script was a mishmash of nothing. We couldn't see how it could possibly be directed, or even played. Then, one day in the midst of our dilemma, a friend called and said, "I hear you're doing *Uncle Tom's Cabin*. My mother-in-law played Topsy for twenty-six years on tour." We welcomed this miracle with open arms and rushed to see the lady. After talking to her, we understood why there was no script. The play was treated as a kind of scenario. The actors in the touring company made up lines and business to suit themselves, and to fatten their parts. If it worked, and if they could get away with it, it became part of the play but was evidently never set down in script form.

The lady we spoke with was still, at the age of seventy-six, a dynamo. She knew everyone's lines and most of the business. It was her suggestion that we have a Black male quartet to sing Little Eva into heaven, and singers and dancers for the plantation scene, which was a completely improvised musical interlude. We approached the local African Methodist Church for help and received wonderful cooperation. This was our first introduction to the Seattle Negro community and it was to lead to a long and productive friendship.

There were more than a few problems with the production, of course. One involved the scene where Eliza, with her baby in her arms, flees the "patarollers" (the dialect word for the patrols) who pursued runaway slaves, following the "drinkin' gourd" to Canada. Eliza crosses a river on the ice floes, followed by the patrols with dogs—bloodhounds.

We searched Seattle and the surrounding countryside. No bloodhounds, not even one. Though we knew that in some of the touring versions of the show spaniels, dachshunds, mongrels, and even Pekingese had been pressed into service, we wanted the scene to be exciting, not hilarious. At last, we met a man who owned a trained tracking dog, a Doberman, well-known for finding people lost in the mountains and elsewhere. The owner, who was also the dog's trainer, was willing to let us have the dog for the show, under certain conditions. The dog was to come to the Playhouse in a taxi and be returned the same way. Our accountant took a dim view of paying taxi fare for a dog, but our canine colleague was essential to the play, so he finally capitulated.

The other stipulation was that only one person was to have anything to do with the dog. The day the owner first brought the animal to the Playhouse, he showed us why this was necessary. While the dog was lying quietly in a corner, the owner told Burton, "Grab me by my lapel." The moment Burton touched the man, the dog was up with one leap, grabbed my husband by the wrist, and held him until the owner gave him the order to release. The owner introduced the actor playing the leader of the patrol to the dog and rehearsed him in the necessary actions. He stressed that no one but this one actor was to speak to the dog or try to make friends with him. I may say that no one particularly wanted to.

Even the taxi driver kept his distance. He would drive to the backstage entrance, open the door of the Playhouse, open the door of the taxi, and leap smartly behind it. The dog would bound out, run straight to his pad backstage, and stay there quietly until he heard his cue, which was the crash of a box. With that, he would leap to his feet, barking and snarling, straining at his leash. The actor would grab the leash and they were off—a good show. After that brief scene was completed, the dog would trot back to his pad and wait for the taxi to come and take him home.

Arnold von Winkelreid (that was the dog's name) never did take a curtain call—his owner had not been able to rehearse him in that. But he stole the scene every night. Even the *New York Times* commented on it. But as actors say, "Acting with babies or animals … you can have it!"

As an audience-pleaser, for some fond memories, and for its introduction to some fine people, *Uncle Tom's Cabin* was an important production for us.

When Paul Green's *In Abraham's Bosom* won the Pulitzer Prize for its New York production in 1932, we asked for and received permission to produce it at the Playhouse. The play's story is laid in the turpentine camps of North Carolina in 1885. Though the Emancipation Proclamation had freed the slaves two decades earlier, peonage still existed. Abraham is the illegitimate son of the White landowner and half-brother to his father's White son. An altercation arises between the boys, and the father whips his Black son to show him his place and to teach him that he can't "get uppity" with a White man. "You've got to know your place, Abe, and I've got to teach you." But Abe never accepts this. He hopes for something better than being a turpentine hand in peonage and longs for an education that could lift him out of the hopelessness of his life. His struggle goes on until he is lynched.

The play needed a Black cast with only two White actors. In order to cast it, we went back to the African Methodist Church. One Sunday, twenty-five people came to hear Burton read the play in hopes of interesting a Black cast in the production. We got not only a cast but a choir and started rehearsal early in October. Rehearsals at first were very difficult as the cast was inexperienced. But they were interested and concerned with the job, and they learned quickly.

All the cast, with the exception of Joseph S. Jackson, who played Abraham, and Sara Oliver, who played his mother, were from the north, and some had been born in Seattle. The area and situations of the play were almost totally foreign to them. Mr. Jackson, however, came from within a few miles of the play's location, and Mrs. Oliver had lived in that area. Although Mr. Jackson was a graduate of New York University and had been in the north for years, he had not forgotten his early roots. And Mrs. Oliver was a tremendous help in teaching the dialect and authentic customs to the other members of the cast. She still spoke as the people in the play spoke, and she knew the customs and behaviour patterns of the people in the area where she was born and raised. Her business with the snuff stick, her prayers, her dancing in moments of joy gave a lively authenticity to the scenes she was in and seemed to communicate itself to the other members of the cast. Alberta Walker, who played Abe's wife, had the spark, the talent, that quality which makes an actress not only a good one but in inspired moments even a great one.

The play opened January 11, 1933. Reviewers, excited by the performance given by these Black amateurs, called it "the greatest triumph of The Playhouse." Audiences came from up and down the coast to see it, many asking where the actors had come from, although most of them had lived in Seattle all their lives. Suddenly, the papers, which at that time would not print photographs of Blacks but only line drawings, were calling them "Seattle artists." Audiences gave them standing ovations and shouted "Bravo" (rare experiences for Seattle) and left the Playhouse as though it was a church.

We used the choir for incidental music in the scenes and between the acts. The concluding spiritual after the lynching was "When the World's on Fire," with its moving lyrics—*don't you want God's bosom to be your pillow?*—sung low and rising to a crescendo at the curtain, which we held for a moment or two. It was an unforgettable experience.

In the spring of 1933, remembering our financial successes with *Peer Gynt* and *Faust*, we decided to produce Gerhart Hauptmann's *The Sunken Bell,* orchestra and all. The musicians' union, always cooperative, made special financial arrangements with us for this production. But all the support from the German community seemed to have disappeared. A strange new wind was blowing in the world; Hitler had come to power. The production was incredibly beautiful to look at, but a crashing bore. Perhaps this was due to my direction, as I was never able to sort out and clarify the German mythology that Hauptman dramatized in his play. The failure of *Sunken Bell* ended our productions of spectacle plays. We didn't realize it at the time, but with the changing world situation, as well as our straitened financial situation, we were moving into the period of the realistic play.

The *Sunken Bell*'s sinking closed the theatre for a few weeks for the first and only time in our history. We began to make preparations for our Summer Festival, reviving *The Living Corpse* and *In Abraham's Bosom*, and preparing a new Ibsen, *The Vikings at Helgeland*. These productions tided us over the summer, and we were able to start rehearsals on our fall production without quite as many austerities as the year before, although we still owed money to the oil and electricity people and wouldn't have heat or light until we settled the accounts.

In our fifth season, we had acquired a small building directly adjacent to the Playhouse for our apprentice classes and extra rehearsal space. This little building, which resembled a Doric temple, had been built originally as a gas control station and we leased it from the Seattle Gas Company for twenty dollars a month. We were particularly glad to have the apprenticeship building at this point, because it was hooked up to another electric light company, one to which we were not indebted. We strung a cable over to the theatre and jerry-rigged one light on the stage and one in the workshop. The theatre log reveals, "It's against the law, but necessity doesn't recognize it, and we're hoping we don't get caught." A day later, the log adds, "We had the gas for the office heater turned on today, but we had to tap the Apprentice Group Building again for the current to run the fan in it."

That was the situation in September of 1933. We opened our sixth season with Björnstjerne Björnson's *Love and Geography*, a charming Norwegian comedy. Björnson was a contemporary of Ibsen, a popular and established playwright when Ibsen was struggling. He recognized Ibsen's genius and was his good friend during those trying years. He was a good friend to us as well, since his play brought in badly needed box office dollars.

We followed this with *Richard III*, our third Shakespeare. There was growing interest in these Shakespearean performances in the high schools of the city. More high schools sent larger numbers of students, and these performances increased our receipts at the box office, which for us was an important consideration. Burton played Richard, and I appeared on the Playhouse stage as an actress for the first time. I played Queen Margaret as a replacement for an actress who had a job that did not permit her to do the matinee performances. Al Ottenheimer, in his log, recorded that I did "a surprising job." Surprising perhaps because I got through it—with my husband waving me out of his way.

For our pre-high school audience we produced J. B. Fagan's *Treasure Island*, with Al directing. Burton played Long John Silver, with a parrot on his shoulder. We had all assumed that the bird was a male; but one morning the owner found an egg in the bottom of the cage. We never did decide whether it was a tribute or a criticism. The play went very well, with good audiences. The Christmas plays always attracted young audiences, perhaps because admission was only twenty-five cents. After Christmas, we produced *No More Frontier*, by Talbot Jennings, a play we did subsequently for the Washington State Theatre.

We went on producing plays and attending meetings and overcoming crises, one after another. Al recorded in his log in 1933, "Things look black indeed. Our history has been one protracted crisis, from which we have [extricated] ourselves by a series of timely miracles. But it will take the failure of only one of these miracles to trip us up. Each crisis is a little more stringent than the last."

By May of 1934, the stringency was acute. We had been unable to raise the money to meet two payments on the bank note and the royalty for our current play was in arrears. The license inspector was protesting because we hadn't paid the city theatrical license, due the previous November. Al recorded one memorable day in the log: "I was awakened by the service of a summons of a suit instituted by the National Discount Corporation against Sam Fitz (our landlord), his deceased wife's estate, and The Playhouse, for our neon signs, of which there are two. On top of that, today we had two other suits threatened but, I think and fervently hope, forestalled for the time being at least." We sent our irate creditors ten dollars apiece, and crossed our fingers for luck.

Other forces, nation-wide in scope, were at work shaping the course that our group was to take. We received a letter from the State Transient Service, which argued the case of the recreational needs of the homeless and dispossessed of the area. Most of the transients who were wandering the nation in search of jobs and security were under twenty-five, "on the bum," in and out of jail, following the seasonal harvest work when there was any to be had. At that time they had no organization interested in their daily problems or able to give them the "respectable" poverty represented by organized charity.

The State Transient Service Director's letter sketched some of the most pertinent facts:

> Due to the pressure of many perplexing problems that confound us in relief administration from week to week, we have found it difficult to make adequate recreational provision for these people as a group and hence this letter to you. I would ask whether you and your associates would be willing, within the coming months of September and October, to arrange for a definite evening's entertainment for the benefit of these

> people. I do not know whether the accommodations at our Central Feeding Station could be made available for this purpose. If not, it may be that you could co-operate with this office to the end that some public auditorium or high school gymnasium might be made available for this purpose. The drab and colorless life led by these people tends to provoke irrationalism and I am of the opinion that if your organization could co-operate with us, as suggested above, that your organization would be making a fine contribution to public service. We are confronted with a rather serious situation in dealing with this group of people who are anxious to return to work and still are denied such an opportunity. It is pertinent, therefore, to endeavor to give them, within the limitations of reason, some of the things the average person has come to regard over a period of years as a standard of human recreation and daily life.

We had no time to arrange special programs, but we could make seats available in the theatre and we did. The street railway was willing to honour transfers for return fares, so all the transients had to pay was the tax on admission. A few lines in Al's log record how we felt and our response to such requests: "We have been doing this sort of thing off and on for three or four years. I can't think of any better use for vacant seats. It would be fine if business was so good that we wouldn't have to call on them for a respectable-sized audience, but there'd always be room for some of them. This is right in line with our recent efforts to work with the social service work that's being done, for all of us are agreed—although Mr. and Mrs. James were the first to recognize it—that in some way the future of the theatre is bound up with this matter of adult education."

We finished the season with *Volpone*, adapted by Stefan Zweig from Ben Jonson's script and we had some censorship problems. There is a scene in the play where Volpone attempts to rape Columba and there is a scream from her window, "Rape! Rape!" We left it in. The Pasadena Community Theatre had changed the line to "Skulduggery! Skulduggery!", but we felt that this was terribly hard to scream and somewhat lacking in accuracy.

Bette Anderson, the young actress who played the part of Columba, said that when her mother and family saw the play they were not in the least shocked. Others thought differently, however, and one man wrote to say that he would never again put his foot in a theatre that would produce such a "scandalously vulgar" play.

We did a Summer Festival in repertory, producing Noël Coward's *Hay Fever*, Jennings' *No More Frontier*, and Ibsen's *Master Builder*. Marijo played Hilda to her father's Solness, the Master Builder, and received exciting reviews. Though she was only fifteen, she was a fine actress and thoroughly professional.

One night, I heard her prompted three times. I was aghast. Marijo had no trouble learning lines. She usually did it in rehearsal. I went backstage and asked, "What happened?" She said, "When I forced Solness to sign the papers of the apprentice, he looked at me and his eyes looked plain crazy. I forgot my lines. I couldn't even hear the prompter." I told her that she wasn't the first actor, or the last, to be actually frightened by another actor's immersion in his role.

During the run of *The Master Builder*, a man spoke to me in the foyer, and said he'd like to meet Mr. James. "Of course," I said. "When the play is over, I'll take you to his dressing room." When he met Burton, the man introduced himself as a psychiatrist, and asked, "Who did you study for the part? Did you ever know a man like Solness?" Burton shook his head. "I didn't need to. It's all in Ibsen's play."

In 1933, the country was moving into the darkest depth of the Depression. The ceremonies for Franklin Delano Roosevelt's inauguration in 1933 had hardly been concluded when a run started on the banks back east and travelled with electrifying speed across the country. President Roosevelt declared a bank moratorium from March 3 to 14 and all banks closed. We had been playing *In Abraham's Bosom* to standing-room-only houses since January, the best sales we had had in a long time. The day of the moratorium, as fast as the office staff could lift the telephone, they got cancellations. The only money people had was in their wallets and no one knew when "normalcy" would be restored. It broke the back of our successful run but as the Irish say, "When God closes one door, He opens another." The door that opened for us then was the Negro Repertory under the WPA—the Works Progress Administration.

President Roosevelt set up agencies in government to try to stem the tide of despair and depression that was dragging the country under. One of these agencies was the Works Progress Administration, directed by Harry Hopkins. The WPA included a section known as the Arts Project that was to deal with all the arts as artists in every category were out of work. Hallie Flanagan of the Vassar College Drama Department was in charge of theatre. When we discovered that this was not to be a "pork barrel" for Broadway and Hollywood, we prepared a brief for what we decided to call a Negro Repertory Company. In order to participate in the Arts Project, our theatre had to provide all facilities for implementation of our project. This meant rehearsal space and theatre space for playing dates and all the physical equipment for production, staging, costumes, and scenery. In the beginning, the government paid salaries only to those on relief. WPA was an agency to employ the unemployed, enabling them to earn money with their skills instead of receiving a dole for doing nothing. Money earned by productions would go into a cashier's fund and could be used for royalties, rents, and equipment.

When the Arts Section was set up, our proposal was accepted. George Hood, former manager of the Metropolitan Theatre, was appointed as state supervisor of the section, Guy Williams was state director, and Burton was managing director of our project. There was a considerable delay in getting started, hindered by the red tape that governments wind around such endeavours, but we were finally given the go-ahead signal. There were supervisors and managers, but no people—as yet.

One day, Mr. Williams called my husband. "Burton, don't you need the money? Get on the project. Come down and sign the payroll."

"I will when you send us the people. Where are they? I work for my money."

We had applied in April 1935 but it was not until September that we began work on André Obey's *Noah*. The play was translated from the French but it served as an excellent vehicle for the Negro Repertory. It is a story of Noah and his animals and the Flood. We used Black music and introduced Black dancing to express the jubilation of Noah and his family when the flood recedes. The cast and chorus entered into the spirit of the thing with zest and gave a very good show. Reviewers expressed amazement at the talent displayed by people "taken from the scrap-heap of unemployment." The reviewer in the *Seattle Star* commented, "This all-Negro cast put on a performance so rich, so full of promise, it was tragic in its implications. Tragic because these people who have so much to contribute have so long been wasted."

Our next play, *Stevedore*, by Paul Peters and George Sklar, was in rehearsal while *Noah* was playing. It was a controversial play about a strike on the New Orleans waterfront and one of our board members resigned over it, saying that he thought the production was very good but it gave people ideas—ideas he could not accept. The ideas he found so onerous were those evoked by the bitter struggle sometimes necessary to build a union, a situation not unknown in Seattle and San Francisco, as well as New Orleans.

Very early in this project, we recognized the dearth of good plays for Black casts, so we began writing our own. After *Stevedore*, we created a musical revue called *Swing, Gates, Swing*, and Theodore Browne, an excellent actor, began writing a play about John Henry, a Black railroad worker who lost his life trying to compete with a steel drill. He called the play *Natural Man*.

We began to arrange Aristophanes' *Lysistrata* for production. We placed it in Ethiopia, as Mussolini was developing his war techniques there for later use in Spain, so the country was somewhat familiar to our audiences. We were in dress rehearsal and just about to open when a major from San Francisco expressed horror to the state supervisor and state director of our project that the WPA would permit production of such a bawdy play. This project always seemed to be involved with military men in one capacity or another. I sometimes wished that somebody would put me in charge of some military operation—I figured I knew just as much about the military as these military men did about the theatre.

A meeting was called. We asked how they could know what they were censoring if they hadn't seen it. Don Abel, state supervisor of the WPA, sent his wife and his secretary to the opening. Another meeting was called the next day. Mr. Abel reported that his wife and secretary said the play was "indecent and bawdy." My husband retorted, "My wife directed that play. Does that mean that my wife's tastes are 'indecent and bawdy,' or that your wife doesn't know anything about theatre and in any event shouldn't be permitted to censor productions?" Aristophanes' two-thousand-year-old comedy, which had opened at the Moore Theatre to capacity audiences, was "clapper-clawed with the palms of the vulgar" and summarily closed in the best interest of the Federal Theatre Project.

Our cast and chorus were all Black, but there had been some White people on the project: Hugo Alde, our stage technician, Roy York, electrician, Virginia Miller, scene designer, and Virginia Opsvig, costumes. Burton had to explain to the supervisor when we started that these were trained theatre people and essential to the project, even if they were White. When we needed White actors in the cast, we got them from the White theatre project or used actors from our theatre. We had to get them accepted by the supervisors, although White actors also needed relief.

The people involved in the White project of the WPA were largely from vaudeville. One of them was Toby Leitch, an elderly man who had been in every kind of theatre known—tent shows, carnivals, medicine shows, circuses, and Toby shows, which is where he got his name. I first directed him when he played the White boss in *Stevedore*. During the early rehearsals, he seemed to be paying very little attention to the script. When I reminded him that his lines had to be learned by a certain date, he said, aghast, "You mean I have to memorize all those lines? Don't think I can. Never memorized a line in my life." Amazed, I asked, "But what did you and the other actors in your shows do?"

"Just made 'em up. Depended on the audience. If they wanted comic, they got comic. If they wanted serious, we gave 'em serious."

This explained the state of the *Uncle Tom's Cabin* script from French's. The actors playing in that show had "just made 'em up" and nobody bothered to "set 'em down." Why should they? They would be changed at the next playing date.

The language in *Stevedore* was a little rough in spots. One of the women in the cast had to say, "I got the red-headed son-of-a-bitch!" She did not think that she ought to say the line and consulted her pastor. He told her that it was all right—she was not saying it, the character in the play was. Toby was shocked, too. He said, "We could never get away with any language like that in our shows, but then this is an Art Theatre." Someone should have written Toby's history. He had a lot to say and was very patient and cooperative in the face of what he must have considered the vagaries of an Art Theatre. He was very helpful, too, when I came to direct the White group. I was having a little trouble to begin with, for they resisted the standards of work I demanded from them. Toby went through the cast and told them, "She's all right. You do what she says. She knows her business."

The success of the Black group was creating friction with the White group, which was doing vaudeville turns in the parks. Annoyed by the publicity the Negroes were getting, they began complaining to Washington that White professionals, some of whom were Equity members, were being denied opportunities that Negro amateurs were getting. So I was asked to take over the White group as well and produce the Living Newspaper: *Power*.

The Living Newspaper was a type of play in documentary form developed under WPA. The first production was called *The Plow That Broke the Plains*, a film by Pare Lorenz with music by Virgil Thomson. It was a story of pioneering the Midwest and the breaking up of the grasslands that resulted in the dust bowls. *Power* had to do with the growing interest in the government's development of electric power through the Tennessee Valley Authority and the Boulder Dam, and was a natural for our area in Washington, which was very power conscious and in the process of building the Ross Dam.

I left the Negro project for the time being and tackled *Power*. I was staggered when I saw the script. There was everything in it—actors playing scenes, film, slides, a chorus, and an orchestra to play Lee Wainer's music. I started with the music, which was far from simple. We had a limited number of musicians on the White project and I had never heard them do anything but background music for the vaudeville acts. They were led by George Metcalfe, a small man who had had a back injury that had left him crippled. I doubted that George and his musicians could do the job. All sorts of solutions were suggested, up to and including renting a Hammond organ. One day, I was approached by Mr. Metcalfe. He said, "I hear you're worried about the music. May I see it?" I had never heard him play anything more demanding than "Pal O' Mine" for the rope artist but I gave him the score. He went over to the piano and played it.

"You can play that?" I asked.

He smiled. "I'm a graduate of the Toronto Conservatory." He took the score, arranged it for the musicians we had on the project, hired some tympani and one or two other musicians, trained the singers, and conducted the orchestra and chorus for the performances.

We got the rehearsals going. If I had had problems with untrained Black amateurs, I had even more problems with White professionals. One man came up to me and asked what mugs I wanted him to use. I didn't know what he was talking about. He explained patiently that he had forty-six mugs and wanted me to see them so I could tell him which ones to use. It turned out that he was referring to the roster of facial expressions that had been his stock in trade as a performer. I told him that he should memorize his lines and say them, and the mug that he wore every day would be just fine.

We needed a large male cast for *Power*, more men than we had on the White project, so I was literally looking for bodies, professional or not. One morning, I came into the building that housed the WPA project, and saw a personable chap mopping the floor. I asked him if he would like to be transferred to the theatre project. He looked startled.

"Oh, ma'am, I can't act."

"We'll see."

I arranged his transfer. His name was James Grahame. When I tried him out, I discovered that he couldn't read. In inquiring about his background, I found out that he had had almost no schooling and had been in the navy for sixteen years. He had a good voice and, fortunately, a good memory. His lines had to be read to him and he memorized them that way. He played the part of Wendell Willkie and looked every inch the man when he was costumed in an elegant cutaway.

When we were in dress rehearsal, the slides which had been sent to us cracked, one after another. The operator told me that they were for older projection machines and the present lamps were too hot for them. A man who happened to be working at some odd job backstage said to me, "I can make you some slides that won't crack in that machine. I used to do the slides for the songs that they sang in the old motion picture houses on skid road." So I gave him a copy of the script, indicated what slides were needed, and he took off. A day or two later, he came back with beautiful slides, some of them coloured, which did not crack and were far better than the ones which had been sent to us. He also became our photographer and got remarkable pictures working with an old-fashioned camera and flashlight arrangement, retouching the negatives. One day, I got a call from Mr. Williams, who was trying to find out if we had been splurging on new photographic equipment. He'd had a complaint from Washington DC about our pictures, "because they're too good!"

Another positive development that grew out of this chaos was the contribution made by the Black group to the White production. We needed a chorus, prop people, and trained stage managers. By now, some of the Black group were pretty good technicians as well as fine actors and I got permission from the directors of the project to put the Negro group on this production. They came over willingly, joyfully, and everybody worked together, Whites taking orders from Black stage managers and technicians, Blacks working amicably with Whites—no Black power, no White power, no tensions, no frictions anywhere, just people joined in the effort of doing a job and doing it well.

The experience of discovering talents among people who had been doing dull, mundane jobs was a constant source of joy to us. To see the colossal waste of such human resources, the most valuable assets to any country, and to realize what could have been accomplished and what this accomplishment could have meant was staggering. In 1969, burned-out cities were being rebuilt all over the country—even in Washington DC—at a tremendous cost to the taxpayer. Contrast this outlay with the few million dollars originally given to the Federal Arts Program. It seems that we can find money for just about anything and everything but people.

We all dreamed of a permanent Federal Arts Project, with a cabinet minister representing all the arts. In the WPA, set up for relief in a stressful time, there were dancers, painters, architects, writers, playwrights, directors, and actors. Orson Welles' Mercury Theatre was one of the projects. It was said that eighty-five percent of the paintings on display at the New York World's Fair had been done on WPA. When, later, some of these paintings were to be sent abroad, Congress objected—they had been done on WPA, so of course they were "Communistic."

How did the newspapers view all this activity in the theatre? With a jaundiced eye! The *Seattle Post-Intelligencer* and the *Seattle Times* opposed President Roosevelt and his policies and the theatre presented a ready target. This was apparently true for newspapers throughout the country. When we presented Sinclair Lewis's play *It Can't Happen Here* with the Black group, it drew a blast from the local papers and others, east to west. What seemed to be controversial was the theme of the play, that Fascism can happen here. All through the rehearsals, we were getting word from Washington: "Cut this speech." "Add this." "Take out that." We finally had to throw caution to the winds and do the play as Lewis wrote it. The play, part of the Federal Theatre Project, opened in eighteen cities on the same evening—the first and only time in theatre history that that has happened.

We seemed to be constantly involved in one problem or another on this project, as the red tape wound tighter and politicians got into the act. At the start, we had one timekeeper, a Black girl who was a University of Washington graduate. Every two weeks, I signed her time sheet and submitted it. By the end of the project, we had three timekeepers, political appointees. Essential people had been dropped from the project to make room for them.

The people on the project were to start work at 10:00 a.m. and stop at 4:00 p.m. I learned about inflexible bureaucracy the hard way, when a supervisor came by and found the group in rehearsal on a difficult bit of business after 4:00 p.m. Against the protests of cast and chorus, I had to dismiss them summarily. At the beginning of the project, the organizers graded people as skilled or unskilled and paid them accordingly. In view of the fact that they were all unskilled, such a situation would have created no end of dissension, so my husband had to straighten it out. They were paid sixty-six dollars a month, later raised to seventy-two. Directors and technicians were first paid seventy-two dollars and later ninety-six dollars a month.

We all learned a great deal. I had never known, before I worked on the project, how easy it was for Black people to become involved with the police. Although we never had any really serious problems, it seemed that practically every day someone was missing from the cast or crew, picked up by a police dragnet. I never met so many plainclothesmen in my life, and I got to know some quite well. The police could hold Black suspects for twenty-four hours and then had to charge them or let them go, which meant that they would lose a day's pay. I remember with gratitude one policeman who would call and tell me that he had brought in so-and-so but would see if he could get him released so he would only lose half a day's pay. In that day, Black people seemed to take it in their stride—not today, not any more. I remember one of the fellows on the project who simply shrugged and said, "Oh, they pick me up whether I'm wearing dungarees or my ice cream pants."

My connection with WPA came to an end when I became so tied up in red tape devised by the administration that I was spending most of my time and energy in controversy over this and that, rather than producing plays. I resigned. In 1936 the United States was pulling out of the Depression. World War II looked imminent, and people were beginning to get jobs creating "the tools to finish the job," as Churchill said in one of his speeches. The WPA was getting the axe, and the first project to be hit in the pocket was the theatre. Anything and everything connected with it seemed to be controversial, and Congress had yowled loud and long about wasting taxpayers' money on the arts.

We met the crises of the distressful years of the Depression and enjoyed the excitement of the excellent work done by the Black people on the project. We maintained our concern for the development of programs for our young audiences. We re-evaluated our approach to the theatre, economically, philosophically, and artistically. We reorganized our sales and business methods and organized weekend workshops to provide training for young people interested in working in the theatre. These workshops enabled us to study and practice a more scientific approach to the problems of creativity. Along with the intensive activity and pressures of work in the theatre, we became concerned with the lengthening shadows of war moving across the face of the world, with Mussolini's aggression in Ethiopia, Hitler and Mussolini in Spain, and the Japanese invasion of Manchuria.

At one time, Joe Hirakawa, who had played the troll king in our first production of *Peer Gynt,* attempted to arrange a trip for our theatre to go to Tokyo to play *Peer.* Joe had been born in Japan but had lived in the state of Washington from his early teens. He contacted Ichigo Kobayashi, known as the Carnegie of Japan, who expressed interest in the idea to the extent of agreeing to finance the trip. At the time, the Japanese were arranging such cultural exchanges as a goodwill gesture. Guests who went on such trips were so lavishly entertained that they came back ecstatic about the Japanese and their hospitality. However, after the Japanese victories in China, we felt that we could not accept this invitation and the obligations the trip entailed, opposed as we were to the aggression in China. So we didn't go.

As Hitler, that "madman with a mission," moved from the Anschluss in Austria to the takeover in Czechoslovakia and threats to Poland, our apprehension increased. But we were totally involved in Spain. We participated in programs to raise money for ambulances, medical supplies, everything, for the money of Republican Spain was frozen in the States. The American government was following the British and French policy of non-intervention. A group organized by Charles Lindbergh and Senator Burton K. Wheeler, called "America First," actively opposed any involvement in the Spanish civil war but the American people were generally critical of this policy, and young people were intensely concerned.

One day, one of my students came to the Playhouse and asked to see me. He explained, "I have to talk to somebody. I won't be in class tomorrow, because I'm leaving tonight for Paris. I'm joining the Abraham Lincoln Brigade to fight in Spain. My parents would never understand." And they didn't. When his father found out, he commented bitterly, "And that's the guy who objected to being in ROTC on campus because he hates uniforms and the military. And now he's off to fight in another man's war three thousand miles away!"

Two of my students and a friend left for Spain, and one was killed at Teruel. The Madrileños, when they saw the ranks of young men marching through the streets of bombed Madrid, cheered wildly, crying "We are not alone!" Years later, when World War II had erupted and the United States was involved, President Roosevelt admitted that his policy with Spain had been a mistake.

Remembering those days, and the Federal Theatre Projects, years, miles and a new country later, I am filled again with dismay at the stupidity of people who can get themselves elected to positions of power that enable them to arbitrate the destinies of others, often without thought or consideration. Hallie Flanagan told the story of a congressman who called her the day after the vote in Congress killed the Federal Theatre Project. He wanted to get his niece on the project. Miss Flanagan told him there was no longer any FTP, that Congress had just killed it. The congressman said, "Oh. Was that what we voted down yesterday?"

The dreams we had had of a permanent Federal Arts Project vanished for good in the "mushroom cloud" of World War II. It was spreading fast from the horizon.

PHOTO 1. In Florence's hand on the back of this photo: *Me! at 19. Taken in Boston while I was at Emerson College.*

PHOTOS 2 AND 3. *This and facing page:*
Burton and Florence, 1916.

PHOTO 4. Florence, Jimmy Cagney, and Marijo, undated. The photo is signed *To Florence B. & Mary Jo. Love to you both, Always, Jim.* Photograph by Clifton L. Kling.

PHOTO 5. Seattle Repertory Playhouse actress Bette Anderson, Florence's colleague and friend, and Florence, undated.

PHOTO 6. Burton and Florence, undated.

PHOTO 7. Portrait of Burton James as Peer Gynt. *Peer Gynt* was the Playhouse's first big production (in 1931) and was revived by the company three times. Photograph by H. E. Addington

PHOTO 8. Florence as director, circa 1940s. Photograph by Hale Van Scoy and Que Chin.

PHOTO 9. The massive outdoor set, more than 150 feet across and 50 feet deep, designed by Ruth Kreps for the 1927 production of Verdi's *Aida*, produced in the University of Washington Stadium by the Wayfarer Pageant Society. Photographer unknown.

PHOTO 10. The Negro Repertory Theatre production of Obey's *Noah*, June 1936. Photograph by Richard Erickson. Washington State Works Progress Administration.

PHOTO 11. The 1936 Playhouse production of *Stevedore* by Paul Peters and George Sklar, a WPA project. Photograph by Richard Erickson. Washington State Works Progress Administration.

PHOTO 12. Aristophanes' *Lysistrata*, set in Ethiopia and produced by the Negro Repertory Theatre at the Playhouse under the Federal Theatre Project in 1936. Photograph by Richard Erickson. Washington State Works Progress Administration.

PHOTO 13. *Prometheus Bound* by Aeschylus, produced at the Playhouse. Burton James (upper right) and Bette Anderson (extreme left). Photograph by Van Ness Studios.

PHOTO 14. *Uncle Harry*, by Thomas Job, performed at the Seattle Repertory Playhouse, 1944-45 season. LEFT TO RIGHT: Betty Hall as Hester, Florence Bean James as Nona, Helen Taverniti as Lucy, Russ Arwine as George Waddy, Bette Anderson as Lette, and Albert M. Ottenheimer in the title role of "Uncle Harry." Photograph by Lawrence R. Novak.

PHOTO 15. A scene from *Calico Cargo*, the Playhouse's original musical (1945) about the Mercer Girls who came around the Horn as brides for the early settlers in Washington State. In the background, wearing a top hat, is Bruno Gerussi. Photograph by Richard Erickson.

PHOTO 16. A scene from the 1945-46 production of *Once Upon a Clothesline* by Aurand Harris. From left, Mr. Cricket (Walter Gyger) and Pinno (Frederic Youens) rescue Pinnette (Beatrice Warren) from the spider's web. Photograph by Peter E. Anders.

PHOTO 17. *San Juan Story*, an original musical produced by the Playhouse in 1947, was based on the famous "pig war." The production enjoyed tremendous success. The actress dancing at centre stage is Martha Wright, who later went on to Broadway and replaced Mary Martin in *South Pacific*. Photograph by Van Ness Studio.

PHOTO 18. The Playhouse production of Benjamin Britten's *Let's Make an Opera*, 1950. Helen Taverniti conducted the orchestra and the audience-chorus. Photograph by Van Ness Studios.

What
HELEN HAYES
Thinks About
Your
Civic Theatre

The Seattle Repertory Playhouse

MISS HELEN HAYES
First Lady of the American Theatre

PHOTO 19. Cover of a flyer with the transcript of Helen Hayes' greetings to the audience at the opening night performance of the Seattle Repertory Playhouse's twentieth season, September 17, 1947.

PHOTO 20. The courtyard of the Seattle Repertory Playhouse.

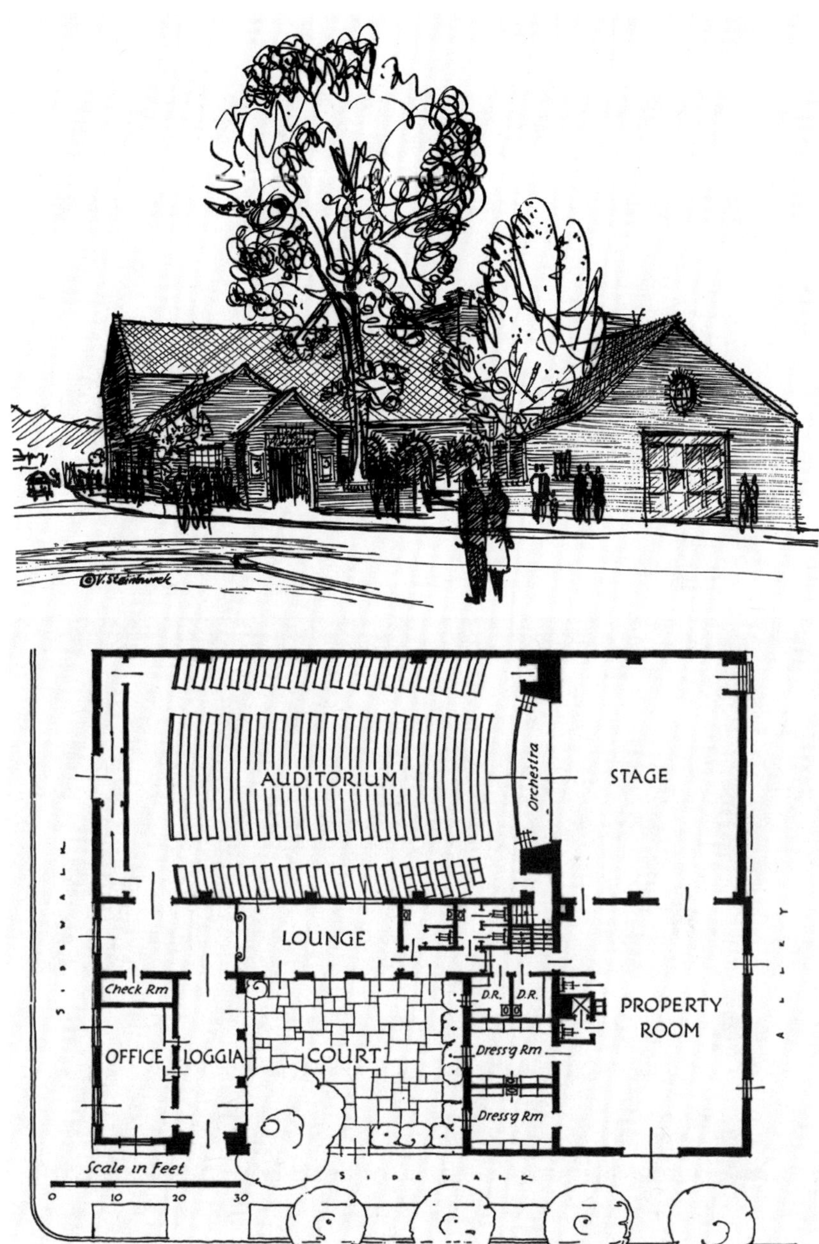

PHOTO 21. Artist's rendering and floor plan of the Seattle Repertory Playhouse.

This and facing page:
Florence James before the Canwell Committee.

PHOTO 22. *Above:* On the stand. Photograph 86.5.30002, Seattle Post-Intelligencer Collection, Museum of History & Industry.

PHOTO 23. *Facing page, top:* Demanding the cross-examination of a witness. Photograph 86.5.30003.2, Seattle Post-Intelligencer Collection, Museum of History & Industry.

PHOTO 24. *Facing page, bottom:* Being escorted out of the hearing. Photograph 86.5.30003.1, Seattle Post-Intelligencer Collection, Museum of History & Industry.

PHOTO 25. On stage at the Playhouse in 1948. Burton and Florence surrounded by part of the flood of newspaper clippings dealing with the hearings and trials of the Un-American Activities Committee. Photograph by Van Ness Studios.

PHOTO 26. Florence and Burton at the Saskatchewan Arts Board Drama Workshop, Qu'Appelle, Summer 1951.

PHOTO 27. Florence and students at Summer School, Qu'Appelle.

PHOTO 28. Florence Bean James, circa 1976.

CHAPTER NINE

To go back a bit, early in the spring of 1934, we had been amazed to receive an announcement of theatre festivals to be held at Malvern and Stratford in England and in Moscow during the first ten days in September. When in our lives had a government anywhere thought it important to present a festival in theatre? And what kind of a festival could the USSR present? Had we not read in the newspapers that art, as well as artists, had been liquidated by the Workers' Republic as something too contemptibly bourgeois for the high ideals and development of a Communist State?

We had long been familiar with the unparallelled contribution of old Russia to theatre, dance, and music. In New York in the 1920s we had seen the Moscow Art Theatre productions of Chekhov's *Three Sisters* and *The Cherry Orchard*, and Alexei Tolstoy's *Tsar Fyodor*. We were aware that this great theatre had somehow survived the revolution. But we also knew that it had involved a cultivated aristocracy and that the masses of the people had made no contribution to its creation and participated not at all in the results. Anna Pavlova and Diaghilev's Ballets Russes, the Moscow Art Theatre, and Balieff's theatre group the *Chauve-Souris* had been enthusiastically received in America. But Pavlova and Diaghilev were dead and their organization of artists scattered. Balieff had last been heard of advertising cheese on the radio in America.

The festival announcements were intriguing in including the familiar names of theatre companies that had flourished under the old regime: Kamerny Theatre, Mali Theatre, Second Moscow Art Theatre (formerly the Studio Art Theatre), and the Bolshoi Opera. But more interesting were the new names: Red Army Theatre, Vakhtangov Theatre, Jewish Art Theatre, The Young Spectator's Theatre, Moscow Theatre for Children, their names indicating they had been created since the revolution. We had long recognized the advantages of being able to do freely what we wanted to do in the theatre in this faraway corner of the country, but we also recognized the disadvantages of being so removed from opportunities of seeing what other theatres were doing. I had often looked at some play I had directed and thought it good, but I longed for some more objective comparison and criticism. So, with the announcements of the Malvern Festival, the Shakespearean Festival in Stratford, England, and most exciting of all, this festival in Moscow, marvellous opportunities were being offered for a very rich theatre experience—if only one could go. But we were deep in the Depression in 1934, and such an expenditure didn't seem possible. Just about this time, I received word that my father's estate—he had died in the fall of 1933—was to be settled. There was very little in the estate, as he had lost everything in the Depression. But Burton said to me, "When you get that money, take it and go to England and Russia to see those festivals. There isn't enough for both of us to go, but you go. It will do us all good."

Marianne King, who had written two plays for us, decided that she would like to accompany me. Many of our friends thought we were insane to think of taking a trip to the Soviet Union. Myron Jacobson did everything he could to discourage me, but when he saw that I was determined to go, he gave me letters to Madame Knipper-Chekhova and some other actors at the Moscow Art, with the strict injunction that I was to deliver them myself—I must not, under any circumstances, put them into any other hands. (As it turned out, I was not able to meet any of Myron's friends, as they were on vacation in the summer of 1934.) I received my $1,200 from father's estate and Marianne and I set out. When we got to Chicago, the city was in an uproar. We had arrived on the day the gangster John Dillinger was shot.

We spent a few days in New York, seeing plays. The night before we were to sail, Marianne called me late in the evening and said, "Have you heard the news? The Nazis have shot Engelbert Dollfuss, the Austrian federal chancellor. It looks like war. Do you think it's smart for us to go to Europe now?"

My answer was, "Let's go. We'll be five days on the ship, and by the time we get to England, things ought to either have erupted or settled down."

They settled down, so we carried on with our plans.

When we were preparing for our trip, the agent at American Express urged us to take the German ship *Bremen*, on which we could travel first class for what it would cost us for second class on the Cunard line. We said "No." Mussolini had been at work in Ethiopia and we suspected Hitler's intentions, though he hadn't yet revealed them in Spain. While we weren't too well informed about what was going on, we didn't like what we did know, and we certainly didn't want to travel on a German ship. We were what was later called "prematurely anti-Fascist."

We spent a lovely two weeks in England, seeing the festivals at Malvern and in the beautiful new theatre at Stratford, as well as plays in London. Early one morning, we boarded the *Siber*, a Russian ship bound for Leningrad and Moscow. We sailed down the Thames, out through the North Sea, and passed through the Kiel canal by moonlight. Not many people were travelling to the Soviet Union then. President Roosevelt had just extended recognition to this Socialist government, having waited about the same length of time it had taken Catherine II of Russia to recognize the United States after the American Revolution. The American Revolution shook every throne in Europe: the Russian Revolution shook the world.

Before we left London, friends of Marianne's warned us, "You're going to be hungry. You'd better take beef cubes, chocolate, and crackers." We did, and left them in our rooms in Moscow. We were so well fed that we actually returned with Intourist food tickets that we hadn't been able to use.

The trip had been paid for in advance and arranged by Intourist—hotel rooms, sightseeing tours, theatre tickets, and a Russian guide who spoke English with an American accent and used American slang. When I asked where she had learned it, she said, "I work for an American road-building firm, and this is my vacation." Things had to be arranged this way, of course, since we couldn't spend any foreign currency in the country and weren't allowed to buy Russian money. Our American money was counted when we entered Russia and counted when we left. I remember that the Customs people, or whoever they were, were fascinated by our silver dollars with what might have looked, I suppose, like an Imperial eagle.

Most of the people on the *Siber*, like ourselves, were going to the theatre festival. All of us were a little apprehensive as to what the accommodations might be. The ship was small, something like the ships that formerly plied between Seattle and Alaska, and the accommodations were adequate. It was there that we saw, for the first time, women sailors working alongside men. Later, we were to see women bricklayers, street cleaners, and, on the train between Leningrad and Moscow, railway maintenance workers.

Before we landed at Leningrad, someone said, "Watch your belongings. They'll steal you blind." We made a mental note. I decided when we docked that Leningrad had the smell of Seattle—lumber and the sea. We were taken to the Hotel Europa and given, much to our amazement, fabulous accommodations. It began to look as if things might turn out all right after all. Later that night I discovered that in the excitement of arrival and Customs, I had left my coat in the Immigration Pavilion. Next morning, I spoke to our guide about it. She dismissed my concern with a casual, "It will be at the hotel when we return from the sightseeing tour." And it was. I erased my mental note about people stealing me blind.

In Leningrad we visited the Winter Palace and the Hermitage Museum with its fabulous collection of paintings and art objects, St. Isaac's Cathedral with its great malachite pillars, and then an anti-religious museum. It wasn't really so much anti-religious as it was anti-superstition, an attempt to eradicate by education the reverence for the most revolting objects that had held the uneducated people of this big country in thrall for centuries. It was at this museum that we saw women soldiers on guard for the first time.

The material things we saw didn't interest us as much as the people we met and talked to, the history, the impressive beauty of the old and the driving energy of the new. Moscow was being built and rebuilt, the subway was under construction, streets were being widened. Everything seemed to be moving at an accelerated pace, and everywhere was the slogan for "Work and Defense."

We arrived in Moscow on September 1, a holiday similar to our Labour Day, but this holiday was for Youth. Returning from a sight-seeing tour, we passed streets where marchers stood preparing for a parade to be held in the evening when work was over. On one street, we saw masses of men and women in work clothes, large boutonnières of red flowers in their coat lapels, the men carrying guns. "Who are they?" we wanted to know. "Just militia men," the guide replied. On another street, there were women soldiers powdering their noses and putting little red pennants on their bayonets, getting ready for the parade. "Who are they?" "Women sharpshooters. See their medals."

Some years after my trip, my husband and I were teaching at the University of British Columbia summer school. Hitler had just invaded the Soviet Union. At dinner one evening, another American teaching with us said, "Well, this is the end of the Soviet Union. Hitler will be in Moscow in six weeks."

I startled the table by announcing with conviction, "Hitler will never get to Moscow. Every man, woman, and child will rise up against him. He's making the same mistake Napoleon made. It's the end of Hitler, not the end of the Soviet Union."

Our co-worker laughed. "I was at a dinner party before I left Washington. I was the only one in civvies. Those military men said, 'Hitler will go through Russia like a hot knife through butter.' They should know!"

I don't know what the American military were seeing in 1934, or what anyone else saw, but I based my opinions on what I had seen for myself.

The streets, the city, the people, everything interested us. As far as we could tell, there were no restrictions at all for us with regard to looking or talking. But we had come to Moscow to see theatre. The first night, we went to the Bolshoi Ballet to see *Prince Igor*, a fabulous production—an orchestra of more than a hundred musicians, ballet, beautiful costumes and decor. We looked up at the royal box, where the Soviets had removed the golden eagles of the czar and put up the hammer and sickle. We thought the people sitting in the box must be notables, but the guide said, "No, just workers." And that is what they looked like, the women in sweaters with white handkerchiefs that looked like tea towels tied over their heads. The guide once commented that in our American clothes and silk stockings Marianne and I looked like peacocks in a hen yard.

One of our most interesting experiences was when we were taken, as part of a large group of festival participants, to meet a Mr. Vontsky, assistant commissar of the theatre. Theatres were under the Commissariat of Education. He outlined the place the theatre held in the Revolution and answered questions about censorship, theatre collectives, and subsidies. When asked if the Russian theatres were censored, he said, "Assuredly. We censor immorality, religion, counterrevolution, and mysticism. No classic is censored, and any play that seems to have merit is first produced before a decision to censor is made. Even though it may contain one or all of the censorable elements, it may have other values which offset the censorable defects."

One such play was Mikhail Bulgakov's *The Days of the Turbins*, first produced at the Moscow Art Theatre in 1926. In this play, the White Army is presented in a sympathetic light and the Czarist national anthem was heard in the theatre for the first time since the Revolution. This was censorable material, particularly in 1926. In the last act of the play, a group of White Army officers seek refuge at the home of the Turbins in the city of Kiev. It is Christmas Eve. They have just fled a disastrous engagement with the brigand troops of Petlura, who operated during the wars of intervention, reportedly financed by the Germans. Suddenly, there is the sound of machine guns and the rumble of gun carriages, which announces another attack on the city. Above the din is heard the "Internationale." Someone gasps, "The Bolsheviki!" "Well," says one officer, "Perhaps they have a plan that will serve Russia." A young officer on crutches, swathed in bandages as a result of the recent battle, says, "Perhaps it's the prologue to a new era." An older man answers, "Yes, perhaps—but for some of us, an epilogue."

I had never seen this play and had heard about the production, with a new young cast, but it was not on our list of festival productions. Late one afternoon, I realized that I had already seen the evening's Chekhov by the Moscow Art when they were in New York. I told the guide that I would very much like to see *The Days of the Turbins* instead.

Throughout the festival, we had been very interested in the audiences that thronged the theatres we attended, obviously working men and women, people who in the old regime could not walk the streets in the areas where the theatres were located, much less enter one of them. Some of the skeptics in our group scoffed at the crowded houses. "Naturally the Soviet government wouldn't have festival guests attending a theatre with a half-empty house." The inference was that these audiences had been rounded up and sent to the theatre at bayonet-point, or with some other dire threat, to create a good impression on foreign theatregoers.

However, when I made my last-minute switch in plans and went to see *The Days of the Turbins*, I found that that theatre was crowded, too. If I had believed that it was for my personal benefit, I would have been awe-struck at the efficiency that could fill a theatre on a few hours' notice, and flattered that they had considered me of sufficient importance to go to such lengths to impress me. I came to the conclusion, not too reluctantly, that the audience was there of its own accord.

We were in Moscow for ten days, and they were packed. We went sightseeing every day and saw some sort of theatrical production every night. About fifty percent of the plays we saw might have been classed as propaganda, but even they had so much that was excellent theatre, were so beautifully acted, and achieved such distinction in production that we, who had too little background to be moved by the propaganda, sat enthralled, laughed with their laughter, and wept with their tears. It is not at all surprising that Maxim Gorky and other playwrights apparently did not feel regimented in writing plays that "held a mirror up to nature" and "showed the very age and body of the time, its form and pressure."

We had long believed that theatre had a contribution to make in helping to make education exciting and could provide emotional content that would interest and excite the viewer, leaving indelible impressions. Theatres were being built in the Soviet Union not only to fill needs but to create them. In the remote reaches of the Republic, in Soviet Asia, the Urals, Siberia, many provinces that had never seen a play or knew what theatre was, we were told that drama was being brought to the people.

I remember a story during World War II, when planes were flying from the USSR to Alaska to pick up materials made available through the Lend-Lease program. Some of the American pilots met their Russian counterparts, who were disappointed when they learned that they would not be able to see American plays or opera while they were on their Alaskan layover, as there was no theatre in the North and the nearest opera was the Metropolitan Opera House in New York City. The Russians were used to flying over the wastes of Siberia where new towns were being built. Whenever they put down, they found theatres, and they couldn't imagine that it would be any different in America.

While producing contemporary plays, the Russian theatre we saw did not neglect the classics, either their own or those of other countries. One of our most delightful evenings was spent at the Second Moscow Art, watching a performance of Shakespeare's *Twelfth Night*. The scenic artist had mounted Shakespeare's fantastic land of Illyria with real joie de vivre. The actors projected the mood of the play that had been created, playing the comedy with robustness and the naive romance with delicate charm. In an address of welcome, one of the directors of the theatre said, "We have a feeling of healthy confidence which goes well with the life and colour of Shakespeare and the vigour of his sonorous voice." At some point during the production, a young Englishman in our group turned to me and whispered, "I think nobody but the English should produce Shakespeare." I replied, "After seeing the productions at Stratford, I think anybody *but* the English should produce Shakespeare!"

Another aspect of Russian theatre that interested us was the attention given amateur theatre groups on collective farms and in the factories. We had an opportunity to get a clearer impression of this when we were at the Commissariat of Education. A young man, recognizing us as Americans, spoke to us in English with a New York accent. After the Revolution, the Soviet government was looking for skilled workmen, offering jobs and possible citizenship to anyone interested. He had been working in a shoe factory in the United States and came as a factory worker to a shoe factory in Russia. He told us he was now attending a Theatre Technicum, learning to become a director. The amateur theatre group in his factory had recommended him, and he continued to receive the wages he would have earned in the factory, plus a small bursary from the government. After two years' apprenticeship in an area designated by the state, he would be free to apply for a job in any area where he might like to live and work.

Probably the most interesting experience we had in theatre while in Moscow was our visit to a production of the Moscow Theatre for Children. They did a charming version of *The Negro Boy and the Monkey*, a pantomime with songs, dances, animated cartoons, and a storyteller. The play was so utterly, completely child-like that it captivated the affection of the adults as well as the children with its imaginative charm. What interested us most was the company's understanding of the child's psychological need to participate in the experience of theatre. During intermissions, the young audience, under supervision, danced, sang, and drew pictures. Every child is stimulated by the theatre to do something on his own and wants to actively create. We had recognized this need during our productions for children at the Playhouse, for it was impossible to keep them in their seats. They would come creeping down the aisles of the theatre, even climbing the steps to the stage, taking curtain calls with the actors.

Natalya Sats directed the children's play we saw in Moscow. She had started this theatre shortly after 1917 and was still active at least until a few years ago. Sadly, many years after that exciting Moscow experience, I met her in Montreal at a conference of the Association Internationale du Theatre pour l'Enfance et la Jeunesse / the International Association of Theatre for Children and Young People. She and her company produced a play for the conference, and I was not impressed. She was still doing proscenium production, while I was involved with theatre in the round and audience participation for children.

At the Moscow Festival, Miss Sats said: "Children are so pathetically certain that what they see is absolutely perfect, we have no right to deceive them. We all know how strong and lasting are the impressions received in childhood. We know, besides, that education is easier than re-education, and that a child's taste in artistic matters can be utterly spoiled for the rest of his life."

It is sadly true that when an adult says, "I don't like Shakespeare," or "I can't listen to a symphony," he is telling the world that his education has been faulty and that somewhere along the line an adult has failed him. Taste is not born, it is developed, in every field in the arts—or even in the matter of food. I saw people in Moscow eating caviar by the tablespoonful for breakfast (a taste I had not acquired), and they were not Russians. With my less-adventuresome spirit in that area, I couldn't even look in their direction while they were happily munching away.

Our curiosity was insatiable. We went everywhere and anywhere that the somewhat limited time of our tour allowed. At the Kremlin Museum we saw the antiquities of the old regime, jewelled harness and weapons, solid gold stirrups and gem-trimmed saddles, clothing embroidered in gold and silver thread, encrusted with pearls and other precious stones. Once during the reign of Elizabeth I of England, someone wrote, "The Muscovites arrived, shedding pearls and lice." Seeing the clothing on display in the glass cases in the Kremlin, we believed it could have been so.

We visited Lenin's tomb and saw the long queues. Because we were visitors, our guide whisked us up to the door, and we were admitted ahead of the line. We saw Lenin in his glass coffin, and I noted that he was a rather short man, dressed in a simple soldier's uniform, with small, delicate hands.

We went to the Ostankino Palace, built by serfs for some prince whose name I've forgotten. It was included on our tour as a point of interest for the festival visitors because it had a beautiful little theatre in which trained actors, dancers, and musicians, all serfs, performed for their master's guests. The guests sat in boxes raised to avoid any contact or possible contamination from the serf artists. When we looked at the theatre, we realized that this architectural feature had given very good sight lines. The effect was almost like theatre in the round. The guide told us that the prince who had built the palace had owned property larger than an area the size of Belgium. The last prince had married one of his serf actresses and been ostracized. We also learned that these White serfs had been freed at just about the same time that Lincoln freed the slaves in the United States.

One day, a Scots doctor in our party asked, "Would you ladies care to see a Propholactoria for prostitutes?" We figured that we were on the tour to be educated, so we answered, "Yes. What is it?" "That's what I'm going to find out this afternoon, so come along." This was an unprogrammed trip. The Propholactoria turned out to be a rehabilitation centre that provided hospital services and education: training in all kinds of skills for factory work, even instruction in driving tractors. The administrator of the institution told us that there were over thirty thousand women engaged in prostitution in the city of Moscow. They knew the exact number because the women had to be registered with the police and carry permits. Women came to the institution voluntarily and could leave at will. Prostitution was not a crime, but anyone profiting from these women was considered a criminal. One thing that especially interested us was the instruction given in the arts. One young lady proudly showed us an invitation she had received from Maxim Gorky to attend a writers' conference to be held later that month.

Few women who entered the institution left before they had been trained for other jobs. As the guide said, "Who would choose to earn a living in a filthy occupation like prostitution? It's all economic necessity." I couldn't help remembering the prostitutes who had been my charges and friends so many years before in New York. They had suffered from economic necessity too, but there had been no Propholactoria for their rehabilitation.

I must stress that our visit to Russia was in 1934. The Russians felt that their Revolution had survived the Allied intervention that followed and was now consolidated. We were treated like guests, not tourists. Everything was done to make us feel comfortable. Our guide became a friend, answering all our questions, and sometimes seemed amused by our naiveté. My friend Marianne and her sister returned to Russia again in 1936 and told me later that everything had changed. Sergei Kirov had been assassinated late in 1934, and the Moscow Trials were beginning. In 1936, Marianne said, they received courteous but perfunctory attention. No one was making friends with foreigners.

We left the Soviet Union after our ten-day visit exhilarated and exhausted because we had seen and done so much but also depressed by the future we could see looming, given the gathering clouds of the Second World War. Emperor Haile Selassie had pleaded his cause fruitlessly in the League of Nations. The world seemed to be in the grip of those who based their actions not on realities but on their hopes, which were fantasies. They were blind to reality: everyone who had anything but butterflies in the head could not fail to see the outcome of such a confrontation, not only for those immediately involved but for the world.

We left the Soviet Union by train, going through Poland, Germany, and on to Paris and Cherbourg to sail for home. Coming down the Ruhr Valley, a man in our compartment said, "Look at those smoking chimneys. I came this way from Sweden last year, and those factories were quite dead. Hitler is making armaments."

"How can he, under the Versailles Treaty?"

The man laughed. "He's making them to go against the Soviet Union."

I thought to myself, "And do the Soviets know it! They're getting ready for him too." One day in Moscow, the guide had pointed out a new school being built so that it could be converted into a hospital. "In case of need," she explained. The Molotov-Ribbentrop pact did not surprise me. The Soviets were buying time. They got it—two years.

When I returned home to our theatre, our audiences may have expected a spate of post-Revolutionary Russian plays. In actual fact, during the next few years we produced only two: in 1935, Valentin Katayev's *Squaring the Circle*, an amusing satiric comedy of two young couples struggling with the housing shortage and squaring everything they did or said with "Can it hurt the Revolution?" In 1944, we did Ilya Vershinin and Mikhail Ruderman's *Counterattack*, a war play. I had not seen either of these on my trip to Moscow.

After I had recovered from the exhaustion and excitement of the trip, I began to sort out my impressions. In England, it seemed to me that the theatres were dull, doing plays that said "nothing to nobody" and which, because of their content, were given dull, unexciting productions. Even at Stratford, Shakespearean performances were pedestrian and conventional.

In the Soviet Union, on the other hand, many of the plans that we had for our own theatre seemed to be in the process of realization. The recognition that theatre was an essential need for the many, not a frill for the few, and the efforts to extend it to remote areas, the work being done for the children and the efforts being made to involve this young audience in the creative process all impressed and informed me.

It is difficult to describe the excitement created by experiencing ten days of fabulous theatre, introductions of *Prince Igor* and *Swan Lake* at the Bolshoi, work at the Moscow Art Theatre and other of the old established theatres, and the excellent productions of the new theatres, many of which had started as amateur groups after the Revolution. I thought of something Lincoln Steffens once said when he returned from the Soviet Union shortly after the Revolution: "I have seen the future, and it works." Then as now, it is not, of course, given to any of us to foretell how far any given future will extend, nor how long its exciting promises will last. My glimpse into a possible future took place in 1934. The future of that day now lies far in the past, and I am sad to say that many of mankind's hopes lie with it.

CHAPTER TEN

At the inception of the Repertory Playhouse, we decided that, as a community theatre, we had a responsibility to the young people of the city. We realized that with nothing but movies to watch (the "talkies" were coming on strong), a whole generation could have no experience of the live actor and the living theatre. In our first season, playing at the Women's Century Club, we produced the version of *Rip Van Winkle* that Joseph Jefferson had created and played in successfully for almost forty years. We went on to do other plays that were enthusiastically received by pre-high school age audiences.

When we built our own theatre, one of the factors that inclined us toward building in the university district, one block from the university campus, was the expectation that the University of Washington, with its more than 8,000 students at that time, would provide a potential audience. One might have thought that natural curiosity, if nothing else, would have led to student attention. But that didn't happen, even though the *University of Washington Daily*, the campus newspaper, reviewed the plays favourably and sometimes with considerable enthusiasm.

We concluded that students, not having had any experience of live theatre, had very little interest in it. If we wanted to correct this attitude, where would we start? How could we gain at least a speaking acquaintance with this young audience?

We decided to go to the high schools. We thought that if we could introduce the state's high school students, at that time some 95,000 individuals, to theatre, and keep at it for a reasonable length of time, a positive attitude toward theatre could be developed. Burton, in an interview with a reporter from a weekly newspaper, once said, "We hope for the time when the Board of Education will ask the Playhouse to do annual productions of classics, to be tied in with the grade and high school curriculum."

No such request came, but we didn't wait for it. When we produced *Romeo and Juliet*, we approached the school authorities, as Shakespeare was in the high school curriculum. These authorities were naturally hesitant about taking such a precedent-setting step and were doubtful of the outcome. But they did agree to a limited experiment—a special weekday matinee for high school students, played during school time. Three schools, those nearest the Playhouse, participated. Tickets were sold through the schools at a twenty-five-cent admission fee. The matinee was at 2:30 p.m. and students were dismissed from school in time to reach the Playhouse. The results of the experiment were a revelation in the eagerness of the students who thronged to the performances and their response in the theatre and in the classroom. Approximately 750 students came from the three high schools in 1931.

By 1935–36, these performances had grown to include every high school and junior high school in Seattle, as well as many separate and private schools; 10,673 students attended the thirty school matinees that season. Then students started coming in from outlying towns. Sometimes a hundred would come a distance of a hundred miles or so in chartered buses, and it seemed that many more would come if they could afford it.

Early in 1935, a committee of the heads of English departments, appointed by the State Board of Education, with W. O. Swenson, the state superintendent in charge of high schools as an ex-officio member, met with Playhouse representatives to discuss further plans. A couple of out-of-town tours were proposed as an experiment. As finances were extremely limited (thanks to the Depression), the Playhouse undertook this touring at its own risk.

We played Shakespeare's *Midsummer Night's Dream* with a cast of fifty, including a ballet corps of twelve and a ten-piece orchestra of first-chair members of the Seattle Symphony performing Mendelssohn's incidental music. We played three matinees in Tacoma and two in Everett, both cities between thirty and thirty-five miles from Seattle. Tickets for all matinees were sold in the schools for the usual twenty-five cents. All we hoped to do was to clear expenses, and we succeeded. We played to capacity audiences.

The enthusiasm of the student audiences for *Midsummer Night's Dream* indicated to the committee that the time seemed ripe to extend this theatre-going experience to other high schools in the state. On the basis of the success of our experimental tour, we approached Dr. N. D. Showalter, state superintendent of public instruction, for sponsorship by the State Board. At this time, we didn't expect any funding, but we wanted the board's sponsorship and its administrative assistance. Dr. Showalter was an excellent, progressive educator, but it took him some weeks to get a favourable reply from his board.

When a pledge of the board's interest and assistance had been obtained, the Playhouse presented a brief and a budget to the Rockefeller Foundation for a grant of $35,000 to initiate the project as a three-year experiment. The foundation had to be assured of two things: the continued interest of the State Board and the standard of our productions. Dr. David Stevens, director of the Humanities Division of the Rockefeller Foundation, sent John Marshall, his assistant director, to interview Dr. Showalter and the state superintendent of high schools, Mr. Swenson, and to see us and our operation. His visit seemed favourable. The sun even shone in Seattle on the day he visited us.

On April 15, 1936, the Rockefeller Foundation gave us a grant of $35,000 to establish a theatre for the high schools of the state, to be called the Washington State Theatre. We received $20,000 of the grant in 1936 to finance office space and meet other expenses involved in setting up the project; in 1937–38, we received $10,000 and in 1939–40, the final $5,000. A separate corporation was set up to receive the grant, which was to be administered by a committee of six, composed of representatives from the State Board, the Washington Education Association, the State Parents and Teachers Association, the Board of Trustees of the Repertory Playhouse, and school superintendents of first and second class districts. The duties of this committee included authorization and audit of funds, passing on matters of policy, coordinating work of the theatre with classroom curricula, authorizing a Research Department with the State Board that would observe and report the activities of the Theatre for publication, informing the Rockefeller Foundation, and developing a long-term program for future development.

The first official activity of the Washington State Theatre was a fact-finding survey of the state that took place from May 25 to June 6, 1936. Al Ottenheimer, our promotional representative, and Hugo Alde, our stage technician, made the trip. Al was to meet with school staff, PTA leaders, and newspaper and radio people, looking for support and sponsors for adult performances, and Mr. Alde was to make a survey of the school auditoriums and stage facilities to enable us to build our sets and meet all contingencies of the tour.

At the conclusion of the survey tour, Al prepared a booklet titled *Washington State Theatre—Theatre for Youth*, attractively designed with a question and answer format and photographs of plays produced by the Playhouse for high schools in Seattle. A statement by Dr. Showalter appeared as a foreword:

> We are about to embark on a history-making project. It is unique in the annals of education and the theatre in America, and we do not know of any place in any country which has been launched under such close governmental direction. The Washington State Theatre's ultimate power for good, the eventual consequences of such an experiment on the whole educational system of America, can only be conjectured, but the prospect is inspiring. It is neither fantastic nor grandiloquent to conceive of it as ultimately achieving a powerful and beneficent influence throughout the nation for culture and education and all the great, good things of life for which we all strive. It is, to speak with restraint, a high and worthy goal, and one fraught with boundless possibilities for the public good.

We decided to open the tour with Shakespeare's *Comedy of Errors*, a riotous farce that could appeal to the most unsophisticated members of the audience. We had initiated our venture with *Romeo and Juliet* and *Midsummer Night's Dream*, and we believed that at this point nothing but Shakespeare would serve this new enterprise. Some of those from the schools on the committee thought that Shakespeare would not interest the students. One man said, "Students are bored with Shakespeare. We are trying to take it out of the curriculum as soon as possible." His opinion notwithstanding, we stuck with Shakespeare. This was to be a theatre for education.

We felt that Shakespeare could be more satisfactorily introduced in the schools before our production with the use of a lesson plan. These lesson plans gave the students information about the cast of characters, their relationships, and so on. They also served to integrate the theatre with the work in the classroom, and in every instance where they were used we had a more responsive audience. The difficulty was that sometimes the lesson plans were overlooked or ignored. We worked very hard to try to make sure that they were used, as we knew that they worked: we had had the plans prepared by a committee of teachers in the high school English departments, including one teacher who was also a Playhouse actress, who were familiar with the work we had done in the local high schools.

A staggering amount had to be accomplished before the opening tour. Promotional and publicity material was designed to appeal to a wide range in the potential audiences. Designs for posters were made with an eye to artistic excellence so they would provide satisfactory examples for art classes. Press and radio releases were prepared for the newspapers and radio stations near the playing centres, to be used by the schools or sponsoring groups. Photographs of the cast and scenes from the play had to be prepared for display in the schools, and mats of these photographs made up for newspapers. The next major step was recruiting actors and business personnel. People who had worked with us for a number of years provided the staff and personnel for this new venture.

All members of the group performed in more than one capacity: the two advance men who arranged the tours also acted in the company for which they had prepared the way. One member was in charge of all radio work at home or on tour, another stage-managed the production, another arranged schedules for truck and cast travel, another prepared daily reports for the office. Yet another kept a critical eye on the performances and prepared an excellent report on the problems encountered in playing for these young audiences and recommended steps that should be taken in acting or directing techniques to eliminate these difficulties in future. His reports resulted in some distinct changes in our approaches to acting and directing.

We realized that actors might still be regarded in some areas as "mountebanks and scalawags," so rules of conduct were agreed upon by the group. No smoking was permitted in or around school buildings, and of course no liquor was allowed at any time. It is interesting to note that these rules were strictly observed by everybody from truck drivers to cast and crew. Later, letters from school people and hotelkeepers testified to the validity of our approach. We were, after all, representing a theatre in education.

Another step in preparing for this and subsequent tours was a trip by Al Ottenheimer to high schools in the state in advance of the playing dates, speaking to school assemblies. On his first trip, he spoke at fifty-nine assemblies to 36,280 students. Toward the end of the project, he was performing the gargantuan feat of addressing eighty-nine assemblies in twenty-four speaking days, to a total of 43,882 students.

There was no talk then of a "generation gap," but whatever gap may have existed, Al successfully bridged it. He talked of the history of the theatre, one of the oldest of the arts, and the significance it had had in the history of civilization, and why the Department of Education was sponsoring it as a necessary step in the educational process. He spoke of the play they were going to see, and sometimes read from it. If the play was by Shakespeare, he gave the students an idea in advance of what the language sounded like when spoken by an actor. Al's talks provided an exciting introduction to theatre for a new, inexperienced audience, and his engaging manner of presentation appealed to the young people, for it was humorous, informal, and unpretentious. He was a great success as a speaker and preparer.

While all this preparation was going on, rehearsals were in progress for *Comedy of Errors*. The Washington State Theatre opened its first tour in Aberdeen, Washington, on November 2, 1936, with a matinee for students and an evening performance for adults. That first tour, we performed in nineteen playing centres, drawing from 143 outlying communities, and about 35,000 students and adults saw the play. Student prices were twenty-five cents, adults fifty and seventy-five cents.

Student tickets were sold in the schools, while adult performances were sponsored, and ticket sales were handled by the PTA and other service groups.

Dr. Showalter once said in a letter to Burton, "We have conserved lumber and fish. It's about time to think of conserving human beings." It seemed to us that we were on our way to doing exactly that.

We received support and encouragement from a wonderful variety of sources. On July 12, 1937, the IATSE (International Alliance of Theatrical Stage Employees) and MPO (Motion Picture Operators) stage hands' and teamsters' locals of the American Federation of Labor passed a resolution commending the Washington State Theatre and recommending that other locals in the state give "aid and espousal." The *Washington State Labor News* of September 30, 1932, carried an article that explains, at least in part, our continuing good relations with the unions: "Mr. James is a gold-edged brother of I.A.T.S.E. Local 15. Nearly all theatres in America similar to The Playhouse, a checkup has revealed, are either non-union or open shop. The Playhouse, however, has been a strictly union house ever since its inception four years ago, employing union stage hands and musicians from the beginning." Without exception, unions everywhere supported us in generous measure, largely unprompted, and gave us special consideration in the matters of wage scales, hours, conditions of work, and general helpfulness. Their support and encouragement were greatly appreciated during the Washington State Theatre tours.

At the conclusion of the first tour with *Comedy of Errors*, plans for the spring tour were underway. The Committee of Play Choice decided that the second tour should be a modern play. The one chosen was *No More Frontier* by Talbot Jennings. It was the story of the pioneering of Idaho, with a locale not far from Pocatello, the town where I was born. When I directed this play, I brought a great many memories of the area's pioneering history to the task.

In the play, two young men prospecting for gold meet and become partners as cattle ranchers; the partnership splits up when one of them decides to run sheep and there is competition over grazing lands. Idaho had marvellously rich soil, so sagebrush was grubbed up and dryland farming began. Though the first crops were planted with the hope that there would be enough rainfall to get a crop, irrigation became a necessity and a great man-made lake was created, with government assistance, at a place called American Falls.

In *No More Frontier*, this lake was on the cattlemen's old ranch, called "Hardtrigger." The two old partners meet again after a separation of many years, when the grandson of one of them is lost in a submarine accident. The other man asks, "What made him want to go to sea?" and his old partner answers, "He was always crazy about that lake. Every Sunday I'd take him out to look at it. He went to see the lake, and I went to remember Hardtrigger. I think that gave him the idea." The two old men sigh, "Well, the frontier's gone—Yeah, gone for good." A young grandson, perched on the porch listening to the mail plane flying overhead, says, "Grandfather, will we ever find a way to reach the stars?"

A nice prophetic ending for a play in 1936 about pioneering. The play seemed a natural for young audiences, with cattle rustlers, cowboys, and Indians, but we found that much of the play's tragic element was beyond the experience of the youngsters. The adult audiences, on the other hand, appreciated *No More Frontier* more than they did *Comedy of Errors*. We frequently heard people in the audience sobbing aloud, as they remembered their bitter experiences as pioneers.

Since there were several scene changes, the playing time was two hours. To ease the wait between acts, we engaged a musical director who travelled with the company and conducted student players, using a musical score that had been sent to any school with an orchestra two weeks before the playing date. School orchestras entered into the experience enthusiastically, for they became part of the performance. This was our first attempt to involve the theatre with other arts that already existed in the school.

The lesson plans were reviewed. More emphasis was placed on social and historical backgrounds, elements of theatrical appreciation, acting, scenery, costumes, and production. We didn't overlook certain aspects of audience responsibility and the contribution made by the audience to a better performance by the actors. At the end of the first year's tour, we had received almost five thousand letters from students and teachers expressing pleasure with the program, but we felt that more carefully gathered information was necessary in order to know for sure whether our "theatre in education" was achieving any or all of its goals.

The students were asking for modern plays. But most available modern plays dealt with controversial matters and had at least a little profanity. After the limited success of *No More Frontier* with high school audiences, we knew that "hells" and "damns" were out. *No More Frontier* had a small amount of such language and a barroom scene. These had been approved by the Play Choice Committee but the rural areas took exception to them. It seemed that our research methods were inadequate.

We approached Dr. Ralph Gundlach, assistant professor of psychology on the University of Washington campus. He volunteered his services, and entered the project with enthusiasm, preparing a questionnaire that would give us some of the answers we needed. The answers on play choice were revealing—the students wanted to see plays about the problems in their own young lives. In our efforts to find plays that met the interests and needs of this young audience, the Play Choice Committee circulated forty-five contemporary scripts to students, teachers, and school superintendents. We were unable to find anything that they didn't class as either silly or cheap.

My husband decided that plays which were contemporaneously valid and suitable would have to be specially written. But then he came up with another, better, idea. Wouldn't it be possible to create a situation that would permit the students to write their own plays? With this in mind, he approached Reed Fulton, the progressive principal of West Seattle High School, and Belle McKenzie, an English teacher in the school, to put a class in playwriting into the curriculum, to be conducted in school time. Miss McKenzie selected students who had shown interest, had some experience in writing and some talent, and encouraged them to enter the class. Some thirty of them met with Burton and Miss McKenzie two class periods a week, and, with the enthusiastic support of Mr. Fulton, a class in creative writing became a reality in a Seattle high school.

One of the students kept a verbatim record of the discussions Burton held with the class to determine the interests of the young people before they put pen to paper. It makes amazing reading thirty-five years later for it reflects the simmering pot now boiling over in the contemporary scene. In determining a theme for a play, they thought at first that Fascism might be a subject, but then they decided that democracy would be a better subject, as they were more familiar with that. They then moved to their immediate experience of democracy in their homes, their school, and the society in which they lived. Burton used a Socratic approach to this leadership task. His questions opened up discussions on every situation or experience that interested them. He listened and they talked. In their struggle to find a theme for their play on democracy, the students discovered that their quest was related to mankind's search to find a viable way of life. They decided to call the play *Search* and to create it in the form of the "living newspaper."

The classes were started on February 10, 1938, and before the play was completed, the term was over. During summer vacation, the students came to the Playhouse and finished their play. It was produced, along with other one-acts, in the fall tour of the Washington State Theatre. The audiences, though unfamiliar with the form, were enthusiastic about the content.

Burton, in a foreword to *Search*, which was circulated to every high school in the state, commented:

> The world has become conscious, as never before, of its youth, and youth in turn becomes conscious of the world in which it lives. Youth today does not rebel from sheer perversity or want of sufficient reason, and does not lack initiative or energy to mold a world after its own desires. Certainly it is understandable that youth today should be bewildered if not resentful. [They say,] "There is so much to be learned, so much to be done." In microcosm, the play *Search* says, in effect, "In this country as in every country, a tremendous task confronts youth, a task of creating a just social order, an economy that will produce and distribute goods efficiently and in accordance with human needs. We seek to build a world in which peace and justice will prevail." Our play *Search* is a contribution to this task.

At the outset of this playwriting project, we didn't really think that it would be capable of more than limited realization, if indeed it worked at all. And we didn't anticipate that results would be of anything more than tentative and, immediately at least, minor significance. Happily, however, the actual outcome immeasurably exceeded our expectations. The play was written by students, dealing with problems and ideas near and important, and to a large extent peculiar, to young people of secondary school age. It was tremendously popular. According to school officials interested in the project, it was one of the most momentous contributions of the Washington State Theatre to the field of education. *Search* released a previously scarcely tapped stream of creative energy and ability, and in the process made a significant legacy to teaching techniques. It was the latter that impelled Dr. Edgar Draper, professor of education at the University of Washington, to begin a similar experiment in classes in other schools in the state the following year, with the collaboration of the State Theatre.

While we broke even financially at the end of our first year of operation, definite deficiencies in budget planning began to emerge. We had counted on the adult performances to carry the weight of the twenty-five-cent admission for the high school audiences. The expected revenue didn't materialize, however, for the adult audiences had had little experience with live theatre, and therefore had little interest in it. We were also troubled by the fact that even the twenty-five-cent admission was too much for many students. In this day of "student affluence" it's hard to believe that many students then did not have a twenty-five-cent piece.* But that was the situation, caused by the effects of the country-wide recession on the state of Washington.

The Sino-Japanese War had curtailed and almost wiped out the chief market for the state's lumbering, the Orient. First pulp and saw mills, then logging camps shut down, and the maritime trades, shipping and longshoring, were keenly affected. In the great apple orchards in eastern Washington, there was a plethora of fruit. Some farmers had thousands of dollars' worth of unsalable fruit in warehouses or rotting on the ground, yet did not have enough money to buy groceries for their families.

In this kind of setting, it came as no surprise to us that many of our high school audience members could not get the money to attend our plays. It seemed that some kind of subsidization would be necessary, reluctant as we were to recognize it. All students everywhere should have the opportunity to see live drama, regardless of their ability to

* Twenty-five cents would have been worth about fifty-six cents in 1964 and $4.10 in 2013.

pay. It was suggested that schools meet some of the costs out of school funds but only in Whatcom County were funds made available to permit every student in the area to attend the performances.

When we were touring in the area of the state penitentiary at Walla Walla and the federal prison at McNeil Island, we played complimentary performances for the prisoners on Sunday afternoons. The warden warned us that prisoners who were bored with "outside" entertainment such as ours could return to their cells whenever they wished. "And," said the warden, "many do!" We were pleased to note that none did during our shows. They seemed to enjoy Shakespeare's *Comedy of Errors* and *The Taming of the Shrew*. We could not play *No More Frontier*, as there was a scene where a cattle rustler is shot, and no guns could be brought into a prison.

There was an interesting aftermath to this aspect of our touring. One December 31st, during the years of the Washington State Theatre, we were rehearsing at the Playhouse when the stage door opened and a young man walked in. He was welcomed by the company with delighted shouts of "You're out!" A member of one of our prison audiences, he had worked backstage on one or another of our productions and was now on his way to a job in Alaska. The company introduced him to me. We were having our New Year's Eve party at our house that evening and I invited him to come and join us. He said, "Oh lady, I can't go to any party. I don't have any clothes but these I've got on." I assured him that party clothes were not necessary, and he came. I remember him standing at a window, looking out at the lights on Queen Anne Hill as the New Year was coming in, and I like to remember him greeting the New Year and a new life among actor friends he had made when we played the penitentiary.

For the first production of the Washington State Theatre's second year, we planned Shakespeare's *The Taming of the Shrew*. While the *Comedy of Errors* was pure farce, the *Shrew* was a comedy with quieter, more serious overtones. The play committee was edging toward a "serious" Shakespearean play. In spite of the unexpected and disappointing failure of the adult performances to meet budget requirements, we reached a new high of 175 towns and cities in the state that year. We also played out-of-state performances in Portland and Pendleton, Oregon, and Lewiston, Idaho, at the request of the school officials in those areas. We were pleased with these latter performances, as it seemed that the project was beginning to fulfill Dr. Showalter's expectations of a "powerful and beneficial influence throughout the nation for culture and education and all the great, good things of life for which we all strive." *The Taming of the Shrew* proved to be the most successful, financially and artistically, of all the productions undertaken, and it was a satisfaction to know that nearly 55,000 students in the state had seen two Shakespearean plays.

It was at that time that we realized costs were rising. Hotel accommodations and meals, production costs, newspaper advertising and printing were all higher. Salaries, which had always been at a minimum, had to be increased. But we tried to balance these unavoidable increases by economies within the company. A tightened touring schedule saved money in salaries and transportation. While the financial picture was neither solid nor bleak, adjustments were in order.

She Stoops to Conquer by Oliver Goldsmith was selected for the spring tour and the performing group agreed that it went more smoothly than those on any previous tour. The thorough preliminary job undertaken in other tours was paying off. Audience response was excellent, perhaps because *She Stoops to Conquer* was on the school curriculum, and perhaps, too, because students were becoming conditioned to a theatre-going experience. William P. Tucker, state librarian, helped promotion by encouraging local libraries to put up displays relating to the play and provide reading lists of related material. He also asked Burton to be guest speaker on a radio program in a series that the state library was promoting.

We opened this play, as was our practice, to an invited preview audience at the Repertory Playhouse in Seattle on February 20. The Mutual Broadcasting System did a state-wide broadcast with the state superintendent of public instruction as speaker and interviews with members of the cast. In spite of new promotional approaches, *She Stoops* did not do as well financially as *Shrew*, but it received the largest number of votes of approval of any play in subsequent questionnaires.

When we started preparations for the third year of the project, our fifth tour, play choice presented the knottiest problem. The students were asking for moderns, but there didn't seem to be any that would be acceptable and would fulfill our exacting conditions of a theatre in education. We decided on four one-acts: Anton Chekhov's *Marriage*

Proposal, Thornton Wilder's *Happy Journey*, because of the interesting production problems—no props, no scenery—*Red Head Baker* by Albert Maltz, a play dealing with school-day problems familiar to student experience, which we had heard first as a radio play and then obtained permission from Mr. Maltz to arrange it for a State Theatre presentation, and *Search*. We called the four-play package "On Stage."

Of the four plays presented, *Red Head Baker* created the greatest interest. It was the first play produced by the State Theatre that had an element of controversy. It is the story of a boy unable to adjust to the authoritarian demands of a grade-oriented school, who succeeds in a school with a more creative, progressive attitude. This was the first time the Theatre ran into even slight censorship from the State Theatre committee. They wanted a scene cut, so that the boy would return to his old school and adjust, with the aid of progressive methods. They felt that the play as written would give the students ideas that would make administration problems more difficult.

The play for the spring tour was to be *Julius Caesar* in modern dress. The play was in the curriculum. The Playhouse had already produced it in this conception and it had been enthusiastically received by audiences. The modern-dress aspect enabled us to translate the power struggle in terms of the present—the takeover by a demagogue and a military clique of an established government. One reviewer wondered why we had used modern dress and not the togas of the period, and accused us of violating the Shakespearean script. For the first and only time in my life, I wrote a letter to a reviewer, asking him to read the play and then to return as our guest to see it again. I pointed out to him that in Shakespeare's own day the play had been presented in doublet and hose. He was generous enough to review it again and recant, saying that modern dress had actually seemed to make the script more intelligible.

By the end of the tour of "On Stage," we realized that we were in serious financial trouble. The Rockefeller grant was running out and the planned adult performances were not meeting our financial requirements. Something else had happened which had a definitely deleterious effect on our project. In the 1936 election there had been a landslide vote for President Roosevelt. Dr. Showalter, a Republican who had run unopposed for several terms, was beaten in that election by Stanley Atwood. Dr. Showalter and Mr. Swenson, who had been closest to us and had the most wholehearted enthusiasm and support for the project, were out. Dr. Showalter died a few months later.

Mr. Atwood and the newly elected superintendent in charge of high schools, Mr. Thorsett, expressed interest in the State Theatre and offered their support. But there was a conflict between the economy-minded governor and the State Board of Education. There were also conflicts in the Legislature and the school districts, conflicts that began to emerge after the election but which we somehow did not attribute to the political situation.

Rockefeller Humanities had made the grant of $35,000 contingent upon the State Board's continued interest in the project. All that was needed to indicate this interest was sufficient funds to establish a Department of Speech and Drama, which would have put the State Theatre's program on a permanent basis. When the governor's budget appeared, it precluded the possibility of this development, and Dr. Stevens informed us with regret of the Humanities' unwillingness to proceed further in the program. The excitement created by the letter from the Rockefeller Foundation giving us the grant to start the Washington State Theatre in 1936 was equalled in intensity only by the gloom that descended when we received their message of regret in 1939. We realized that the Washington State Theatre was doomed and the Playhouse threatened.

One day soon after that, we met in the offices of the Theatre to make plans to save the Playhouse and to try to retain use of the space we had renovated for the State Theatre operations. We needed this additional building for rehearsals, costume, and prop storage. We realized that any future we could devise would be dependent on our own efforts, with the help of those associated with us. Collectively, we decided who should and would remain on the staff of the Playhouse, and who should seek employment elsewhere. Those who were selected knew that they were accepting an immediate future of extreme austerity. But no one refused, and somehow we managed.

There was no time to waste, so in January 1939, the Administrative Committee of the Washington State Theatre sent word to the sponsoring high schools of the state that the spring tour of *Julius Caesar* would have to be cancelled in all communities to avoid incurring further deficits, a figure that now stood at $3,000. (The Repertory Playhouse eventually managed to pay off this debt.) The Washington State Theatre had failed financially, but its contribution to the young people of the state had fulfilled our most extravagant expectations. Most undertakings of this type have problems to overcome, but those associated with our effort seemed more acute than usual and the project could scarcely have been undertaken at a more uncertain time from a historical point of view. We had, however, brought good theatre to over 95,000 students, and over the years many people would meet us and say, "I'll never forget the day you came to our school and I saw Shakespeare."

All the projects proposed as a result of the initial experiment seemed realizable and never had so much been undertaken by so few in so short a time. We realized halfway through the three years that we should have planned on a five-year experiment—we might have avoided the political situation that wrought such havoc with our efforts. And we might have realized earlier that the adults we were counting on for financial assistance to make low student fees possible suffered from the very lack of experience in theatregoing that we were hoping to obviate through the State Theatre.

We made other valuable contributions to the schools of the state. The Works Progress Administration was building schools at this time and our technicians, with their expertise in auditorium requirements, met with school staff, architects, and electrical companies, helping to avoid many costly mistakes. The experiment of the writing course in the West Seattle High School encouraged my husband to recommend more such courses, to be set up with fellowships or bursaries where the student showed talent.

As Gloria Ann Hewitt said in her 1960 thesis for a Master's Degree in Drama at the University of Washington:

> The State Theatre's greatest achievement lay in the realization of Burton James' ideals of integrating drama with education. Perhaps it is an overstatement to assert that Burton James was a prophet. But today, thirty years later, there is a growing realization that such experiences by the State Theatre are a vital part of every child's education. Too often these experiences are not provided, and it will take a leader with the vision of Burton James and a company with the dedication of the Washington State Theatre to provide them.

CHAPTER ELEVEN

This seems a good point to define the word "theatre"—"not what it looks like, but what it is," as Burton once put it. A building that contains a stage, an auditorium, and the necessary physical equipment to put on a show is not necessarily a theatre. A theatre is, first of all, a group of people, of artists, if you will—actors, scene and costume designers, lighting and construction technicians, musicians, and a director or directors—all dedicated to producing, honestly and beautifully, plays of merit.

To what extent do theatres today conform to this definition?

When I went abroad, there were pitifully few such theatres in England or America. Today, on this continent, with the successful advent of regional theatres such as the one I was associated with—the Globe in Regina, Saskatchewan—this concept has begun to take hold. I believe that it is these regional theatres, and not the commercial theatres in the larger centres, that are developing the ensembles to create truly good theatre.

A commercial producer in America, heading for Broadway, usually selects a play, not because it is good, but because it will make money. He collects a group of actors, people who want jobs and whose appearance seems to fit the parts, among them a star or stars (often movie actors or actresses, because their names are usually better known to the public and therefore have greater box office appeal); a director who has never seen most of the actors before and whose connection with the production frequently terminates on opening night; scene and costume designers; and a technician to light the play.

Before or during rehearsals, the play may be "doctored" by someone not at all familiar with the author or his intentions but who is supposed to know what Broadway likes. And if these changes are not enough, the "angel" gamblers who have backed the play see rehearsals and have a go at it too. When the play is deemed ready for production, a theatre is rented. It may not be the right kind of theatre for this particular play, but if it's available at the time required, it's used.

If such a mélange achieves success, it is sheer accident and, success or failure, the results are equally hard on the actor. If successful, he or she goes on and on, night after night, for months—even years—in deadly repetition, often in a part of no particular distinction. Great ability can scarcely survive such success, and for young talent, it is death. If the play fails, as it often does overnight, the actor is back going the rounds, looking for another job. If, during a reasonably long run, some distinction of style and harmony of purpose is achieved as the result of the association of the component talents, these talents are dissipated at the end of the engagement. Instead of being conserved as an experienced and efficient unit for the purpose of establishing true theatre, the group is scattered in the inevitable search for further employment.

On my trip abroad in 1934, one of the first things I discovered in Moscow was that no such haphazard arrangement would ever be mistaken by the Russians for a theatre. When we entered a playhouse there, we were immediately conscious of the intentions, imagination, and discipline of the director and his group. No two theatres looked alike; each had a definite, separate distinction of its own. A theatre, we always felt, should be the most attractive building in the area, exciting even to look at, and should have a personality of its own when you entered it. This understanding of what theatre should be motivated all we did throughout the years.

As students in Boston, Burton and I had been introduced to the idea that life and work should be based on a philosophy, so it was inevitable that we would search for a philosophy as the basis for our work in the theatre. We found it in a statement by Julius Bab in an article in the *Encyclopedia of the Social Sciences*: "A theatre, in the true sense of the word, is a unity, at the core of which is the living community finding some vital part of itself reflected in the creations of the dramatist and actor."

The living community meant for us the *total* living community, anybody and everybody who wanted to work in it in some capacity or be an audience. All kinds and conditions of people worked in our theatre, from the society matron who came to rehearsals in her limousine driven by a liveried chauffeur, to the little man selling papers at the Pike Street Market, who had no telephone and no address because he lived in Hooverville, the shanty-town of the Depression.

We wanted our audiences to be composed of the total community too, which was one reason for keeping admission prices within the range of everybody's pocketbook. My husband frequently said, "People should be able to afford theatre." And when it was not possible for them to meet even this modest price of admission, we gave them tickets. I remember one evening I was standing in the box office when a man slipped up to the ticket window. He was eating something out of a brown paper bag, probably his dinner. Hesitantly, he said to the attendant, "I've gone by this place a lot of times, and I thought that someday I'd like to see a play, but I can't afford to go because I'm unemployed. But I'd particularly like to see this play, and somebody told me that sometimes you give people tickets. If you could spare it, I'd really like to have one for this play."

The box office attendant promptly gave him a "comp" and said, "Give this piece of paper to the man at the door. The play begins at 8:30. I hope you enjoy it." This was not an isolated incident.

Everyone connected in any capacity with our theatre had an attitude of gracious service toward the public. Once, our custodian, sweeping the sidewalk, was approached by a young man who said, "I'd like to meet someone in charge here. How do I go about it?" The custodian replied, "Just knock on that door. Mr. or Mrs. James are around. Just ask to see them." It was just after the Second World War; the young man had been demobilized and was looking for somewhere to put his feet down. He wanted to be an actor but, as he told me later, he had been rebuffed so often that he felt he did not know the right approach to those people he called the "big shots." Dominic Nigrelli turned out to be a very good actor. He worked with us and later went to Hollywood where I heard he appeared with Mario Lanza in *The Great Caruso*.

We believed in the creative capacity of those who came to the theatre to work, whether as actors or in any other function necessary to the running of a theatre, and we believed that it was an opportunity and an obligation to assist in developing this capacity to the point where it could be identified as talent.

In 1942, on a grant from the National Theatre Conference, I travelled down the Pacific Coast and as far east as Texas and up through Utah to see community and university theatres. In Seattle, we frequently had fact-finding visitors who came in on the morning plane, took notes in brief interviews they had with us and our staff, and left in the afternoon without seeing either a rehearsal or a play. Then they went home and wrote us up. We often wondered, when reading what they had to say about us, where or how they got their ideas. So, when I went on my trip, we decided that I would come back with as much factual information as I could get, as well as my impressions of what I saw. We prepared a questionnaire. The first questions on my sheet were "What is your philosophy of theatre?" and "How do you implement it?" To my great surprise, these questions upset the interviewees so much that finally I had to put them down at the end of the questionnaire. One man, a Russian émigré directing a play at Baylor University in Waco, Texas, shook his fist at my handbag, which happened to be a beautiful shade of red, and screamed at me, "Philosophy? Stalinist culture! Bolshevik nonsense!" At the other end of the scale were those who shrugged, "Philosophy? Oh, I suppose I must have one. Never thought of it."

At Stanford University, I had the pleasure and good fortune of meeting Dr. Harold Chapman Brown, formerly head of the Philosophy Department but retired when I saw him. I showed him our questionnaire. When he came to the two offending questions, he asked me what response I had received to them. When I told him of my experiences, he said, "The word 'philosophy' threw them. People think philosophy is something you get degrees in. All you really want to know is 'What do you want in your theatre, and how do you go about getting it?' If they can't answer the first part of the question, they'll have no answer for the second."

Dr. Brown gave me a booklet, "What Is Philosophy?," based on one of his lectures. I found certain quotations from it very helpful: "You can't escape philosophy, whether you want it or not, for you are bound to have opinions about the world you live in, and what you want out of that world. This is your philosophy. Philosophy is not, as is often assumed, something highly abstract and aloof, but the most concrete intellectual activity of mankind." And he concluded with a quotation by G. K. Chesterton, "We think that for a landlady considering a lodger, it is important to know his income, but still more important to know his philosophy."

One of the most crucial areas in the operation of our theatre was play selection. Selection is a vital matter, whether you operate on a hit-and-miss basis of "what the public wants" or a planned program of plays to attract the widest possible audience. The difference in these two approaches is a philosophic one—producing plays to make a lot of money or producing plays that have real merit and should be done whether or not they are box office successes. Play selection presented problems for us not only at the Playhouse but also in the Negro Repertory and the Washington State Theatre. Each theatre's selections presented unique and different problems for vastly varying reasons.

When you sell subscriptions, it is necessary to offer variety. Even the Canadian Stratford Festival Theatre eventually realized that it could not go on producing only Shakespeare. They had to include other and different kinds of plays to gain and hold the interest of their audiences. The first three plays we offered our Playhouse subscribers in 1928 had variety. All were contemporary, but were quite different in content.

The classics are classics by virtue of having qualities that have stood the test of time, but the fact that they are classics is sometimes seen as diminishing their popular appeal. It was our experience, however, that the classics always attracted the largest audiences to the Playhouse and did the best business. With few exceptions, we never had "standing room only" for even the most attractive modern comedy; we did sometimes have capacity audiences for modern controversial plays such as *In Abraham's Bosom*, *Stevedore*, *Little Ol' Boy,* and *Waiting for Lefty*. But we regularly had standing room only audiences for our productions of the classics.

Our play selection in the first two or three years of the Playhouse tended toward the romantic, but looking back on it now, I think we must have sensed that there were two kinds of romanticism, as described by Maxim Gorky in "How I Became a Writer":

> Within the romantic school one must again distinguish two sharply divergent tendencies; passive romanticism which either attempts to reconcile people with reality by coloring it, or else attempts to divert people from reality and lure them into fruitless preoccupations with their own world with thoughts about "the fatal riddle of life," about love, death, about problems which can never be solved by speculation and contemplation, but only by scientific research. Active romanticism, on the other hand, attempts to strengthen man's will to live, to rouse him to rebellion against reality with all its tyrannies.

We believed in, and produced, plays of "active romanticism."

Controversy was the keynote of the work of playwrights in the 1930s. Recognition of social and economic inequalities served as a basis for the work of such playwrights as Eugene O'Neill, Clifford Odets, Paul Green, Lillian Hellman, and others. Our first production of a play that could definitely have been considered controversial was Paul Green's *In Abraham's Bosom*. This play, whose plot I've outlined earlier in this book, was applauded as a great play in Seattle, but it would not, at that time, have been given a production in the South. It is only when the theme of the play touches a live nerve of the living community that it becomes controversial, and it is a commonplace that plays that are controversial in one period come to be accepted in another as great drama. Practically all of Ibsen's plays created controversy. *Ghosts*, for example, led to uproars and protests in London and New York when first produced because it dealt with the unmentionable subject of inherited syphilis. One London reviewer said that Ibsen had "emptied the sewers of London" into the theatre.

In 1934 we did another potentially controversial play, Albert Bein's *Little Ol' Boy,* which dramatized the brutalization of "problem" youngsters brought into the jurisdiction of a reformatory. Because we needed young people in the cast, I approached principals and teachers in the high schools of Seattle. The students they recommended had to be top-flight in school in every way. Though they were bright, talented, well-behaved boys, when we photographed them during rehearsals in their reform-school uniforms against the brick wall of the Playhouse stage, a tougher-looking group of youngsters could scarcely be imagined. From their ranks came some of our company's best actors, among them Marcel LePlat, later known as Marc Platt, ballet master of the Monte Carlo Ballet, and Howard Duff and Stacy Harris, well-known radio, television, and motion picture personalities.

We visited a reform school near Seattle to get impressions and background. When taken for a tour of the institution's cow barns, I noted the exactly measured quantities of food in each stall and wondered if the supervisors' knowledge of the youngsters' needs was as precise as it was for the animals. Albert Bein had drawn on his own experience for his play—he had been an inmate in a reformatory in Tennessee for two years. This institution later used Bein's play as "corroboratory evidence" in a campaign for state legislation to provide new and better facilities for reformatories.

Our production of *Little Ol' Boy* got very favourable responses from the press and audience. Sermons were preached on it. Women's clubs, the Seattle PTA, even the mayor and his wife, participated on committees to promote the production. We received such recognition for doing a play that, however well or ill it might have fared at the box office, should have been produced.

Though Seattle audiences applauded plays exposing injustices in a Georgia turpentine camp or a Tennessee reformatory, we cut a little closer to the bone when we produced Eugene O'Neill's *The Hairy Ape.* We had long considered this play to be a truly important contribution in the field of drama. O'Neill was then receiving attention as a superlative American playwright, and his plays had also been produced in England, Russia, Germany, and the Scandinavian countries. Shortly after we produced *The Hairy Ape,* he was awarded the Pulitzer Prize for drama. O'Neill, more than any other single American, was giving a new life and a new significance to the American theatre.

But a production of *The Hairy Ape* by the Playhouse presented a problem in casting the part of Yank. It was not until Jack Rustad joined us that we began to think seriously about producing the play. Jack was of Scandinavian ancestry, over six feet tall, bull-chested, husky, and blond. His father had been a deep-sea skipper, and Jack and his elder brother had shipped out as able-bodied seamen and worked as stevedores as soon as they were big enough to do so. The shipboard setting of *The Hairy Ape* was thus a natural environment for Jack. He had tremendous vitality and when he boasted of his physical prowess and cowed and quelled his shipmates, his physique made his statements and action seem easily possible.

The play is laid in the days when ocean liners were fired with coal by stokers such as Yank. When the lady from First Class insists on seeing the stoke-hole, she faints, frightened by the grease, dirt, and sweat of this great man. Paddy, one of Yank's shipmates, says, "She tought you was a great hairy ape, escaped from de zoo." This is a traumatic experience for Yank, who now believes that he is not what he thinks he is, not even a man. He is seen by others as an animal, an ape, and he belongs nowhere.

Rustad did an excellent job with the character of Yank; he looked the part, and acted it. My main problem was to keep him within the confines of the play. One reviewer commented on a bit of Jack-created action when Yank receives his card from the IWW secretary. "He holds it like a foreign thing for a moment in his great paw, then digs in his trouser pocket and says, 'Four bits? Is dat all?' It is one of the most heart-gripping, moving things I have ever seen in the theatre."

What Yank received for his fifty cents was a red card in the Industrial Workers of the World, the "Wobblies," a name bestowed on them by a Chinese restaurateur who was unable to pronounce "IWW." They were attempting to organize the migratory workers, the "working stiffs" as they called themselves, into One Big Union. During World War I, lumber prices soared astronomically but wages and working conditions remained unchanged. The Wobblies had no difficulty organizing, but when they called a strike in 1917 and ten thousand "working stiffs" downed tools and walked out of the camps, what sympathy they had from the general public evaporated. Someone said it was "more patriotic to kill a 'Wobbly' than a German." Anyone caught carrying a Wobbly card was in for a very tough time. So the red card in *The Hairy Ape* touched a live nerve in certain segments of the community.

The play received a mixed reception. Everyone praised the production, but many criticized the play itself and the Playhouse for doing it. One of our own board members remarked, "It was a beautiful production, but aren't you afraid it'll give people ideas?"

The sprinkling of dissent over *The Hairy Ape* turned out to be a mere summer squall compared to the storm that broke over our heads when we produced Clifford Odets' one-act play *Waiting for Lefty.* My husband often read some interesting play or other material to our Sunday night supper guests. In 1936, *Waiting for Lefty* had just been published and one evening he read it to our guests, who happened to be our colleagues at the university. At the conclusion of the reading, everyone clamoured for a production. But the play was only a one-act and not suitable for a six or seven-week run—audiences then were even less accustomed to attending productions of one-acts than they are now. We figured that it would cost about $85 to mount one performance, but our friends volunteered to sell the tickets and meet any deficit, so we agreed to do a single performance.

Even before the play opened, storm clouds began to gather around us. As the ticket sale was in the hands of a committee, tickets were not available at the theatre box office. This was standard practice: when groups took tickets for a performance or a block of seats, they sold them and only the unsold tickets were returned for box office sale. But in the case of *Waiting for Lefty,* gossip built this into some sort of conspiracy.

At the same time, several seemingly unrelated incidents were taking place that would eventually bring the roof down on our collective heads. As few people travelled to the Soviet Union in those days, I was asked to speak on my experiences there to any number of organizations and clubs—the Junior Chamber of Commerce, the Elks' Club, women's groups, and many others. Among the requests was one from the Unemployed Citizens' League. This group had organized the first self-help arrangements among the unemployed in the United States in the dark days of 1931. As I had not refused anyone who asked for my services as a speaker, I did not consider refusing to speak to them, even though I was warned that the audience might contain some political heretics and agitators. So on a rainy night, I went to a gloomy hall on the Skid Road in downtown Seattle, and spoke. When I talked about the theatre festival in Moscow, I got a bit of heckling about the political aspects, but I honestly told the hecklers that I couldn't answer their questions because I didn't know anything about Russian politics.

Once before, after I had spoken about my trip at a large dinner attended by some members of our Playhouse Board, one of them, a very nice man, put a friendly arm about my shoulders and said, "You make that speech too well. You're going to get people to like the Soviet Union." And that seemed to be a mistake, for it showed up in the furor over *Lefty,* with certain segments of the public drawing particularly dire conclusions from my speech to the Unemployed Citizens' League.

As well, that fall, we had rented our theatre to a church group whose minister had been asked to resign from a fashionable Seattle church because some of the more affluent members, who disagreed with him, were leaving the church and taking their support with them. What the issue involved was, we neither knew nor cared. A committee from the breakaway church offered $50 a month in rent for the use of the theatre for Sunday morning services, an offer we accepted gratefully because we were having a real struggle just to meet current bills. When we began receiving telephone calls at the Playhouse complaining about the "Church of the People," as it was called, I went to a Sunday morning service to see and hear for myself. The minister was speaking on Abraham Lincoln, a seemingly safe topic but, as a noted politician once said, "Mention Lincoln, but don't quote him." Our rental to this group, done quite innocently, later added fuel to the fire.

The production of *Waiting for Lefty* was a tremendous success. Many of the audience members had been out to dinner and arrived in evening clothes to immerse themselves in Odets' story of a taxicab strike, told sympathetically from the viewpoint of the strikers. It was an exciting experience for audience and performers alike, with great empathy developing as the play progressed. When the climactic cry, "What's the answer?" rang out from the stage, the audience response came back, "Strike! Strike!"

Al Ottenheimer wrote in his theatre log that night, "It was electric! You could feel the tingle in the audience, the excitement which welled up and surged across the footlights. The audience, apparently, was wildly enthusiastic at the close of the performance, giving us five curtain calls and lingering in the theatre and in the lounge to discuss the show."

Since there was only one performance of *Waiting for Lefty,* and censorial effects accruing from it lasted for nearly a decade afterward, it is pertinent to note that, from those who actually attended, there was no protest. It is pertinent to note, too, how we who were involved in the production felt about the play. In the same log entry, for January 12, 1936, Al admitted the bias of Odets' play, but emphasized its solid artistic qualities:

> It has a message, a bitter tirade against racketeering in trade unions, and, likely, something of a Communistic bias, but the play transcends these. Its dramatic excellence, excitement, and power cause these other considerations to fade into the background. *Waiting for Lefty* admirably fulfils a quotation Brooks Atkinson adopted from one of his correspondents in a recent issue of the *New York Times*, to this effect: "The propaganda play ceases to be propaganda when it becomes good drama." The universality of the drama, emotion, passion in *Lefty* make all other considerations of small consequence.

The ax fell on us on the fifteenth of January, three days after the play's Sunday performance. Al was making his usual rounds of the newspaper offices with Playhouse press releases and received a cool reception when he reached the *Seattle Times*, the city's most influential evening paper. His releases were refused and he was referred to Carl Brazier, then the managing editor. Nothing could be accepted from the Repertory Playhouse, he was told, until he had talked with Brazier.

Al reported after his interview with the managing editor that he had never in his life, at least to that time, received such a going-over. "I managed, strangely enough," he said, "to keep my temper. I asked repeatedly what I could do to clear the matter up, but all defense was waved aside." Brazier kept insisting that the Church of the People had sold the tickets for *Lefty*. They hadn't, of course. They had had nothing to do with the production and the minister himself was not even in the audience to see the play.

When the newsman barked at Al, "Don't give me a lot of theoretical stuff about your right to play any plays you want to," Al asked, "Is freedom of speech, of which the papers make so much, and freedom of the press, which they so vigorously defend, also 'a lot of theoretical stuff'?" He didn't get an answer.

As the capper, the newspaper executive charged that the most horrifying of all our crimes was that we had "incited people in evening clothes to riot." I gathered that he felt that if I had incited the members of the Unemployed Citizens' League to riot (he had also reamed Al out because of my "political" speech to that group), it would have been bad, but when you incite people in evening clothes to riot, you are really climbing into revolution. And of course, in a way, I suppose he was right. When people in evening clothes demand change, you may get it.

The upshot was that for the next decade the Seattle Repertory Playhouse was never mentioned in the *Seattle Times*. When it was absolutely unavoidable for the paper to give a report on some recital or other event that happened to have taken place in our theatre, it was simply referred to as "a theatre at 41st and University Way."

As individuals, our names were not printed in the *Times* until the Washington branch of the House Un-American Activities Committee got into action. Then, our names made headlines. When Burton died, no mention was made in his obituary of his ever having had any connection with the Playhouse. The whole thing had definite overtones of Orwell's *1984*. The press, always very vocal in defending its own freedom of expression, knows exactly the pressures to apply when someone else chooses to exercise the same prerogative.

We received many letters about *Waiting for Lefty*, both for and against. A surprising number of the complaints came from people who said that they would never support the Playhouse again. In checking our subscription lists, we found that few if any of them had ever been in our theatre, and none of them, as far as we could ascertain, had ever been subscribers. They were still prepared to tell us what we could or could not do. Some letters came from people who protested the production of a play whose name they didn't even know.

But many more came from people who applauded our efforts, though most of those hadn't seen the play either. Word had gotten around, and if we'd had the money to spare, we'd have loved to do *Lefty* again, to respond to audience demand. It seemed as though we could have filled the theatre several times over with enthusiastic theatregoers. But it just wasn't possible.

After Al's experience with the *Times*, we expected repercussions from our board and from members of the audience who'd actually been there to see the play. Surprisingly, none came from the board (at that time, at least), and we received many letters of enthusiastic support from all kinds of people who had been in the theatre that Sunday night. One prominent politician wrote, "My conservative mother-in-law enjoyed the play immensely." A civil engineering professor wrote, "How can we know the theatre unless we see the contemporary plays, and what else could the contemporary playwright concern himself with but the suffering which has been too common during the last decade among the working classes, and the way this suffering has awakened people to an understanding of the real causes of poverty in this country?" (If only it had!)

Rumours circulated, charges were made, some of them openly, most of them whispered. Our board held a meeting to discuss the "lefty" eruption and arrived at the consensus that, though wholly unintentional, the circumstances surrounding the performance were open to misinterpretation. A resolution was passed not to sponsor the Habima Players in Odets' *Awake and Sing* but to rent them the theatre instead, which might or might not have been a compromise. Al Ottenheimer summed up the meeting in his log: "The Board has taken no stand on the matter of whether we do the new things in the theatre with a social aspect or not."

One well-meaning friend suggested that we do things like *Little Lord Fauntleroy*, "because you can get away with things like that." Instead, in May 1936, we produced George Sklar and Paul Peters' *Stevedore* with the Negro Repertory group. This was a production that might have been expected to arouse controversy. Where the theme of *Waiting for Lefty* was racketeering leadership in trade unionism, the theme of *Stevedore* was the dock strike in New Orleans. Seattle was no stranger to waterfront problems or striking longshoremen, and Harry Bridges was building his International Longshore and Warehouse Union on the Pacific Coast into a force to be reckoned with. One might have supposed that a play about the struggle to break a strike and destroy a waterfront union would have had repercussions, but protests about *Stevedore* were comparatively mild, though we did have one resignation from our board. It may have been that, since the locale of *Stevedore* was New Orleans, it seemed remote from similar issues in Seattle.

How do you deal with a situation that involves you in controversy with your public, whether with "patriotic loyal Americans" who protest the production of *Waiting for Lefty* or with moralistic patrons who denounce a production of Stefan Zweig's arrangement of Ben Jonson's *Volpone* or Dorothy Parker's *After Such Pleasures*?

Al once replied to a critic of one of the above persuasions:

> Only two things are taken into consideration when we choose a play. One: Is it significant for some phase of life and literature? Two: Will our audiences like it? *After Such Pleasures* was chosen because Dorothy Parker is one of the most representative and important figures of contemporary American literature. You may not agree, but that is the evaluation of the world's critics. We felt that this, plus the fact that we ourselves consider the sketches highly amusing, justified the production. Outspoken, yes—somewhat vulgar, yes. But so, plainly, are the phases of contemporary American life which she reports and holds up to the purgatory fire of ridicule.

I believe it is fatal to compromise your insights in order to acquiesce to the demands made on you. There is only one way to respond, blunt though it may seem: state your case and hope the playgoer will acknowledge your integrity and arrive at an understanding of your standards. Otherwise you will be producing plays written about nothing for nobody. It seems strange to me now to remember the difficulties we had over controversial plays that touched on moral issues. I am sure no one today would raise an eyebrow over Zweig's *Volpone* or Parker's *After Such Pleasures*, when *Hair* presents actors in the nude and four-letter words creep into almost every playscript. Playwrights reflect their age, and time sorts the value of their contribution.

In our twenty years of productions, there were only a handful of plays that our audiences, or the community at large, found "controversial." If some portion of our audiences reacted with "I won't put my foot in your theatre again," others kept coming, or started coming, because of the interest engendered by the controversial plays, particularly those with social content.

Seattle was a very union-minded town then and several unions began buying blocks of seats and then entire houses for their members. These were for a variety of performances, not just the "controversial" plays. Progressive leadership in the unions began planning educational and cultural programs for their membership. When the head of the meat-cutters' local wanted to buy a performance for his union, one of our board members, a banker's wife, protested.

"Why do meat-cutters want to come to a theatre?"

"Why shouldn't they come to the theatre?" Burton replied. "They won't bring the entrails with them."

Her opposition to the whole idea was so strong that she resigned.

Someone once said that there must be a climate for the arts. We found the climate very favourable in Seattle and in Washington as a whole, I think, as the heritage of decades of struggle by dedicated, forward-looking, imaginative people to achieve a viable existence in their environment. The arts advance in such struggles. It is a precondition not only of artistic advance but of artistic survival.

It delighted us to see unions concerning themselves with our theatre. We wanted the theatre to be part of the living community. We were in the community—how could we not be of it as well? So we went on producing plays that we thought all kinds and conditions of people in our growing city should see.

CHAPTER TWELVE

We had a slogan at the Playhouse: "Keep the Doors Open." This referred not only to our audience policy but to our backstage policy as well. We had a nucleus of perhaps a dozen "regulars," including Burton, but when anyone approached us for an opportunity to work at the theatre, we took their name and address and when we were casting a new play, all of these people were sent notices for the play reading and asked to try out for any part they thought they might like to play.

When we were planning our new season in the fall of 1934, I had seventy-two people sitting on the stage waiting for a chance to do something. I knew nothing of the capabilities of most of them. It was then that we decided to provide workshops on Saturday and Sunday afternoons for people who were willing to accept the discipline of learning the essentials of something they thought they might want to do. Only those really interested would come to the workshops, and the dilettantes and those only vaguely curious would eliminate themselves. Our teachers were members of the Playhouse company. Classes included the philosophy of theatre and makeup taught by Albert Ottenheimer, body movement taught by Louise Hastert, speech by Frederick Patterson, and acting techniques by myself. Everyone, regular members of our acting group and our newest recruits, took part in these workshops.

We had long ago rejected the idea that acting was something that could not be taught. For centuries, actors have tried to understand, even to codify, the processes by which they learned their craft and developed their art. Art and craft are separate but definitely related. The imaginative powers of the actor and his craftsmanship are completely dependent on each other.

There is a persistent view that the ability to act is the result of inspiration, beyond the range of question and investigation. This view was summed up in all its majestic vagueness in an answer given by Orson Welles to a question asked at the conclusion of a lecture he delivered at the Actors' Lab in Hollywood. A young actor said, "But Mr. Welles, don't you think that acting can be taught?" It seemed to me that Welles had already answered the actor's question in his lecture, to the effect that if you can act, you can act, and there is nothing to worry about. Nobody can do anything about it except you, and perhaps God. But he chose to deliver a Wellesian reply: "How can you calibrate the aura of the Holy Ghost?" Perhaps he believed what he said, but his reputation for painstaking study and effort, beginning with his astounding success as actor and director in *Citizen Kane*, would seem to deny this.

Sometimes it seems to me that successful artists have done as much mischief in this area as anyone, perpetuating the myth of the rarely endowed, the "unique soul." Perhaps their struggles have been so painful, so arduous, that they have come to feel their position, however secure, must be the result of efforts beyond themselves, of the supernatural. Or perhaps they simply wish to discourage competition! Our competitive society is not a particularly friendly one, in any respect, to struggling artists, and successful artists may feel that their continued success depends more on a relationship to God than to others. They may feel their accomplishments are the result of intuition and inspiration. Stanislavski and his followers attempted to perfect a method to create by will conditions favourable for the appearance of inspiration, but as theatre critic George Henry Lewes once said, "Trusting to inspiration of the moment is like trusting to a shipwreck for your first lesson in swimming."

Many actors and directors learned their craft by watching other actors and directors at work. André Antoine (1858–1943), founder and director of Théâtre Libre and later director of the Odeon, the second most important theatre in Paris, had little formal education but a vast enthusiasm for the theatre. He first became a member of a claque at the Comédie Française and later joined the theatre as a supernumerary. In this way, he was able to watch actors and directors at work. While a clerk in a gas company, Antoine organized an amateur group and began to put into practice his own thoughts on the problems of acting and directing. He believed that the art of the actor should be based on "truth, observation, and the study of nature." His ideas were so revolutionary that when he founded the Théâtre Libre and performed there as an actor, he actually turned his back to the audience, an unheard-of action in that day. Going to his theatre was referred to, jocularly, as "going to see Antoine's back."

His innovations included changes in staging and scenery. He was immeasurably helped by the new playwrights Ibsen, Eugène Brieux, Gerhardt Hauptmann, and Tolstoy, for productions of their plays needed "naturalism." He was so successful that he influenced the work of the German Meiningen Theatre, which in turn served as inspiration for Constantin Stanislavski and Vladimir Nemirovich-Danchenko when they founded the Moscow Art Theatre.

Antoine learned his craft by observation. Sir Henry Irving had been a dresser for some actor and studied him. Edwin Booth, the great American Shakespearean actor, watched his father, Junius Brutus Booth, who was reputed to be an exceptionally fine actor. My own experience in the theatre has always involved me in the teaching process. My first directing was of amateurs, and amateurs have to be trained. I brought the same attitude to this activity that I did to directing—however effective I might be, I never knew enough and always wanted to spend time exploring new approaches and techniques. I never gave up my quest. Never!

When I first started to teach, I tried to use the practice and precepts I had learned at Emerson, those of the nineteenth-century Frenchman François Delsarte (1811–1871). Delsarte went to the Conservatoire in Paris, studying to become a singer. Through faulty instruction, he lost his voice and turned to teaching, becoming the leading speech and voice teacher of his day. He was dissatisfied with the actor training techniques of his time and set down methods of his own which, unhappily, were just as mechanical as those he criticized. You could still find second-hand books on "Elocution" based on the Delsarte methods, complete with pictures of ladies wearing what appear to be bed sheets, doing Delsarte exercises illustrated by lines from plays: "Down on the knees for Supplication," stances for Anger, attitudes for Love, etc., each with the proper facial expression to accompany them ("Mugs," as my Federal Theatre actor called them), and descriptions of what the voice should sound like: "Gay, soft, charming voice for Love," "Hate, sharp and sullen," "Grief, dull and languishing," and so on.

In my day, Delsarte's exercises were widely accepted in the United States, not only for actors but for anyone who wished to acquire "charm, grace, and a fine carriage." Delsartian exercises became clichés, the hackneyed expressions and broad gestures of the melodramas that were so popular at the turn of the century ... Theodore Kremer's *Bertha, the Sewing Machine Girl,* Lillian Mortimer's *No Mother to Guide Her,* and Owen Davis's *Nellie, the Beautiful Cloak Model.* Delsarte served me well when I came to direct these plays, for I had been well-schooled in his gestures. We didn't "ham" them, but played them seriously, as they had been played in the days when they were popular, and the audiences loved them. More than one member of audiences at these performances complained about people who laughed "when it was all so sad."

All these exercises, so diligently practiced in the classrooms of my youth, never seemed to be referred to in the rehearsals of the scenes and plays at Emerson. They were taught much as the steps in classical ballet are taught and were expected to come into play when you needed them. Then I began rehearsing plays at Lenox Hill and soon abandoned them as completely impractical. I had to trust instead to my instinctual knowledge, for I had no other guides.

I knew good acting when I saw it. What impressed me most about the work of the Abbey Players when I saw them on their New York visit was their seemingly effortless simplicity. These actors were once amateurs and what Lady Gregory and W. B. Yeats had done to develop them to this point of artistic achievement interested me.

I think my philosophy of actor training begins with an essential belief in the potential creativity of anyone who has ever approached me seeking the opportunity to do this work. I knew nothing of the capacities of the twenty-five Black people who came to the Playhouse one Sunday afternoon for the first reading of Paul Green's *In Abraham's Bosom.* When it came to casting the play, I had to judge their capacities, aptitudes—in essence, whatever had brought them there. What brought them there was the urge to do something they had possibly wanted to do all their lives. I recognized their essential creativity and never doubted my ability to open that "horrible, horrible cage, that utterly horrible cage," as Vincent van Gogh once described it, that imprisoned the creative urge.

This urge, this aptitude, is essentially what a person is born with—the mental, nervous, and muscular abilities that fit someone for a given activity, such as acting. This inheritance can grow by being developed, or deteriorate by being neglected or mistrained. To this degree it is subject to teaching and experience, but its quality and degree vary from person to person. It is a native attribute of the individual and cannot be taught into existence. It can only be built upon.

The other element of the actor's ability or urge can be taught and can be developed by use and experience—technique. I think it is clear that you cannot make a good or gifted actor out of everybody. While the native aptitudes of many individuals are much higher than most people, including themselves, suspect, and certainly high enough to make an actor of sorts out of almost anyone of "normal" faculties, the level of proficiency will still differ greatly from person to person.

There are thus two factors that combine to make an actor (or any other artist, for that matter): native aptitude and the degree to which it has been developed, and the technique available by virtue of study, training, and experience. Vary the degree of either of these elements and you change the result.

There is a third element that belongs in this formula—opportunity. And this, it seems to me, may be the most important element, for without opportunity (access to training and a chance to use skills) neither aptitude nor technique is of much use. Times without number I have had anxious parents ask me if I think one of their offspring has any talent. I have always answered, "I don't know. Only the individual and God know that, and we can't concern ourselves with it. What we can do is provide the opportunity for training, experience, and discipline, and then we will all know." I've always thought that talent, or even genius, is the result of all these elements working together. C. G. Jung once said, "It is not Goethe who creates *Faust*, but *Faust* which creates Goethe."

When I started my work at Lenox Hill, I was dealing with a group of young people who wanted to act in plays. I had rejected the techniques I had learned at Emerson but knew of no other approaches to actor training. I had, however, acquired an excellent background in literature at Emerson, and our classes in interpretation had provided insight into the meanings and intentions of the author. And I had learned, through the scenes and plays I worked on in college, how to develop stage action. So I read the script of whatever play we were working on carefully, including stage directions given by the author. For the rest, I had to depend on intuition, an instinctive sensitivity to the actor's needs—and a great enthusiasm for the task.

I was immediately concerned with the problem of young actors' lack of physical competence. Stiff with fright, their voices were almost a whisper, their arms and legs were independent appendages. A person in that state has no equipment for the gigantic task of being in a play, and in my Lenox Hill days, I had as little equipment to help. Very few books or studies on actor training were available to help me with my problems until Louis Calvert's *Problems of the Actor*, published in 1918, came to hand. Calvert received his training and experience in England and, as he said in his preface, he was merely setting down his experience, after forty years as an actor and director, for whatever help it might be to a young person wanting to make a career in this profession. He notes, too, that the laws of playmaking had been codified by critics such as Aristotle and, in Calvert's day, William Archer—men who had never written, or presumably produced, plays. Textbooks on music, painting, sculpture—in fact, all the arts—had been written by practitioners. Only the fundamentals of the actor's craft seemed missing.

As I wrote this chapter, I tried to remember what was involved in my early struggles to acquire the skills for my task. When I thought of Calvert's book and read it again, I was amazed at the marginal notes I had made so many years ago. I had taken the first steps to the right approach. Calvert's book did not give specific directions but outlined the essentials that I, working in the dark, needed to carve out techniques I would find useful. These were humanity, a real interest in people, imagination, enthusiasm, and a sense of humour. Burton and I assessed our qualifications, which encouraged us to believe that our aptitudes and background had given us some preparation for the job. We proceeded, through success and failure, to discover our own techniques—our own "Method."

Today, there are hundreds of "how to" books, many of which had been resting on dusty library shelves, now resurrected, translated, collected, edited, and published, that meet the need Louis Calvert tried to deal with when he wrote *Problems of the Actor.* In 1936, the first issue of *Theatre Workshop*, a quarterly magazine that dealt with all phases of theatrical activity, from actor training and directing to scene and lighting design, was published. The first article in the first issue gave me my first definite answers, the one, two, three steps that Stanislavski in *My Life In Art* calls "the solfeggio for the development of creative feeling and experience required by the actor." The article was by Josef Rapoport, a director in the Vakhtangov Theatre in Moscow, a post-revolutionary theatre created by Yevgeny Vakhtangov, who had studied with Stanislavski and had worked in the Moscow Art Theatre.

Rapoport confines the first exercises to the five senses—sight, touch, smell, hearing, and taste. For the first, sight, I used an antique silver Chinese bracelet that I had had for years and which is on my wrist as I write this. The bracelet consists of seven frames and in each of which is a Chinese flower or leaves. I asked each student in turn to look at the bracelet. To begin with, no one actually looked at it; instead, they acted out "looking." Without exception, they tried it on, waved it about, and really saw nothing. I called a student back and said, "Identify the plant in that particular frame of the bracelet." At once, he concentrated on the one frame, all tension gone in the process of accomplishing the task. What Rapoport called his "organ of attention" was focused on the object. He was not trying to do something about the task—he was doing it.

At the conclusion of the exercise, the whole class gathered around the bracelet, talking about it, asking questions, moving freely without tension or pretence, all attention focused on the simple object—in short, with all the freedom they lacked while doing the exercise. This experience was repeated again and again through the years, with different groups, different ages, different degrees of aptitude.

The smell and taste exercises provided interesting experiences too. I used saucers of brown liquids—black coffee, soy sauce, Worcestershire sauce, vanilla. All looked the same, but all had different smells and tastes. For hearing, we listened to our own breathing, then all the sounds in the room, then outside the room, then every sound that could be heard anywhere—birds, planes, dogs barking, and so on. For touch, I gave them a piece of material while their eyes were closed and asked them to determine what the material was—its texture, length, shape, quality. I developed an interesting exercise around a nail file in a leather case, with the students asked to discover all the 'feels' in that object. A student once said to me, referring to the many kinds of exercises we did, "This is [illegible]ing?" I replied, "Not quite. But it's the beginning, and everything you are doing is a stage task."

When an actor acquires this simple "solfeggio," numberless problems in an acting task are avoided, chief among these being the actor's tendency to generalize instead of concentrating on the particular elements in a scene. I was once sitting near enough to watch the eyes and face of a young actor playing the part of Dunois' page in Bernard Shaw's *Saint Joan* during the important scene in the play when the wind, which Dunois has been praying for, changes. The young actor's immediate stage task was to look for birds. As Dunois looks, the trees move in another direction. He sees it, he feels it—the wind has changed. What was the actor doing? Waiting for his cue—nothing more. He blurred the whole climax of that scene. Imagine what it would have been if he had completely realized his action. Excitement, tempo, mood, action would have followed. Without him, the climax could come only from Shaw's lines, and the text in any play is never more than an element of the performance.

Once, on a tour of Thornton Wilder's *Our Town*, a local fireman had to sit on the stage near what was to be imagined as the kitchen door of the Gibbs' house, which of course in *Our Town* isn't really there. Every time the actress playing the part of Mrs. Gibbs opened that imaginary door, the fireman moved his legs, as if he thought they might be in the road of the door, so complete was the actress's action. The fireman's reaction was a source of amused satisfaction to us.

When I first started teaching in the Playhouse classes, the students and I found improvisations unsatisfactory, for I gave the students themes to develop into scenes. They started with dialogue and had soon talked themselves out of both steam and believability. It was not until I started with activities that they were able to develop meaningful action. Dialogue then followed. I changed my approach and, in the beginning, I gave a student three unrelated activities, such as counting money, taking off a shoe, using a Kleenex. The student had to build a stage action from these activities. Then I paired students, each with three different activities. They had a few minutes to decide who they were, what their relationship was, and where they were. From this they developed a "stage attitude." In these improvisations, they had to find justification for each activity separately, then link them in one general justification. They found these justifications through their imagination or what Rapoport called "creative fantasy." Creative fantasy is an endowment that can be developed, enriched, by reading all kinds of material—novels, biographies, the sciences—and by observation of the world. All artists must have a rich imagination, actors especially, for they are entirely surrounded by fictions, make-believe, which they must endow with believability. Every movement, even a glance, a pause, must have a justification derived from a true-life situation, projected by memory, enriched by imagination.

Sarah Bernhardt said, "An actor must be—if not a scholar or a learned man—at least what used to be called an 'all-round man'; that is, he should not be inferior in the manner of acquired knowledge to the average of mankind." This acquired knowledge enables an actor to project himself, through his imagination, into the consciousness of another human being and the situation in which he finds himself. Rapoport's article showed me the way to deal with projects that had been troubling me for nearly twenty years and provided invaluable help in dealing with the problems that arise in directing a play. Best of all, he provided a vocabulary, which the acting profession, unlike the other arts, had lacked. I was able to relieve the tensions of young actors with these simple exercises, which gave them a feeling of accomplishment and me a way to approach problems that needed an immediate solution.

I once had a memorable experience with a young actor so overcome with tension that it could have ruined his career as an actor and even affected his life. He had been demobilized from the armed services after spending some months in a Japanese prison camp and had returned to the University of Washington, intending to get a degree in Drama, and been cast in a play there. For no apparent reason, he began falling on stage, then off stage, over anything or nothing. A member of our company happened to meet him the day the university director had relieved him of his part in the play and the head of the Drama Department had advised him to drop Drama and get his degree in Speech or English.

When I met him, he told me that he had seen a doctor who found nothing physically wrong but thought that the tensions of his adjustment to civilian life, with the added tension of the work he was doing, were too much for him. The doctor, too, advised him to drop Drama. This was the spring quarter at the university and I was casting for an old-fashioned melodrama, which had a character who was a drunk. I suggested to the young actor that he drop Drama for that quarter, and, if it interested him, take the role of the drunk in our play.

My first direction to him was, "When you first step on that stage, fall. Fall all over the place. Fit it into the character. You have been trying not to fall—now do it at will." Other members of the cast knew his situation and heard my direction; he had sympathetic confrères and a concerned director. He told me that when he fell he forgot his lines. Being the kind of play it was, and the kind of character he was playing, it made little difference. As he worked on the part, he developed some beautiful action using the falls, and he didn't forget his lines. The day I saw him riding a bicycle through heavy traffic on University Way, after he had once told me he was afraid of crossing a street for fear he would fall, I blessed Rapoport and thought, "Ah, Theatre!"

All our actors participated in our workshops, for they agreed with the general approach in our theatre—as Henry Adams said once, "The man who knows enough knows how to learn more." Working with other directors and teachers, I learned to use music to establish situations: you are walking barefoot on hot cement, soft grass, a sandy beach, deep mud, in a blizzard, across a flimsy bridge over a deep chasm. These exercises were especially helpful in handling a large group, for each student could find his own experience unobserved by others. When I had problems in directing plays, I devised improvisations in the workshops to solve them. We frequently improvised scenes that the author of the play had not included in the script, but which had to have taken place.

Throughout my life as a teacher and director, I looked for any contact or experience that would increase my abilities to do this work. In

1951, I came across an article by Mao Tse Tung in the British magazine *Labour Monthly*. In the article, called "Concerning Practice: The Connection Between Cognition and Practice," Mao noted that some knowledge is known only empirically, that is, through study, experiment, and experience, and discussed the scientific whys and wherefores of this process. I found his discussion enlightening, for it clarified some pertinent problems and illuminated the heart of the learning process. How does this learning process function and how is it applicable to the actor's learning processes? "The first step in the process of cognition is contact with the external environment, the stage of sensations, that is, sense perceptions." (I like the word "cognition," used interchangeably with the word "knowledge," for it seems to have an extension that "knowledge" lacks.) "The second step is the summing-up of the materials of sense perceptions, setting in order—and rearrangement—the stage of concepts, judgments, and inferences, the development of theories, the application of rational knowledge. The important third step is practice, without which no theory, no matter how good it may be, can have significance."

When actor and teacher accept the conditions of their work, eliminate superficial, mystical thinking, and call on history, science, philosophy, and literature to aid them in their efforts, realizing that the stage of sensations with which they begin their work is undoubtedly a reflection of the reality of the existing world—that sensations can be understood and evaluated, and serve as a basis for rational knowledge, and that theories of work can be developed and tested in practice—they can then evolve an approach to the learning process of the actor. If they reject this, they can only repeat their mistakes, and in their frustration, question not the learning process but their own capabilities, their talent—"If I had what it takes, I'd be able to make it."

If student actors realize that they are learning to do a job governed by certain laws that can be investigated and used, and that accurate results can be achieved, confidence returns and with it that special condition, the "creative mood," without which no creativity is possible. And having found it once, students can learn how to find it again and again.

I once read a statement by Peter Brook, the eminent English director, to the effect that he hated theories. "They freeze things. They sit on you like an unnecessary false nose." But it seems to me that Brook had a theory, the theory that he hated theories. How else can one start but with a theory? And how can one understand it, practice it? For that, one needs to be free and critical. Theories need not grow into dogmas. John Howard Lawson reminds us that "In saying that inspiration can be understood, we must not jump to the conclusion that it can be catalogued," and that the practical approach to the theatre must not be confused with an easy approach. *Ad astra per aspera* Carl Sandburg translated as "to the stars by hard ways." The way of the student actor is not easy, but that is as it should be.

Most acting one sees today on the American stage, and I am sorry to say also on the Canadian, deserves little more than a casual glance. Good acting demands and gets a penetrating look. Young actors graduate from a drama school or university acting course, join Equity, consider themselves professional actors, and seem more immediately concerned with pay rates and working conditions than with the development of their craft and art. They seem not to realize that they have only knocked on the door and that an arduous, painstaking journey through that door lies ahead of them, a long way ahead, toward a time when they can be considered a good and possibly a great actor.

CHAPTER THIRTEEN

Directing seems to require a Superman (or perhaps a Wonder Woman!). The most exacting demands are in terms of natural ability. The director must be energetic, enthusiastic, inspiring, authoritative yet not didactic or autocratic; impartial, fair, honest, stable, reliable, and firm. On the other hand, he or she must be gentle, human, tactful, and diplomatic in the extreme. The director must be discreet, dignified, and cautious but not superior or haughty; patient, tolerant, understanding, broadminded, open to suggestion, wise, progressive, and intuitive. Few positions require such contrasting qualities. A director must be idealistic, yet practical. A director must have business sense and training.

This creature has emerged as a defined entity only in the last half-century. In the past, there must have been someone in the player group who put the thing together, someone who moved the actors about the stage, "kept them from bumping into each other," made decisions about scenery, costumes, lights, etc. Perhaps a stage manager who said to a new young actor, "Just go on, young man, and Mr. Booth will find you." All the young man really needed to know was to keep out of centre stage, where Mr. Booth would be. Leading actors often did not rehearse with the cast and sometimes did not see them until opening night.

Shakespeare knew something of the business of directing actors, and his speech to the players in *Hamlet* is perfectly valid as directorial advice today, except the line "Speak the speech as I pronounce it to you." Today of course we believe that no director should speak a speech for an actor—the actor must determine that for himself. But in Shakespeare's day not all actors could read, so they had their parts read to them and memorized as they went along.

In 1865, Squire Bancroft and his wife, Ellie, directed the Prince of Wales Theatre in London, and Samuel Butler directed the theatre at Sadler's Wells. At the turn of the century, Sir Henry Irving held the difficult position of actor-manager at the Lyceum in London, as did Edwin Booth in his theatre in New York. Sir Laurence Olivier tried to do the same much later without success at the St. James in London. A London reviewer noted that scenes Olivier directed and did not appear in achieved the distinction that scenes in which he was playing lacked. I can understand this, for in my infrequent acting experiences at the Playhouse, I found it difficult to drop the mantle of the director. My husband would remind me, "Stop directing, you're acting." Trying to be creative as an actor and critical as a director at the same time is just too conflicting a job.

I remember well when and why I became a director. There were always more women than men in any theatre group I was associated with. Someone had to take charge, and I was available, not being needed on stage. *How* I became a director, I don't quite know. Jean Gascon, a Canadian actor and excellent director, described this learning process as "a kind of osmosis." At Emerson, we were directed by our teachers in plays that somehow got produced, how I can't remember. The greatest emphasis was on interpretation. In our senior and postgraduate years, we were required to produce scenes from plays. We never received any instruction in how to go about this but managed to get them lighted, costumed, and on the boards. Perhaps we imitated our teachers.

I think the reluctance to teach theatre skills must have been the result of the Puritanical attitude toward theatre so prevalent then; Emerson was careful to avoid being identified as a training school for theatre. The Boston Theatre had once circumvented the Puritan-propagated suspicion of the stage's moral propriety by calling itself a "Museum and Gallery of Fine Arts." One floor was stocked with monstrosities, mummies, and some pictures, and performances given in the "spacious music hall" above were called "moral dissertations." *Othello,* for instance, conveniently became an "uplifting colloquy on the evils of jealousy."

It was at Emerson that I first found myself in the position of a director, though in all probability the term hadn't even been coined then. Robert Frost's collection of poems *North of Boston* had just been published and included a poem called "The Death of the Hired Man." Perhaps Frost was thinking about writing plays and wanted to see how this dramatic poem would work when staged. At any rate, he approached the school for a group of young actors to play in it. I don't remember whether I was assigned to it, or, always keen for adventure, volunteered. But I remember very well the excitement of working with young Mr. Frost, who ran up and down the aisle of our auditorium, helping us make his poem into a play.

When we came to cast it, all our available male students seemed too young for the part of the husband. One day, Thomas Watson appeared—perhaps Frost persuaded him to come. This was the same Thomas Watson who had worked with Alexander Graham Bell in the creation of the telephone, the first person to hear and answer the thing when Mr. Bell, calling from another room, said "Come here, Watson. I want you." Mr. Watson was a very nice elderly gentleman, infinitely patient with my fumbling efforts to direct him. The production pleased all of us, but doesn't seem to have stimulated Robert Frost to become a playwright, although the dialogue in his poems talks.

Burton's interest in scene design and lighting, subjects never touched on at the school, improved our productions of scenes or plays when, as a student, he took on the limited facilities at the old Hemingway Hall in Boston. When Burton and I got to New York, the drama group at the Lenox Hill Neighborhood Association provided the opportunity Sir Tyrone Guthrie recommended for a young person wanting to become a director. He said, "The only way to learn how to direct is to ... get a group of actors simple enough to allow you to direct them, and direct." This is an excellent suggestion for how to get started, but the learning process involves a great deal more—time, for instance, and the urgency to learn and never stop learning, and a realization that you never, *never* know enough.

When the opportunity to direct presented itself, I had some knowledge of plays acquired at Emerson and a way with people. I was energetic and enthusiastic, and able to create excitement around a project. And I seemed to the actors to know what I was doing. But who and what is a director? I had an empirical approach to the problems of directing, and I knew it—what worked was right. But what to do when something did not work! I recognized my limitations and constantly worked and studied to find more definitive answers to my problems. I read and reread a number of books, some of them quite simple and titled *Fundamentals of Play Directing, How to Produce a Play, The Art of Directing Plays,* and so on, written by people of experience and reputation in theatre. I found the books confusing, to say the least. There were chapters on mood, tempo, timing, blocking, pause, picturization, and much more. These books emphasized the need for what seemed to me to be the various elements of the well-produced play and then provided arbitrary, mechanical devices for achieving them.

I was in the favourable position of being able to apply and practice as I studied, for from Cornish School days on I was constantly involved in directing a play or plays; later, at the Playhouse and the university, two and sometimes three at the same time, vastly different in scope and content, each demanding a different approach. It seemed to me that even if all the devices suggested in the books could be understood and applied, a director would still be far from his objective—a well-produced play.

The confusion of opinions merely emphasized the comparative newness of our struggles to better understand our medium and to try to formulate laws governing the process. Our attempts were so new that we had difficulty understanding each other, for there was no precise, generally acceptable terminology. In my early experiences as a director, I studied the play and lectured to the cast on the author's biography and intention in writing the play, the meaning of the play, and so on. Later, at the Playhouse, I demanded that the actors do this research and bring their insights and opinions, based on knowledge derived from their study, to our reading rehearsals and play analyses. This enlarged our thinking and stimulated our imaginations, and we were able to come to conclusions that were understood and agreed with by everyone involved. Before this, I had done a great deal of demonstration to stir the actors' imaginations, suggesting appropriate action. I later found this approach a waste of time. A director who demonstrates badly does little or nothing to stimulate the actor, and a director who demonstrates well frustrates the actor. In either case, the director is showing a result and demanding it of the actor. I once saw a two-hundred-pound man galumphing about the stage to show a fourteen-year-old girl how to come in "like a summer breeze." Sometimes a good sense of mimicry on the part of the actor produces an immediate result, but it is no base for growth and will harden into a cliché or be discarded as of no further use.

I am writing here of our philosophy, theories, and practices as we developed them over a period of years in a situation particularly favourable for this kind of work. When we had our own theatre, and a group of people working in it who were dedicated to development and growth, we had opportunities to experiment with theories and test results. These people, members of the staff and others who looked on the theatre as an avocation, spent long hours in discussion and classes.

In 1935, *Theory and Technique of Playwriting* by John Howard Lawson was published. It begins:

> Technique is often used in a narrow sense, as meaning simply the ways and means of getting various effects, the illusions by which the artist intrigues his public. I use the term as meaning the whole relationship between the artist and his material, the sources from which the material is drawn, the process by which it is organized, the standards by which the finished product is judged. An inquiry along these lines must be both specific and general; it must include a comprehensive answer to the troublesome questions which relate to the meaning and function of art. Is it possible to approach these questions from their technical side, from the point of view of the working craftsman? Can such an investigation yield accurate, provable results?

Lawson begins with the idea that there are accurate, provable results in the field of play-writing. We were searching for the same kind of thinking as a guide to the very practical problems of acting and producing in a theatre. Our thinking led us to some very definite conclusions: acting and directing can be learned, given aptitude for this kind of work. There are unknowns, but no unknowables. We believed that the process of learning to act was a knowable, get-at-able process, that failures and successes encountered in the process could be judged and evaluated every step of the way. Acting is an art, an art derived from life and the effort to transform life on this earth. It is done in a very real place called a theatre, for real people called an audience.

Where and what is the director in this process? Alexander Dean says the director is an interpretative artist, while the playwright and the actor are creative artists. I disagree. I believe that the result of the creative efforts of all three interprets the author's intention and the play's meaning for the audience, who in turn participate in creatively interpreting for themselves the significant meanings of the play. Any work of art shapes, forms, and develops feelings; influences thinking and beliefs, and actively assists in the process of transforming life, making it possible, following Hamlet, to "throw away the worser part of it, and live the purer with the other half."

To say that it makes no difference whether the feelings engendered or thoughts stimulated by a work of art benefit or improve humankind is to say that a work of art is a thing apart from life. We work in art, and art in us, for the betterment or detriment of each. Hitler's dictum of what was good art for Germany became bad for both Germany and art. He was able to destroy in a relatively short time the great creativity of a nation that had produced Goethe, Beethoven, Mendelssohn, and Schiller, and in his own day Reinhardt and Brecht.

The director's creativity is no less than that of the playwright or actor. As the director reads the play, he or she hears the lines spoken, sees the colour of the costumes, the movements and attitudes of the characters, and the general feeling and mood of the whole thing. She feels the heat of Verona's summer: "The day is hot, the Capulets abroad, and if we meet we shall not escape a brawl"; or the gloomy foreboding of the lines in the opening scene of *Hamlet*, "Tis bitter cold, and I am sick at heart." The director must be a person of imagination. Alexander Birrell once said of such a one that he can "hear the tinkle of Rebecca's camels or the laugh of Eve."

The director's concept of the play stimulates the imagination of the scene designers, costume designers, makeup people, electricians, and even more, the actors. Every detail of a production is in the director's hands. A very practical attitude toward budgets is required, as well as a complete knowledge of how to get what is needed and, if that cannot be obtained, how to achieve the desired end with what is available. I have never found that working on a budget, no matter how limited, really deterred me from my objective.

At a time when some of the most pressing bills had to be paid, we put ourselves on a cash basis for productions at the Playhouse. My costume designer would say, "Okay, Mrs. James. Before I spend a cent, I'll look in the 'rag bag'," meaning the costume closet. Nothing was ever thrown away until we got all the good of it. We frequently had contributions of things from people cleaning their garrets and basements, some of them lovely things. We often wondered why they would want to dispose of them.

Once, when we were producing Albert Bein's *Heavenly Express*, the scene designer was dressing the set and called me in to look at it. I said, "It's good, all but the curtains. They're too clean."

The set was the interior of a boarding house near a railroad, catering to trainmen and tramps. In the day of the coal-fired engine, curtains in such a location would never be clean and fresh. I said, "Get that carton of old curtains out of the prop storeroom." Somebody had donated a box of worn, ragged drapes, and it had been duly put away until it would be required.

The scene designer objected to my choice. "But those are faded and filthy." "Let's hang them and see." We did. The curtains were faded and filthy, but right—not only right, but beautiful, with the light shining through them.

I was fortunate at the Playhouse in having stage carpenters who were excellent craftsmen, even when they had to "make over" and "make do"—Hugo Alde, who constructed the sets for *Peer Gynt*, *Faust*, and *Romeo and Juliet*, in fact all of our shows of the thirties; then Al Johnson, who later was responsible for the sets for *Carousel*, *Kiss Me, Kate,* and other Broadway shows; later, Frederic Youens, who went to work with the stage design and construction department at Carnegie Tech, and Ernest Watson. They were newcomers to this work and they designed and constructed imaginative sets for Arthur Laurent's *Home of the Brave*, Harry Brown's *A Sound of Hunting*, and Aurand Harris's *Once Upon a Clothesline* and *Circus Day* for the Children's Theatre, to mention only a few. In an established theatre such as ours, where it was possible to accumulate and store valuable props and scenery, it was not too difficult to work on limited means.

It was our practice, after the play was cast and in first rehearsals, to have what we called reading rehearsals for ten days to two weeks, depending on the kind of play it was. Scene designers, costume designers, and actors participated, and it was in these rehearsals that the designers, before they put pencil to paper, became completely aware of the dimensions of their problems. Ernest Watson, who designed the set for *Home of the Brave*, realized in the reading rehearsals that he had the problem of two short scene changes for the doctor's and the major's offices. He designed a flat with a door in it that looked like the rear of a Quonset hut, one side painted green for the major's office and the other white for the doctor's office. With the lights dimmed down on the permanent set, which suggested the jungle locale of the Second World War's South Pacific island-hopping, this flat could be flown very quickly.

In the commercial theatre, where the director and actors are hastily assembled, time for rehearsals is limited—four to six weeks at most—so long reading rehearsals such as we enjoyed would not be possible. For one thing, prohibitive costs for actors' salaries would prevent it. But we had a closely unified group of people who had worked together for months or years, and we found these rehearsals saved time and increased cohesion. No one felt incidental to the effort, or that being cast in a small part meant that they were unimportant.

In our reading rehearsals, we did an analysis of the play, which we called the "break down." Everyone involved in the reading rehearsals understood that they were subjective and Lawson's book was of inestimable value in helping us to understand and place subjective and objective work in their proper relationship. What do I mean by "subjective and objective work"? Subjective work involves the study of the play as a whole and, if it is a classic of the magnitude of Goethe's *Faust* or Ibsen's *Peer Gynt*, a study of the author himself, his period, his life. For these two plays, the director and the main actors spent months preparing. We also had to prepare the playing script, and this cannot be done haphazardly. An analysis of a play greatly facilitated this work, and we were able to get what you might call a blueprint—the author's intention in writing the play, its theme, the author's success or failure in developing his theme, the selection and use made of character and situation.

I remember very well Irwin Shaw's horrified exclamation over an analysis we made of his play *Gentle People*. His comment was, "How can you act a play when you tear it to pieces? Doesn't this kind of work destroy your inspiration?"

We didn't believe it did. We were bringing our thinking to bear on the problems, so that inspiration could flow more freely and from a sound base. I don't think it is dangerous to a production for a director to understand the social framework of the play, the thinking of the author that suggested the theme, and the author's treatment of the theme in all its strengths and weaknesses. I have directed plays for which the author had written no climax, made the climax an offstage noise, or even written an altogether different climax than his theme, character, and situation demanded, perhaps because he (or, horrible to contemplate, the play doctor) thought it more dramatic. Lawson says, "The climax is the highest point of tension, in terms of action." Sometimes the title indicates the climax, as in Arthur Miller's *All My Sons*, when the father says, "They were all my sons," just before he leaves to commit suicide.

Recognizing these problems early in the rehearsal is a help, rather than a problem. After all, inspiration is no gossamer thing that will vanish if scrutinized. Inspiration is the result of a number of things, not excluding a lot of hard work. "Conscious method is not an enemy of inspiration," as Lawson so admirably points out, "and does not originate in one man's illumination"—particularly not in the theatre, dependent as it is on the effort of playwright, players, technicians, and audience working together creatively for a given result. Inspiration is the synthesis of these many elements and is achieved as a result of complete analysis, which clears the way.

During this period of rehearsal, actors were able to visualize their characters, feel them, hear them, see them, and find justification for their activities and attitudes. I think of this as a period of germination, or gestation if you prefer. We remembered Anton Chekhov's dictum, "Read my play. It's all in the play." We were particularly careful to read and understand the author's stage directions and whatever descriptions were given of characters and the situation in which they were put. In a well-written play, the descriptions and directions are vastly important to the meaning and development of the play. I dare anyone to overlook or ignore one of Chekhov's directions.

I remember the difficulty one actress, playing the mother in *All My Sons,* had with Miller's stage direction "she presses her hand to the top of her head." The direction is given not once, but many times. Performing the action simply because the author said to do it made no sense, and at first the actress couldn't fathom it. When she was able to organically realize the significance of the activity of pressing her hand to the top of her head, she had penetrated the emotional and psychological state of the mother and achieved a physiological adjustment to this action. I emphasize the words "organically realize": in order to organically realize, she had to know all the facts in the life of this character and sense imaginatively and emotionally the meaning of that gesture on this particular day in her life.

What facts do we know about the mother in Miller's play? She knows that her husband is guilty of selling defective aeroplane motors to the military. She is burdened with the knowledge of her husband's guilt and another person's punishment for it. She rationalizes her desire not to know, not to believe, by believing that her son Larry, who has been reported missing on a bombing mission, is not dead. If Larry is not dead, then none of the twenty-one pilots killed in the defective planes are dead. If they are not dead, then her husband could not have been guilty, and it is all a mistake. Throughout the play, she struggles to make her rationalization stick, but nature is not so accommodating and there is a physical toll—she has persistent recurrent headaches. Even when she is free of them, she worries that they will return, so she constantly nurses her head.

As a result of discussion and analysis, the actress playing the character of the mother understood the significance of Miller's stage direction. When she was able to objectify this direction in terms of action, she conveyed this meaning to the audience. This combination is what I understand to be subjective and objective work in the theatre. Actors fail when the subjective work is neglected or overlooked, or when their skills are insufficient or their abilities to objectify or translate in terms of action are undeveloped. Too often the director or actor concentrate on externals, what we called in our theatre "playing results." No amount of direction, such as "Take the speech faster," or "You haven't got the mood," will produce right results. I don't direct "results"—this scene is joyful, that scene is gloomy. These results must be achieved in direction. A mood is a result.

I recently watched a young director directing Harold Pinter's *The Homecoming*. There is a point where one actor is speaking to two other characters in a scene and realizes that he is not communicating at all, for there is no answer, no response. After each sentence, he pauses for an answer. That is Pinter's stage direction, and Pinter's pauses are not holes in the script. They require meaningful action. The young director, working with his character, was shouting, "Pause. Now a little louder. Pause again." I consider this approach abortive. A better way would be to help the actor to understand that the character expects an answer, waits for one, but none comes. In his effort to communicate, he would inevitably speak louder, in a greater effort to get some response. I think that a more organic result would ensue. The actor would be speaking from his frustrating effort to communicate and not from a director's direction.

At the Playhouse, we saw firsthand how an actor's incorrect approach to a speech not only put a scene off but affected the last two acts of a play. We were producing William Saroyan's *The Time of Your Life*, which is written in five acts. We broke for a long intermission at the end of the third act, and the play resumed with the policeman making a longish speech to Nick the bartender. The opening of the fourth act just wasn't working. It killed the last two acts. After watching the performances for several evenings, I questioned the actor playing the policeman. He was very sympathetic to the character he portrayed, was impressed with the speech, and loved the scene.

So, we went back to the analysis. What were the events of this particular day? Why had he come into the bar? Where had he come from? We established that the policeman is on duty on the waterfront because his friend the longshoreman is on strike. His relief arrives, so he comes to Nick's bar for a glass of beer. He knows Nick, likes and trusts him. On this particular day, the head of the vice squad has decided to get a little publicity for the coming election by persecuting prostitutes. The policeman hates this man and the vice squad. As he enters Nick's bar, he meets two prostitutes who are impudent to him simply because he is a policeman and they identify him with all their persecutors. At this point, the policeman, with the glass of beer he can't enjoy, "blows his top" to Nick. He came to the bar not to make speeches but to find relaxation in a glass of beer. Simple as that is, it is spoiled for him, and his speech, an angry protest, results. Once he understood all this, the actor playing the policeman realized that he had been simply delivering a speech and changed his interpretation. The scene, and consequently the play, changed. Tempo, always a result, increased. Movement developed, meaning was revealed, the extension necessary to the dynamic development of the play toward its climax and conclusion were achieved.

A graphic example of a director's failure to define his objective, which led to his failure in directing an actor in his task, was once given me by a prominent Hollywood director at Warner Brothers. I was watching, with considerable interest, the shooting of a scene for a movie, the name of which I probably never did know. Shortly after shooting started, word came from the front office that Mr. Warner had seen the rushes of a scene shot the previous day and didn't like it. The director immediately dropped the scene he was working on. Props, lights, cameras, sound trucks were rearranged for retakes on the previous day's scene. While all this was going on, no one bothered to ask (nor was the information volunteered) just *what* Mr. Warner didn't like about the first version. It was enough that he didn't like it.

When the actor got into place, the director said, "Now, Mr. Gardiner, make this good." I cannot imagine a direction less likely to get "something good" out of an actor. Good for what? In this case, it was to be good for the front office.

The scene they were shooting was a simple one. The character, a bush pilot, sits near his plane in a wilderness, drinking a cup of tea and reminiscing about his home in England. It could have been the easiest, most relaxed thing in the world, but for two straight hours there were "cuts" and "takes" and "retakes," with the director urging the actor to look up, look down, look away, say it softly, say it louder, and there was a good deal said about mood. In the end, I never saw two more angry, frustrated men. The actor, whose only task was to drink a cup of tea and reminisce nostalgically about his English home, was intent on murder, if I read his flashing eye and flushed face correctly. The director, with thoughts of pleasing the front office, was in the same frame of mind. I never did hear if Mr. Warner liked the results of that afternoon's work. He may have, for all I know. But if the camera recorded what I saw, it was an afternoon of wasted effort.

What was wrong with this director's approach was that without knowing what was really wrong with the scene, let alone knowing why the producer didn't like it, he could never go about getting it "right." The producer might not be able to tell the actor what was "wrong"—it could happen. His direction, "Make it good," directed the actor's attention toward what would have been the result if the actor had taken the necessary simple steps.

First, the activity of drinking the cup of tea. It is clear that the cup of tea stimulates the character's memories of teatime in England, evokes emotional responses, and it is out of these emotional responses that he speaks. The actor's immediate concentration should have been on the tea: its smell, its taste, the memories it conjures up. Then, when that activity was completely realized, he could speak from it.

It is important, rewarding, and simplifies larger problems of directors and actors to use the actual props and complete activities suggested by the play early in the rehearsals. As a matter of fact, it is an interesting, revealing task for the actor to list, scene by scene, the stage directions and descriptions given by the author for his character. (I am referring here to the *author's* directions, not those in the "playing version," which is generally published with the directions of some later director or directors.) Doing this, certain patterns of behaviour emerge, which give clues to the character's activities that result in a "stage attitude."

When a character is developed around given activities, as for example Eddie mixing drinks in Garson Kanin's *Born Yesterday*, I had fairly exact replicas of the glasses and bottles that he would be using, complete with liquid (non-alcoholic, of course) contents. These were provided early in the rehearsals. His adjustments, concentrated as they are on small menial tasks—running errands, answering the phone, but particularly mixing and serving drinks almost continuously—establish his character and his relationship to the other characters early in the play. His character is established through the performance of these tasks. The actor then has no major adjustments to make in switching to somewhat more elaborate bottles, glasses, and bar appointments in the actual production, because he is accustomed to using approximately the same thing in rehearsals.

Earlier in my directing experience, I permitted actors to pantomime such activities in the earlier rehearsals, often with painful results at dress rehearsals. An actor who has the task of mixing drinks, filling glasses from full bottles, putting in ice, finds the actual job quite a bit different from merely waving his hands in the general direction of his tasks. It takes more time, for one thing, and the handling of heavier, bulkier, *realer* objects where thin air has always been destroys the believability of the situation. Instead of a character doing a job he has done for years, it becomes an actor fumbling at a bit of stage business.

I never really understood why a well-rehearsed play could go to pieces at dress rehearsal until I read the story of Dr. Pavlov and his dogs, and his findings on the conditioned reflex. I then realized that preparatory rehearsals were a kind of conditioning, and I had been changing the equations at dress rehearsals. I found it helpful to the actors to provide proper conditioning to stage tasks, with props, costumes, trains, hoop skirts, swords, canes, and so on, as early as possible in the stage rehearsals, so that there would be as few adjustments as possible needed in the dress rehearsals.

When Toby Leitch was playing the boss in *Stevedore* in the Federal Theatre, during rehearsals he would go about the stage muttering to himself, "Business with eye glasses. Business with letter." I finally asked him what he was doing, and he said, "Trying to remember my business." I said, "Well instead of saying 'business with,' why don't you just put on your eye glasses and read the letter?" He did it, and then said, "Now why didn't I think of that before?" He was amazed that it worked and was better and easier. It also helped him to remember his lines, which he had trouble doing. He had found that suiting "the action to the word, the word to the action" was as good as Hamlet said it would be when he directed the Players.

In the last act of *The Diary of Anne Frank*, Mr. Frank, the only person in the group to survive the death camps, returns to the garret where he and his family and friends had lived for so many bitter months. When I directed this scene, all I could get from the actor playing Mr. Frank was an entrance from backstage. He brought nothing with him.

So, at one rehearsal, I put all the other characters on stage in places where he would remember them to have been. Mr. Frank entered and looked at them, one after another. At a gesture from me, they quietly left the scene. When Mr. Frank saw the diary and Anne's white glove on the floor, picked them up, and began to speak, the scene had the necessary emotional impact. After rehearsal, the actor said to me, "My God, a trick like that made my blood run cold!" A trick, perhaps, but it stimulated his imagination and triggered an emotional response that we both wanted.

Because we were working in our own theatre, the stage rehearsals were on the stage of the theatre where they would be played, and we tried to have the scene set exactly as it would ultimately be in production. When the actor, with script in hand, has a fairly clear idea of what he is doing, why he is doing it, and, most important, knows his relationship to other characters in the play, by the time we begin stage rehearsals, "business blocking," as it is called, becomes a simple matter. When an actor enters the scene with the subjective work already done, the mere action of stepping into the scene begins the step-by-step process of the character's development. This development changes and grows as it is objectified. As this work is not being done only by the actor but is a collective effort involving the cast and the director, transformation of the actor into the character is possible, inevitable, and the play is translated from literature into theatre.

When the synthesis is really complete—play, actor and audience—you have that much-to-be-hoped-for result, an inspired performance. I emphasize the audience, for more times than I can recount, I have come backstage after a performance to express my satisfaction and pleasure at the evening's work, and when I said, "Excellent tonight," the response would always be, "Wonderful audience!" A "Dionysian unity" had been achieved with the audience, that important entity in a living theatre, about which so little is known scientifically.

During the life of the Washington State Theatre, with Dr. Gundlach's help we began to undertake a scientific investigation into this hitherto practically unexplored field. It must have been, as nearly as can be ascertained, the first study of its kind in an English-speaking country. In 1970, the International Theatre Institute with centres in fifty-five countries around the world also did an intensive study of this important phase in the life of all theatres. Norris Houghton, who visited us during the time of the Washington Stage Theatre, recorded his impressions in his book *Advance from Broadway* as follows: "I should like to return to Seattle in another three or four years, for I believe that if the artists in the Repertory Playhouse can keep their number intact, they may have grown into a company with a forceful and incisive theatrical style. At least their studies are heading them in that direction."

Sadly, by the time Mr. Houghton might have returned, the Playhouse had closed. We were not given time enough to make his rosy predictions come true.

CHAPTER FOURTEEN

As the 1930s drew to an end, the dark clouds of the Depression began to lift. People were getting jobs making armaments for the impending conflict we all knew was coming. Austerity in the James family increased, for in 1938 I was fired from my teaching job on campus, after eight years in my position. The Drama Department called my dismissal "reorganization." We believed, however, that the director of the Drama Department, Glenn Hughes, hoped that my dismissal would cripple us financially so that we would have to leave Seattle and seek employment elsewhere. The move, however, backfired. Following my dismissal, Sophie Rosenstein and Wilbur Sparrow, two other teachers in the Drama Department, resigned and the students staged a strike. The students were protesting the loss of their teachers, but they were also protesting the fact that they were required to act in the Studio Theatre on University Way. This was a small building a block away from our theatre, which Hughes had renovated in 1932 when he failed to get the Playhouse.

The students objected that they were being typecast and were required to spend money they could not afford to provide their own costumes, for the plays done were mostly moderns. The slogan devised for the Studio Theatre stressed gaiety in the theatre, and the students' slogan for their strike was "It's Not Gay!" (I hasten to add that the expression had a much different connotation in 1938 than it would have today!) It was a very successful strike, probably the first of its kind on any campus in the United States, for the Board of Regents ordered the Studio Theatre back on the campus.

Mrs. Rosenstein and Mr. Sparrow went to California, where Mrs. Rosenstein became test director for Warner Brothers. She had played Ase, Peer's mother, in our first production of *Peer Gynt*, and the Nurse in *Romeo and Juliet*. Mr. Sparrow was soon in the army, serving in the Pacific, where he was stricken with an Asiatic virus and came back a very sick man.

In 1939, we at the Playhouse met Ernst Gebert, a refugee from Hitler's Germany and, so he said, a former conductor at the Berlin Opera. With him as music director, we opened a new and different phase of work in our theatre with the establishment of a production unit, the Lyric Theatre. In that season we produced Gioacchino Rossini's *Barber of Seville*, with a lovely Japanese girl as Rosina. We also did a modern version of Johann Strauss's *Die Fledermaus*, for which I wrote the libretto. Another modern version of that opera, called *Rosalinde*, was later done in New York—not with my libretto, for I never bothered to copyright it.

The casts for the Lyric Theatre productions came from Cornish School, the Music Department of the university, and music studios in and around Seattle. The singers were delighted with the opportunity to sing opera, Mr. Gebert was a good conductor, the Lyric Theatre was gaining recognition, and we were pleased to have this kind of production at the Playhouse. Ernst Gebert was, however, a difficult, unpredictable, uncooperative person, quite unlike Myron Jacobson, who was a martinet when it came to his work but a pleasure to know and most helpful and understanding when we were involved in problems for a production.

During this period I directed, with Mr. Gebert, Giuseppe Verdi's *La Traviata*, with Jarmila Novotná and Richard Bonelli of the Metropolitan Opera in leading roles. This was performed at the Moore Theatre, because Cecilia Schultz, manager of the Moore, had provided the financing. We were preparing Wolfgang Mozart's *Magic Flute*, for which I was writing an English libretto, when Mr. Gebert decided that Seattle was too small for him, and departed for Hollywood. We never heard from, or of, him again.

We had this experience many times during our life in the theatre. Young actors whose talents had been developed with the discipline and training of the Playhouse decided that Hollywood or Broadway needed them and left to find fame and fortune. What contributed to these youngsters' discontent was the difficulty of earning a proper living in the theatre and the reports of fabulous money being paid elsewhere. Also, no less a factor, was the lack of recognition given performers in Seattle. No actor or actress ever really felt that their work was tremendously important to the community. Sometimes, yes. To some segments of the community, yes. To the rest of us in the company, yes. But the general feeling was perhaps perfectly exemplified by an experience my husband had when, after some performance, a lady came backstage to express her admiration and said, "You are such a wonderful actor, Mr. James. Why don't you go on the stage?"

We were working, keeping the doors open, and looking toward the day when the blight of the Depression would lift and, with a group of talented, trained actors, we would be in a position to provide some security and to pay adequate, if not fabulous, salaries so that they could make a life for themselves in the theatre. (We never paid salaries at the Playhouse until we were able to pay everybody the same amount, minimal though it was.) Some left, some returned, but many stayed. And with our workshops, we were developing new, fresh, vigorous talents. What we never lost was a feeling of solidarity, of loyalty—not to us, but to an idea, without which no organization can really survive. Once a member of our board said, "I wish I could get my staff to work for me the way your people work for you." I replied, "They aren't working for me. They're working for themselves."

At this time, of course, we were certainly aware of the lowering clouds of war, although the United States didn't become actively involved until 1941. A few years previously, we had made friends with a Japanese lady studying at Cornish and invited her for Thanksgiving dinner. At the dinner table that evening, we talked of the Sino-Japanese War. She said, "In Japan, we are very afraid that this war in China will escalate to the whole Pacific. The military are very ambitious. They want all of China, Singapore, Hawaii, the Philippines, and Australia." It sounded laughable, but we were aghast all the same.

"That would mean war with the U.S. and Britain."

"Of course," the lady said. Had we never read the *Tanaka Memorial*? "It's the Japanese *Mein Kampf*." We had not read, or indeed ever heard, of it, but had the State Department ever read it either?

We had built the theatre, survived the Depression, created the Washington State Theatre and the Negro Repertory, survived the loss of those theatres, and also survived, however slenderly, the loss of our paying jobs. With the advent of war, we entered the busiest years of our lives.

One Sunday morning, I had been listening to the New York Philharmonic on the radio. I had to get to the Playhouse for my Sunday workshop, so I snapped it off and hurried to the streetcar. When I alighted, someone from the Playhouse met me with the news. "The Japanese have bombed Pearl Harbor. We are at war." It was December 7, 1941, the "day of infamy."

I was not surprised, remembering the Japanese lady's warning. And hadn't we been anticipating it, consciously, subconsciously, for months and years? We had protested the mountains of scrap iron being loaded for shipment to Japan. Seattle was tearing up its streetcar tracks, New York was tearing down its elevated railroads. Harry Bridges, president of the Longshoremen's Union, had said, "That scrap will come back to us some day in the bodies of American boys." When Dutch Harbor in the Aleutians was bombed, some GIs from the New York area warned, "Duck, you guys. Here comes the Sixth Avenue El!"

The next day, December 8, we were blacking out windows, shielding all exposed lights, and installing special lights and a warning system at the Playhouse in case of bombings. Everyone was convinced that bombings were inevitable, for at that time it looked as though Seattle would be a prime target, with the Todd Dry Dock, Sand Point Naval Base, Bremerton shipyards, and Boeing all easily accessible to bombing raids.

Shortly after war was declared, the number of male members in our acting group was decimated, as men were drafted for the armed services. I frequently cast a play not knowing whether the men in the cast would finish either rehearsals or the run before receiving their "greetings from Uncle Sam."

Once, in dress rehearsal, I had to recast the play. While I was mulling over this problem, a young man came to the box office window and asked to see me. He had just been turned down for the armed services because of a recent motorcycle accident. "They told me maybe they would take me later, but I've got to do something right now. Could I be in your theatre?" I said, "You're in it. Come backstage." I shifted the cast, put him in a small part, and he didn't do too badly. He ultimately developed into a very good actor. It was not the first time, or the last, that I pressed available males into service as actors. I used to say, "Somebody up there looks after fools, drunkards, and people who work in theatres!"

Along with running the theatre, it wasn't too long before we were involved in all kinds of activities for the war effort. Our first concern was for the young people who were leaving us for the far corners of the earth. Anyone over eighteen who could pass the physical was away. We started a newsletter, the "Playhouse Communiqué." It carried stories about what was happening back home, quotes from the reviews of the current show, news about marriages, births, and the addresses of their buddies elsewhere. Frequently we would get a letter from someone saying, "I'm pushing out, but my buddy would like to be on the mailing list. He's been reading my newsletters, and he feels he knows you." When the war was over, some of the boys who demobilized in Seattle came to see us as friends, even if they'd never been there before. They looked on the Playhouse as home.

Every Christmas, we sent parcels to all of them, the items recommended, the weight and size just so. A lieutenant-colonel who had once been on our board said that the only parcel he received from Seattle at Christmas was from the Repertory Playhouse. Sending our Communiqués and preparing the packages for Christmas were two of the highlights for us in this grim period.

Once, the bread of hospitality that we extended to GIs in our area came back to me as cake. During the war I was on the Travelling Fellowship for the National Theatre Conference. I got off the train one rainy night in Austin, Texas, tired and hungry. It was wartime, the trains and hotels were very crowded, and if you missed a room reservation by even a short while, it was given away. My train was very late and I knew that my room must be long gone. As I stood there debating whether to spend the night in the railway station or in a hotel lobby, I heard my name called. A delegation was there to meet me. I was given supper and whisked away to spend a delightful three days as the house-guest of a member of the university staff. When I expressed my gratitude, and some surprise at their overwhelming courtesy to a total stranger, they replied, "Do you think we in Texas are less hospitable than you at the Playhouse in Seattle are to our GIs?"

While I was in Austin, the director of the Fine Arts Department arranged a meeting for me with his students, who were interested in developing something similar to the Washington State Theatre. Because of the depressing memories of our experience with the effects of changing political situations, I recommended, "Ask for a grant for not less than five years—even better, ten. Give yourselves time."

During the war period, we were individually and collectively engaged in intensive activity, even with our depleted personnel. We did forty-nine performances for army camps and various service groups, nineteen special events, eleven Victory Square programs, sixty-eight radio programs, worked on War Chest campaigns, and sent out Communiqués every month to eighty-four men and women in the armed services. All but the radio programs were done on a volunteer basis as our contribution to the war effort.

Doing the shows for the armed forces, the people from the theatre met some of these servicemen. As I never minded people watching rehearsals, it was not unusual to see men, Black and White, in the uniforms of the various services, sitting in the theatre at rehearsal, waiting for the actors to go out for coffee. They were, of course, invited to the cast parties. No person in uniform was ever refused a ticket, and comps for admission were available at the PX's. One evening, going from the front office to back stage, I saw a young sailor looking at the pictures on display in front of the theatre. He stopped me and asked if this was a movie theatre. I said, "No, it's a legitimate theatre—live actors acting a play. Would you like to see it?"

"Yes, ma'am."

I explained that the play started at 8:30. I said I'd take him backstage, and when the house was opened, I'd take him into the theatre. When I went to collect him, some time later, I found him dressed in work clothes, helping to set up the stage. He had seen the girls and Burton setting up and started to give them a hand. Burton said, "This dust isn't good for navy blues. Get the boys in the dressing room to give you some work clothes." From that night on, on his days off, he would come to the theatre and help backstage or in any other spot where help was needed. He was stationed in Bremerton, on the *Yorktown*, which had been damaged by a kamikaze attack.

I began using men from the armed services who were stationed in or around Seattle. Several of them had had experience in theatres similar to ours and were pleased to get out of uniform and work with a theatre again. A couple of them turned out to be very good actors, relieving my casting problems a bit.

We had a memorable experience with a show we did to recruit workers to build the B-27s at Boeing. The show was the responsibility of the military and was done in the university stadium. Bob Hope was master of ceremonies, and General Hap Arnold was the speaker. One of the high points of the show was a dramatized attack by GIs coming in from Lake Washington in assault boats, with a fleet of planes flying overhead. The floor of the stadium had been so thoroughly mined by an over-enthusiastic dynamiter that when the mines went off, they blacked out more than a thousand lights. The mines were blanks, but the smoke was real. For a few minutes things were tense in the crowded stadium, but a light wind cleared the smoke and the show went on. It cost the army $8,000 to put the stadium back in shape—but then, the military always has money.

Everything had to be synchronized by my husband, who was stage-managing the show. A major who was in charge of some military phase of the affair rushed up to Burton. "Mr. James, General Arnold has arrived. What can we do? Shall we bring him in?"

"No, Major. He's fifteen minutes too early. He's got to come in with the band, on the nose for the broadcast. "

"But Mr. James, you can't keep a General waiting." "Just a minute, Major." Burton turned to one of the Playhouse actresses who stage-managed the entrance where the General waited. "Aristelle, go to General Arnold's car, explain the situation to him, and ask him to wait for his cue."

Miss MacDonald went to the General's car, and he was very nice about the whole thing. He said, "Don't worry, young lady. I'll just wait right here, and you tell me when to come in." My husband reported back to the Major. "It's all right, Major. General Arnold says he'll wait."

A nice dramatic moment occurred when Bob Hope said to the audience, more than ten thousand of them, "When the lights in the stadium go out, everybody strike a match." The lights were doused, the huge arena was in total darkness, and when the audience struck the matches, it lighted the entire area. "You see," said the master of ceremonies, "That's what can happen when people do something together."

Recruiting must have been successful, for the B-27s got built, and the "darned big things," as a little girl called the planes, got into the war. Roosevelt was getting the fifty thousand planes he asked for.

Another special event was a show for Civilian Defence, a dramatization of what could happen in a bombing raid, how civilians under attack should act, and how to deal with incendiary bombs. We built a house and burned it down.

With all this work for the war effort, we were still putting on our productions for adults and for our youth audiences. Christmas and Easter matinees were devoted to the children. For our adult audience at this time we did a most successful production of *Lady Precious Stream*, a translation of an old Chinese play by Xiong Shiyi. The play was done for China Relief, with the active interest of the Oriental Society and the Chinese community, who loaned us fabulous costumes for the play. Two Chinese actors, one an actor of male roles and Chin Shu Yin, an actor of female roles, directed the cast in the formalized techniques and manner of acting in the Chinese theatre.

At the same time, we were running *Family Portrait* by Lenore Coffee and William Cowen, a very moving play about the family of Jesus, the brothers and relatives attributed to him in the Gospel of St. Mark. *Family Portrait,* while it was very successful, puzzled a good many of our potential theatregoers. I remember that a number of people who phoned to find out what was playing at the Playhouse wanted to know if it was a comedy, and when informed that it was based on the life of Christ, muttered, "Oh no, I don't think we'd be interested in that" and hung up.

Our Communiqués to the GIs carried this slogan, "Take it easy, but take it," for we believed that, as one of the songs in our first revue said, "laughter is a weapon, too." We had started preparing material for a musical revue early in 1942, with words, skits, and music all prepared by members of the group and one or two interested outsiders. We opened the show with the full cast on stage in work clothes, singing "Let's Get to Work." This revue, *Thumbs Up!,* was so popular that other groups in the country requested permission to produce it. In 1945, as it seemed that the war was coming to an end, we wrote and produced a revue called *Here Comes Tomorrow.* With Dmitri Shostakovich's stirring song "United Nations on the March" ringing in our ears, we dramatized our hopes for a united world, brotherhood, and peace. We felt we had had enough.

But that was not to be. Other forces were at work preparing for the police actions and other undeclared wars that have haunted and tortured the people of the world until we look at each other and wonder if we are as civilized as we think we are.

After the successes of *Thumbs Up!* and *Here Comes Tomorrow,* we decided to do a musical with a book. We cast about for a story and finally settled on the story of Asa Mercer and the Mercer Girls. A Seattle pioneer, Asa Mercer had decided that the Northwest would never be really settled until women came to establish homes and families. Women were getting to California, which apparently seemed an easier trek, even through Death Valley, than going to the Northwest around the Horn or over the mountains. But Mercer believed that women would come to the Northwest if some way could be provided to get them there, and he thought that government ships, standing idle in eastern ports now that the Civil War was over, could be used.

Lumberjacks and trappers in the area were as keen as Mercer was to establish a more stable way of life, and provided the money for a trip to Washington. Mercer finally got his ship and began to recruit interested women, who had to have excellent character references as well as education and certain skills.

He was about to sail triumphantly back to Seattle when James Gordon Bennett, editor of the *New York Herald*, published an article that almost sank the whole venture. Bennett described, "This designing scoundrel, taking these lovely ladies away from families and friends, to 'a fate worse than death,' to a place with the well-nigh unpronounceable name of Se-at-tle." Furious families descended on the ship to snatch their daughters out of the clutches of this monster, but some of the women elected to stay and made the trip.

This true story provided excellent material for our libretto, which was again a joint effort, organized and edited by Al Ottenheimer. In the group were Florence Stewart and Pearl Albino, very good lyricists, and superlative musicians Helen Taverniti and George McKay, who was in the Music Department at the university, to set the words to music. We called the musical *Calico Cargo*, from a statement made by the captain of Mercer's ship, who said it was the first time he had rounded the Horn with calico as cargo and marriage as a market. The show opened our 1945 season and played fifty-three performances in fifteen weeks. It was revived subsequently and had a further production in the summer of 1969 in Bellevue, Washington.

The night we opened *Calico Cargo,* a gentleman and lady in their eighties whose memories went back to the period in which our show was based were at the premiere as our guests, The lady said that she was a child, twelve years old, in a blockhouse a little north of Seattle during the last Indian attack on the settlement. The gentleman, Mr. Denney, told us that when he was six weeks old his family had come up from Olympia by boat and landed at Alki Point. His mother's milk had dried up and as she sat on the beach crying, unable to nurse her baby, an Indian woman approached her. When the mother explained her difficulty, the Indian woman went away and came back with clams. Mr. Denney said, "I was raised on clam juice, as there was no cow nearer than Olympia."

After the success of *Calico Cargo,* we planned another musical in 1946. This was *San Juan Story*, based on the pig war in the San Juan Islands. Just before the American Civil War, American farmers had become a thorn in the side of the British Hudson's Bay Company in the San Juans. The border in the San Juans had never been clearly defined, and when, one Fourth of July, the British saw the American flag flying over what is now Friday Harbor, they brought in the British Marines to establish their territory. The British were sensitive about borders. They remembered 1812, when the Americans had decided they needed Canada.

While all this was going on, the Hudson's Bay factor's pig got into an American farmer's potato patch and the American shot the pig. The factor tried to arrest the farmer and bring him into British territory at Victoria for trial. However, with the dreadful conflict of Civil War going on at the same time, the struggle between the American farmer and the Hudson's Bay factor on a remote island seemed very small potatoes indeed. The people on the island, left to their own devices, found that they had more in common than they thought. The British bought produce from the Americans. The Americans hired an English teacher from Victoria. They invited each other to the national holiday celebrations, the Fourth of July and the Queen's birthday, and they made peace. Several years later, William I of Germany settled the boundary to the satisfaction of the British and Americans alike.

The theme of our musical was "the people make the peace." We added a fictional love affair between the factor's daughter and the American farmer's son. Martha Wright, a charming girl and a very successful singer on radio, played the part of the daughter. *San Juan Story* was her first stage experience. Some years later, I saw her when she replaced Mary Martin in the Broadway production of *South Pacific.*

To our amazement, *San Juan Story* provoked controversy. After the demise of the Washington State Theatre, we had continued doing matinee performances for the city's high schools of any classic or play we thought might interest them. They had seen and enjoyed *Calico Cargo* and were preparing to come to *San Juan Story*. The Junior League was sponsoring this, and one day a committee from the League came to see us. They had been to the *Post-Intelligencer* with their promotional material and been told by someone at the paper that *San Juan Story* had fourteen subversive incidents in it!

The *Post-Intelligencer* had mentioned in particular the song that closed the show. This was "It's One World, Boys," sung by a double male quartet composed of the British Marines and the American soldiers on guard at what was called the "marker tree." During the conflict, any British or American who dared put one foot over the line at the marker tree ran the danger of being shot. In the song, the boys sing of their homes in England and the United States, concluding with the double quartet singing "It's One World." The idea and the title for the song came from a book that Wendell Willkie had written, *One World*, based on his experiences during a trip around the world as a roving ambassador for President Roosevelt.

When Burton heard that the *Post-Intelligencer* wished to censor the script, he was adamant. "Not a line, not a comma, will be changed.

The *Post-Intelligencer* doesn't censor our scripts." We played the show without incident, and I am certain that no one was subverted by it.

In the spring of 1950, we were fortunate in obtaining the rights to produce Benjamin Britten's *Let's Make an Opera*. It was a delight to work on. It is an opera within a play. In the first act, a group of people decides to make an opera, a collective effort done in much the same way we did our own operas. The second act is the dress rehearsal, and the third act is the opera itself, called *The Little Sweep*. It was scored for a six-piece orchestra of first-chair musicians from the Seattle Symphony, conducted by Helen Taverniti. We needed a conductor who was prepared to improvise, for during the intermission the audience learned the songs and then acted as the chorus, so every night there was a different chorus.

The musicians enjoyed working on the opera, for they were part of the show. In the dress rehearsal they were in work clothes. Then, for the last act, the opera, they dressed for the occasion. Actors, orchestra, and audience gave a rousing performance. Frequently people waiting for a streetcar just outside the theatre, hearing the music, would come into the foyer to ask what was going on, and they were invited to drop in and see.

When the war in Europe was ended and the Nazis defeated, we expected further conflict in the Pacific with the Japanese. But after the fearful bombing of Hiroshima and Nagasaki, the war was over, and the men started coming home. There had been casualties among friends, but none in our immediate group, and, to our great satisfaction, not a single mental casualty. Actors are often considered temperamental, perhaps even unstable, characters, but our actors survived the dangers and rigours of their various experiences very well.

Our concern for these returned servicemen was immediate—how to get them back into the demanding activities of the theatre and civilian life? Arthur Laurent's *Home of the Brave* provided an excellent opportunity. It was a play laid in the South Pacific, dealing with the military problems of jungle fighting as part of the strategy of island-hopping warfare. It was an all-male cast—in fact, an all-GI cast, except for the doctor, played by Al Ottenheimer.

Three young servicemen who had never been in our group before joined us, including one young Marine who had spent twenty-seven months in the Marshall Islands and knew the very special techniques for jungle fighting. Someone congratulated me on my direction, wondering how I had coped so well with the technical problems. I hadn't, of course—I had had the help and expertise of the United States Marines.

The play was about the war, but there was also a theme of ugly anti-Semitism that complicated the dangers and added to the problems of men in this perilous situation. The play was an immediate success, and had an excellent therapeutic effect on the cast involved. We did two other plays about the war: *Counterattack* by I. Vershinin and M. Ruderman, translated from the Russian, and Harry Brown's *Sound of Hunting.*

CHAPTER FIFTEEN

Once the war was over, the problems created and intensified by the war effort began to emerge. No state had been more changed by the war than Washington, whose population had grown by more than half a million as men and women flooded into industrial plants and shipyards. Migration prompted by military and industrial activity had profoundly disturbed established community life—assimilating thousands of strangers could not be accomplished painlessly in so short a time. Newcomer and resident alike were affected, and in some instances there was open hostility.

Winning the war had taken priority over everything else. Communities had had to mobilize for the emergency tasks of housing and integrating the new population into community life. Cities and towns, government and private organizations had girded themselves for the job. Various government organizations, such as the United Service Organizations (USO), a federation of private agencies, the Recreation Division of the Federal Security Agency (FSA), and the Federal Public Housing Authority, focused their attention on war-affected communities. The USO organized programs for military personnel and industrial workers. The Recreation Division of the FSA assisted towns and cities in organizing programs and also helped obtain federally financed recreation buildings and other facilities, and the Housing Authority developed active recreational programs in its housing projects.

Early in this effort, local, state and federal governments, as well as private agencies, realized that recreation had a vital part to play in winning the war. An example of this was an interesting experience for us at the Playhouse. We were performing an old-fashioned melodrama, a summer show called *Bertha, the Sewing Machine Girl,* complete with olio entertainment—miscellaneous songs and variety acts done after the intermission. One day, two men in uniform came to the Playhouse office, asking us if we would do the show in Hanford, Washington. We readily agreed, as we had been doing shows for the armed services from the beginning of the war.

This, however, seemed to be something different. We were to go to Ellensburg, where we were to be met and change to army trucks and buses that would take the cast, scenery, and props to the hall in Hanford. We were to stay in the hall, where meals would be served to us by army personnel who would also help with the tasks necessary to get the show on. We were not to mention this trip to Hanford to anyone. We were aware that it involved some kind of top wartime secret, but how top a secret we did not know until after Hiroshima, when Hanford was mentioned as one of the places where the parts for the atom bomb had been made. The tedium of isolation had to be relieved, so recreation became a factor.

In the process of mobilizing their recreational resources, communities unified their forces and had an opportunity to observe the effectiveness of community-wide programs, bolstered by good leadership and adequate financial support. At the end of the war, these agencies began to wind up their affairs and terminate the recreational work. Federal funds were withdrawn and communities were left without the necessary finances and advisory help to maintain facilities and carry on adequate recreation programs. Yet the community problems created by the war did not disappear; they only became more acute.

As one of the actors in the cast of *No More Frontier*, Burton had toured the state of Washington in the 1930s and had been impressed with the interest and enthusiasm of many of the people he met for something comparable to our theatre to be developed in their communities. These people, sponsors of the tour for adults, were members of church groups, service clubs, and women's organizations. They talked of the needs their young people had for opportunities to engage in some kind of cultural programs in an organized way. Sports in school were usually organized, but everything needed more and better facilities. What they seemed to need most was leadership, perhaps some kind of central organization that could provide consultants to evaluate and coordinate activities as well as indoor and outdoor recreational facilities.

Burton, remembering the needs, interests, and concerns of these communities before the war and apprehensive that programs acquired during the war would be abandoned and the facilities fall into disuse and disrepair, decided that something must be done. He asked for a grant from the State Legislature of 1945 to do a recreational survey of the state. This forward-looking legislature appropriated the funds and directed the Hon. Belle Reeves, secretary of state, to make such a survey, which was to be directed by my husband. Burton engaged Dr. Duane Robinson as research director, Jack Kinzel to serve as field representative and to write the report, and hired the other personnel necessary. The survey was called the Recreational and Cultural Survey of the State of Washington and was begun in January, 1946.

Aristotle once observed that "the aim of education is the wise use of leisure." Recreational and cultural resources contribute to constructive leisure. They include material assets such as community playgrounds, swimming pools, and community centres, as well as funds to support them. They include civic groups, youth organizations, and other groups. They take into account less tangible assets of skills, interests, attitudes, leadership, and community traditions.

Technological advance (whereby machines took over more and more actual labour, a process accelerated by the war effort) and the increasing efficiency of the workers themselves had shortened the working hours of homemakers, factory workers, and farmers, giving all segments of society more leisure. But the very changes that had given more leisure had destroyed the base of traditional leisure activity. Spontaneous and informal neighbourhood life, formerly a major focus for leisure, had largely disappeared.

One of the strongest characteristics of pioneer days in the West was a sense of neighbourliness. The reasons were partly economic and partly social. People were short of funds, short of help, and short of equipment; hence, the natural tendency was to work together, to play together, and to make one's own amusement. Now composite schools were taking the place of the little red schoolhouse, which had provided the centre for culture and recreation for small towns and villages. As society became more settled and urbanized, common interests gave way to special interests. Instead of being participants in organized sports, people became spectators in stadiums.

How did the survey get its facts? In cooperation with civic groups in thirty-nine Washington communities, it gathered facts about indoor and outdoor recreation facilities, youth and adult organizations, recreational and cultural groups, commercial recreation, and many other items. Each community also assisted the survey in evaluating its total recreational picture, including programs. Taken together, the thirty-nine communities revealed common accomplishments as well as needs.

The fieldwork on the survey was a tremendous task, and without the help of hundreds of people who spent thousands of hours of diligent, conscientious work, a task of such scope could not have been accomplished. Hundreds of conferences and community meetings were held in every part of the state. Findings and conclusions were referred to the people again and again for evaluation and comment, which served as a continual check on the work being done.

The survey found that, rather than constructive activities, what was emerging were undesirable leisure-time pursuits that could and did develop into problems. First, there were acute handicaps facing young people. These were especially complex for the children of migrant families, living in trailers and all sorts of temporary dwellings. Juvenile delinquency was soaring upward in all strata of society, marked by an increase in alcoholism and sexual promiscuity among teenagers. The story is far too familiar—truancy, school dropouts, vandalism, too much spending money, too little parental control and supervision, and too little community understanding and help. Young people felt that they were isolated. The survey also found that little or no provision was made in communities for adult and senior citizens' groups, thus further dividing the common interests that integrate communities. Survey findings demonstrated that, on the whole, desires for unified programs for recreation were far ahead of any provision made to meet them.

The survey noted the effect that the growing problem of pollution had on the recreational resources of the state. At that time, its chief concern was with water pollution. Atmospheric pollution from industries and pollution from insecticides had not yet emerged as threats. Water pollution was affecting large areas of river and lake recreation grounds, which were already shrinking through private ownership. The survey found, after examining all the essential elements for creative leisure, that Washington's recreation and cultural resources were potentially great and the greatest of these resources were the people struggling with the many problems of building a creative leisure-time life for themselves and their children.

It was the survey's considered conclusion that communities should expect their needs to be met by state government, which should accept the fundamental responsibility of serving them in recreation as fully as it did in other fields. The committees who had given so much of their time to the work of the survey indicated their willingness to accept responsibility for their share of the work to follow, but they needed authority. They required funds and guidance and these could only come from state involvement in the problem.

The concerns expressed by towns and cities in the state of Washington in 1946 have now become the concern of the nation, indeed of the world, demanding solutions.

The survey's report, "*Recreation for All*," was presented to the 1947 legislature. But this legislature was in no mood for culture or recreation. They did not move on the survey, but they did set up the Un-American Activities Committee, with a budget of $158,000.

CHAPTER SIXTEEN

Robert Cromie, late editor of the *Vancouver Sun*, asked me how we were financed, and I told him of our problems and how we met them. He laughed, and said, "Have you ever read Luther Burbank's *The Harvest of the Years*? I'm going to send you a copy. Read the chapter on his work with cactus. That will tell you what I think of you and your operations, and what accounts for your success." He sent the book and I have always remembered the message. Burbank said that the cactus has adaptability. It seizes life,. "adjusting itself to apparently impossible circumstances and doing the right thing at the right time and in the right direction." That was us, all right.

In the spring and summer of 1947, we began plans to celebrate the twentieth anniversary of the Seattle Repertory Playhouse. We were at work on *San Juan Story*, an original show—book, music, and lyrics were all the collective work of the group. The material had been organized into a three-act musical drama by Walter Gyger and Al Ottenheimer. Gyger had been in Burton's playwriting class in the West Seattle High School, had been in our workshops, and had developed into a very good actor.

In twenty years, we had realized many of the objectives we had set for ourselves in our initial planning, even without the $50,000 Johnsrud had insisted we would need. We had developed an excellent theatre for the very young audience. We had created the Washington State

Theatre for the high school groups. We had produced plays that had involved, either as audience or actual participants, members of every ethnic group in Seattle, including the Indians. We had produced nineteen original scripts; we had toured the Northwest; we had produced with notable success the great classics—Shakespeare, Ibsen's *Peer Gynt*, and Goethe's *Faust*. We had developed a good school of theatre, which included actor and director training and all the skills necessary for the management of a theatre. We had created children's classes with a sound educational basis. We had made intensive contributions to the war effort, and we had done a survey of Washington that would enable another agency, some years later, to program leisure and recreational activities for the state.

Over the years we had developed a philosophy that enabled us to meet exigencies and to turn them to our advantage. We had survived the loss of our building, the loss of jobs at the university, the loss of the subscription sales that had provided our working capital, and somehow managed to live and work. We met many difficult situations that eventually came to seem salutary, for they strengthened our will and determination and were as nothing when we were able to chalk up a victory, and we usually did just that.

When we failed, we would carefully consider the reason for failure, and its extent. A failure can be a wonderful learning experience, sometimes teaching more than a success. Over the years we constantly re-evaluated our business methods and studied the problems of acting and directing techniques, philosophically and artistically.

During the Depression, we realized that subscription sales would no longer provide the working capital we needed, so we began a program of advanced sales of complete houses or blocks of tickets to labour, business, and service clubs. A club might buy the house. They could then sell the tickets to their members for any price they chose and use what they earned as a fund for one of their special programs. Or they could invite members of their organization to the play as a good-will gesture. Each spring a large supermarket bought three nights for their employees. As these were to be family nights, we planned a production that would be suitable for them and at the same time maintain our standard.

We sold blocks of tickets, twenty-five, fifty, and one hundred, to organizations with two-thirds of the price of the tickets going to us and one-third to them. This way, by the time we opened the play we were able to judge where we stood financially. Sixty-five or seventy percent pre-sold would mean security, and the drop-in ticket sales would be velvet. Over the years we were able to gauge the taste of these organizations and approach them for sales with some confidence. We were almost always successful—but there was the occasional exception to the rule, as we discovered when we sold Dorothy Parker's *After Such Pleasures* to a women's group that, as a body, was not amused!

By 1940, our weekend workshops had developed into a full-time day school for students, mostly high school graduates who wanted to make theatre their profession. They received instruction in speech, acting, history, body movement, makeup, philosophy, fencing, and creative writing on Mondays, Wednesdays, and Fridays. On Tuesdays and Thursdays they worked in the box office or on ticket sales, or backstage on costumes or sets. We were introducing them to total theatre, which would enable them to make informed decisions on what particular field of theatre, if any, they wanted to make their profession. In 1944 the Junior Chamber of Commerce provided scholarships for high school graduates to attend our school. When the war was over, Congress enacted the GI Bill of Rights, which enabled returning servicemen to finish their education. Our school was accredited, and its activities were developed around a two-year course. Students were constantly engaged in our theatre activities. They watched rehearsals, acted as prop people, came on in crowd scenes, played small parts, and were cast in more demanding roles as their skills and talents developed.

The men and women of the Playhouse were remarkable people. They worked well together, cementing friendships that have stood the test of time, or at least the test of forty-plus years. To them, the Playhouse was not just a place, a passing fancy, or a whim. It was something more, something that was integral to their lives, something that they cared very deeply about, and worked incredibly hard for.

When in 1936 the deepening pressures of the Depression closed in and the financial situation became even more acute, the working force of the Playhouse group seemed to be handed more and greater responsibilities by the board. The workers decided that something in the nature of a guild was necessary and formed a group with a chairman and a set of rules or bylaws. This organization called itself the Organized Workers of the Seattle Repertory Playhouse, or OWSRP. They planned committees to assist in promotion and sales, and to determine policies and other matters of general importance to the group as a whole. It was decided that anyone who had actively worked in the Playhouse for a year in any capacity could apply for membership. This organization never outgrew its usefulness, and the democratic process at work stood the Playhouse in good stead during the war years and the darker years ahead.

Sir Tyrone Guthrie, in his autobiography *A Life in the Theatre*, commented that a theatre, no matter what its glamour or level of subsidy, can be weak where it should not be weak, at the heart. We had created a theatre with a strong heart. We had developed "group communication" between people who were all intent on one purpose and in achieving that purpose had built cooperation in an extremely competitive area, the theatre, and in a culture whose dominant philosophy is competition.

During this period, we revived our Sunday evening performances. They were sometimes a "table reading" of a play that would have been of limited interest for an audience over a run, that was impossible to produce with our attenuated personnel, or that would have been so expensive a production that we could not afford it. Sometimes the evening was a production of one-acts, largely original, or some classic such as Aeschylus' *Prometheus Bound*.

In our table readings we used a commentator, who set the scene and read the necessary connective links that kept the play moving. These readings were carefully cast and rehearsed. In later years, I've had people say to me, "When I saw Mr. James in *Cyrano de Bergerac...*" and when I reminded them that it was a table reading they were remembering and that we had never produced *Cyrano*, they would stare in amazed disbelief. "Well, I'll never forget it. I could have *sworn* I *saw* him!"

We had some exciting experiences in those years when our theatre played host to travelling artists, particularly the folk singers—memorable evenings with Pete Seeger, Earl Robinson, and Woody Guthrie. Sometimes these performances were done as benefits for the artist or to assist in some cause in which we were interested. One evening, Earl Robinson gave the first public performance of *The Lonesome Train*, which Norman Corwin later produced on CBS. The working title of this musical documentary was *Abe Lincoln Comes Home Again*, for it was the story of Lincoln's funeral train as it travelled from Washington, DC, to Springfield, Illinois. The words of the documentary were written by Millard Lampell, the music was by Earl and was sung on the broadcast by Robinson and Burl Ives. This performance was a benefit to assist Hugh De Lacy, then working in the shipyards, in his successful candidacy for the House of Representatives.

One day, a battered old car, threatening collapse at every gasp of the engine, drove up to the Playhouse. A young man carrying a guitar stepped out, dressed in the attire embraced by the youth of today, but not so usual then. It was Woody Guthrie. A performance was given for his benefit, and George Taverniti, who had an uncanny knowledge about cars and how to give even the saddest case a new lease on life, took over Woody's vehicle. Guthrie gave a most successful performance and came home with us afterward, sitting on the floor of our living room, repeating his repertoire into the early hours of the morning. Two songs I remember from that night so long ago were "Talking Union" and "This Land Is Your Land," which much later became a sort of theme song for young people in both the United States and Canada.

Guthrie said, "My songs tell you something you already know." He told us that he had bought his young son Arlo a guitar. His wife thought it too expensive for such a small boy, but Woody said, "We'll start him with the best and he can go on from that."

When we planned our twentieth anniversary at the Playhouse, we wrote to our friends, asking them to sponsor the event. Guthrie wrote back, "I don't want to sponsor the Playhouse. I want to marry it."

On the evening of September 17, 1947, we opened the season of our twentieth anniversary with the production of *San Juan Story*. On this occasion, we had received local and national recognition, telegrams and letters, and a particularly heart-warming message to the audience and to us from Helen Hayes, first lady of the theatre, live via magnified long distance telephone from New York:

> Hello, Seattle.
>
> Hello, Burton James—and the Repertory Playhouse. This is Helen Hayes. I'm so glad to be able to talk with you,

especially at this time. I wanted you to know, at the very outset of your Twentieth Anniversary Season, how we feel about the Seattle Repertory Playhouse, and the wonderful work you're doing.

I felt a wire or a letter wasn't enough, so I'm calling you right from my dressing room in the Broadhurst Theatre, on 44th Street, just off Broadway. A few minutes ago, the curtain came down on tonight's performance of *Happy Birthday*—and in a few minutes more, the curtain will be going up on the opening of your twentieth season, which, I know, will be a happy birthday for you, for the Playhouse staff, and for Seattle audiences.

...

To paraphrase Walt Whitman: "Great Audiences make Great Theatres." The Seattle Repertory Playhouse has helped to build the audiences which, in turn, have helped the development and growth of the theatre.

I'm greeting you, not only for myself, but for our national theatre organization, ANTA, A N T A, which stands for the American National Theatre and Academy. The other board members join me in heartiest congratulations. That includes our president, Vinton Freedley—Gilbert Miller—Richard Rodgers, producer of my *Happy Birthday,* Raymond Massey, Rosamond Gilder, George Freedley, Brooks Atkinson, Robert Sherwood, and many others.

We feel that you are an important part of the national theatre, and that your theatre leadership and pioneering in Seattle is setting a wonderful example for communities in other parts of the country.

In fact, ANTA is holding up the achievements of the Repertory Playhouse to stimulate and inspire other companies. We admire your pre-sales program, which enables whole groups of people to buy tickets in advance at a discount. And we're grateful to you for allowing us to give out information on how it functions, to theatres in other parts of the country. When your kind of cooperation is extended, as it should be, between all the theatres, whether they're community, professional, or academic, then we'll begin to have a national theatre that will enrich the lives of all the people of our country.

Many of us associate your city with the last frontier. And now we have other frontiers of a different kind. The Seattle Repertory Playhouse is pioneering among the social and cultural frontiers of the human spirit. You are held in high esteem—and greatly admired—throughout the theatrical world, commercial as well as non-commercial. You're building the kind of theatre that brings satisfaction to the people of the audience and people of the theatre.

I'm spending my lifetime in the American theatre, and its health and welfare are subjects of deep personal importance to me. I believe I could sum up my sentiments like this: Our theatre is better, finer, fuller, because for twenty years, there in the farthest western reach of the United States, the Seattle Repertory Playhouse has been striving and struggling and pioneering and building. Our theatre is the richer for your effort. Our country is a better place to live, because of you.

Here's to the next twenty years—and HAPPY BIRTHDAY.

The next twenty years.

It seemed that night as though we could do the next twenty years "standing on our heads," after the way we'd persevered and come through the first twenty. But we were wrong about that.

In 1948, not even twenty months later, the Un-American Activities Committees got into action. We were on our way out.

CHAPTER SEVENTEEN

In January 1947, our state legislature had set up the Joint Legislative Fact-finding Committee of the State of Washington to inquire into subversive activities in the state and report back to the 1949 Legislature. The committee was chaired by State Senator Albert F. Canwell. This interim committee received the approval of the State Supreme Court, by a divided opinion, and was in business.

The resolution setting up this fact-finding committee on un-American activities directed the committee to investigate all groups who "under the cover of ... the bill of rights seek ... to destroy our liberties and our freedom by force, threats and sabotage, and to subject us all to the domination of foreign powers." The resolution further directed the committee to investigate the activities of groups or organizations or educational institutions "supported in whole or in part by state funds" "whose membership includes persons who are communists, or any other organization known or suspected to be dominated or controlled by a foreign power...."

This madness hadn't sprung to life full-blown in the State of Washington, of course. It had been building and growing, fomenting in the frenzied situation that existed all over the country at that time. World War II had ended on May 8, 1945, when the German generals, in the presence of American, British, and Soviet generals, signed the terms of unconditional surrender. On September 2 the same year, the Japanese acknowledged defeat. Fascism was beaten. Hitler and Mussolini were dead. Though it had been costly, the Allies had achieved their victory.

Churchill, at the time of the signing of the unconditional surrender of Germany, sent this message to Stalin: "Future generations will acknowledge their debt to the Red Army as unreservedly as we do who have lived to witness their proud achievements." During the conflict, on February 23, 1942, General Douglas MacArthur said, "The world situation at the present time indicates that the hope of civilization rests on the worthy banners of the courageous Red Army."

However, in spite of these tributes to the Soviet Union that recognized their contribution to our common struggle, it wasn't long before we were being urged to go at it again, to set up the same kind of situation that created Fascism, brought Hitler to power, and inevitably resulted in World War II. Not quite a year after his glowing message of thanks to Stalin, Winston Churchill mounted a platform at Fulton, Missouri, beside President Truman, and called for an extension of the anti-Communist faction that he had helped to construct after World War I to meet "the growing challenge and peril to Christian civilization" from atheistic Bolshevism. In the halls of Congress and in the press, the call went out. The name of the game was "Let's get tough with Russia now." We had the atom bomb. What were we waiting for? The Soviet Union would not be able to make it in ten years.

As it turned out, they made it in three, which only added fuel to the anti-Communist crusade, which by then was in full swing.

On January 3, 1945, at the opening session of the 79th Congress, Representative John E. Rankin, in a surprise legislative coup, put through a bill creating a permanent House Un-American Activities Committee under the nominal chairmanship of Representative J. Parnell Thomas. Thomas had been a member of the Un-American Committee, chaired by Representative Martin Dies, who since August 1938 had carried on a ceaseless, virulent campaign against everything forward-looking and progressive on the American scene, calling all such efforts Communist-motivated. The people engaged in these activities, individually or in groups, were labelled by Dies as out-and-out Communists, Communist dupes or fronts, and agents of a foreign power. Dies and his "sordid procedures" left the scene in 1944 when three members of his committee were defeated at the polls and Chairman Dies announced that he would not run again. Following his later service on the Rankin Committee, Dies Committee member J. Parnell Thomas served a sentence in a Connecticut jail for petty peculations. Two of his cellmates were reputable Hollywood writers, sent there by his Committee.

With the advent of Rankin's House Un-American Committee, state committees proliferated like poison mushrooms. Washington State's Canwell Committee made headlines from the very beginning. The news media announced breathlessly that the first targets of investigation would be the Pension Union and the University of Washington. Shortly after the Supreme Court decision that approved the committee, the Washington Pension Union found itself under attack.

The senior citizens of the state had organized themselves some time before into an effective working union. They had persuaded the state to raise pensions from $30 to $50 a month and to institute the first comprehensive health program in the nation. This program enabled all pensioners to receive full medical and hospital care, including medicines and appliances, with freedom to select their own doctors. The Pension Union was also involved with other pressing issues of the time—more aid to schools, better social security, fair employment practices legislation, and better veterans' bonuses—and could always be counted on for strong support in any issue for the benefit of the state and the nation.

The Canwell Committee victories in the Pension Union hearings were small, although the legislature that set up the committee had reduced pensions and deprived pensioners of the right to choose their own doctors. It was not until the trials under the Smith Act some years later that the leadership of the Pension Union came under direct attack.

This first hearing by the Canwell Committee seemed to be a "try on." After the Pension Union hearing, the committee brought up its big guns to take on the University of Washington. Investigators began to prowl the campus. Among the faculty, intimidation (threats of subpoena, loss of jobs, and blacklisting) was freely used to get individual professors to admit to membership in the Communist Party and to name others as radicals. The quality of teaching, writing, or research of the professors was only lightly questioned. Instead, the investigators were intent on identifying those who were active in their union and in university affairs or had been active in any liberal, social, or political organization. Canwell announced in the press that there were 150 such subversives on the campus, and that his committee would find out the facts about them.

The university administration forbade any public attack against the committee by faculty members. The faculty was assured that members' rights would be protected, but that nothing should be done to jeopardize the reputation of the university. This tactic, plus the intimidation applied by the investigators, successfully kept the faculty divided, silent, and paralyzed, innocently hopeful that the whole thing would blow over. The University of Washington was the first educational institution in the country to give aid and comfort to an investigating committee.

Assurances and protestations notwithstanding, on June 19, the last day of the spring quarter in 1948, the committee delivered subpoenas to twenty-five or thirty professors and three members of the Playhouse staff, for hearings to begin on July 19, a time when faculty and students would be scattered and disorganized.

During the Pension Union hearings, with the great build-up in the press about subversion on the campus, no mention had been made about subversion at the Playhouse, which of course was not a part of the university at all. Our first intimation that we were to be involved came when we were rehearsing for our summer show, Charles MacArthur and Ben Hecht's *Front Page*. As it was a newspaper story, we approached the Newspaper Guild to take one of the playing nights, and they asked for the opening performance. A short time later, we received a letter cancelling the arrangement. Al Ottenheimer called one of his friends in the guild and asked the reason for the cancellation. In the best cloak-and-dagger tradition, the friend asked Al not to come to his office but to meet him for coffee in a restaurant. There, Al was told that the heat was to be taken off the university and the Playhouse was to become the committee's prime target.

At this time, the university was building a medical school, the largest such school under one roof, costing about six million dollars. The Board of Regents were worried that it would be difficult to staff the new medical school if it were bruited about that the university was a hotbed of subversion. The man from the guild told Al that the Regents had approached the committee with the request that they lay off the university. As the university administration had been so agreeable and helpful to the committee, it was apparently not difficult to get

Canwell's cooperation. Investigation of the university shifted into low gear and a new target had to be found to provide the same publicity.

It served no purpose for these small-time politicians to investigate some card-carrying Communist making speeches nightly on Skid Road. Canwell was more interested in getting publicity than in investigating subversion. He hungered to be a United States Senator. Some inspired person or persons apparently chose this auspicious moment to point the finger at the Playhouse. We fit Canwell's requirements: we were "almost university," we were actors and therefore somewhat suspect to begin with in some minds, we had certainly been active in various "Union, University, liberal, social, and/or political affairs" over the years, and we were newsworthy people whose faces and names were regularly seen in public.

So one day in June, two men carrying handsome briefcases drove up to the Playhouse in a shiny car, armed with subpoenas for Burton, Al Ottenheimer, and myself. We were commanded to go to the "146th Field Artillery and remain there until discharged by the committee."

On the grim morning of June 19, 1948, we, along with forty other people, sat in a barracks-like room behind ropes, guarded by city and state highway police and some soldiers, to listen to "friendly witnesses" (friendly to the committee) brought in from all over the country. These witnesses were all professional anti-Communists: J. B. Matthews, former investigator for the Dies Committee; Howard Rushmore, a New York reporter for a Hearst newspaper, and George Hewitt, the sole witness against me, who said he had been a Communist for eighteen years and in the Soviet Union for two and a half years.

We listened to their shabby fabrications of crimes we might have been able to commit, had we had the opportunity, such as dynamiting the Seattle waterworks. It was an interesting comment on the characteristic thinking of these witnesses that they would think of dynamite, then a tool of construction, as a weapon of revolution, long before it became a later generation's symbol of protest.

We had hired a lawyer, having been told that it was most unwise to go before this committee without legal aid. Our lawyer, Cliff O'Brien, told us to answer no questions on our activities or beliefs, that the First Amendment of the Bill of Rights guaranteed freedom of belief and assembly. Or, we might refuse to answer under the Fifth Amendment, guaranteeing the right to be silent, which protects the individual against self-incrimination. We chose to answer under the First Amendment, rather than the Fifth, for the words "self-incrimination" seemed to us to indicate guilt of some kind.

We, like many people, did not know the history of this amendment, so bitterly fought for by Thomas Jefferson and others to secure its inclusion in the Bill of Rights. The cogency of the Fifth Amendment was demonstrated at these hearings, for one of the university professors invoked it and was therefore not indicted for contempt of the committee. It did not, however, save his university position, for he was dismissed by the Board of Regents. Ironically, the chairman of that Board of Regents, Dave Beck, boss of the Teamsters' Union, some years later was indicted for crimes that sent him to McNeil Penitentiary; he used the Fifth Amendment more than a hundred times during his defense.

Witnesses friendly to the committee spoke without hindrance and with legislative immunity, telling scurrilous stories of crimes committed, or about to be committed, by the forty people subpoenaed by the committee. We sat behind ropes, guarded by police, and were not allowed to object or answer this ridiculous testimony. The papers carried the witnesses' tales with banner headlines such as "Playhouse Red Recruiting Centre."

When George Hewitt was on the stand, he told the committee that he had met me in the Soviet Union in 1933 (I was there in 1934) and had been told that I was a guest of the Soviet Union and had been ordered by Stalin to start the cultural revolution in the Northwest, which led to my production of *Waiting for Lefty* in 1936. When I could take no more of this preposterous fairy story, I rose to demand that the man be cross-examined.

Canwell's gavel hammered me into silence, while he shouted, "We'll have no Communist speeches at this hearing!" He ordered me out of the hearing. I tried to leave unassisted, but two policemen took my arms, and I was carried from the room. When my lawyer tried to speak in my defense, he was thrown out, too.

Later, at the trials, when Canwell was questioned about lawyers at the hearings, he said, "Oh, half the Bar Association was there." Which may have been true, but at one time there was only one lawyer left *in* the hearings, while the rest were out in the corridors, having incurred

Mr. Canwell's displeasure. The two policemen who hauled me out were very nice—they looked embarrassed, put me in an air conditioned room, found me a chair, and said they hoped I'd be comfortable.

We charged Hewitt with perjury, proven by his own testimony, but before he could be served, he was off on a plane to the Congressional hearings in Washington, where he was to appear again and again as a responsible expert witness, at a tidy daily stipend.

For five days we sat at these hearings. Then they were over and we were dismissed, coming home to read the blazing headlines in the newspapers. Canwell had saved the State of Washington from the machinations of university professors, respectable citizens, and three Playhouse actors. No one need fear the domination of a foreign power any longer.

In our summer show, *Front Page*, there was a line of dialogue when an irate editor, trying to train a rookie reporter in how to write a story, says, "How many times do I have to tell you nobody reads the second paragraph—all they read are the headlines!" Ironically, it was the same in our case. The public saw the headlines and skipped the paragraphs that might have cast some doubt upon our "guilt."

After the hearings, the mother of a friend called and asked me to spend some time at their cottage, at Home Colony, thirty-five miles from Bremerton. She thought I needed a rest, and said that if I were interested her husband would pick me up that evening. The holiday was a delightful respite, and I thoroughly appreciated the heart-warming concern of these people for anyone who needed help.

I had been there only a few days, unwinding and renewing my resources, when a lady from the store at the foot of the hill came to the cottage to say that I was wanted for a very important long-distance call. The only telephone was on a counter in the store, so there was no privacy about the phone call, which was from my lawyer, telling me that I had been indicted and had to be at the county jail before six that evening. He told me that I was out on $500 bail, but not to worry because somebody had put up a property bond. However, I had to be at the jail before 6:00 p.m. or the police would come for me.

I explained that I was thirty-five miles from Bremerton, had no car, would have to take an hour's trip on the ferry—and would probably have to wait for the bus in the morning to get to Seattle from there.

Before I got back up the hill to the cottage, three cars drove into the yard, offering to take me to Bremerton or wherever else I wanted to go.

I was at the county jail by 9:00 the next morning under my own steam and the steam of my friends, to be fingerprinted, mugged, and numbered. I can't remember the number they gave me. I should, I suppose, for not many people in my position, in that day, had that experience.

I didn't know who had put up the bond for my bail, but I was out and had to wait for the trial dates in the fall. The six people who had been indicted were a mixed lot. There were two university professors, a health officer who had reported unsanitary conditions in the kitchens of a swank Seattle club—he had been cleared by the Civil Service Commission in order to get his job and had taken the loyalty oath, but that didn't seem to count for much now—Al Ottenheimer, my husband, and myself. The charge was gross misdemeanor, "contempt of the state Un-American Activities Committee for willful refusal to answer a proper material question," which was what Canwell laughingly called "the sixty-four-dollar question"—"Are you now or have you ever been a member of the Communist party?"

Before the trial dates were set, Prosecuting Attorney Lloyd Sharett called our lawyer and said that if we would come down and plead guilty and pay a $25 fine, we would be spared the ignominy of trials. We were in no mood for that kind of cooperation with this contemptible committee. We had been given no opportunity anywhere to answer the lies told about us by paid witnesses and headlined so luridly in the press. We felt that our only recourse lay in challenging the legality of the committee and its procedures in the courts. So, with greater confidence in the courts than our later experience warranted, we told the prosecuting attorney what he could do with his "guilty" pleas, and went to trial.

What had we and the Playhouse done to merit this attention from Canwell's Un-American Committee? We had produced all kinds of plays, some controversial, that "gave people ideas," in the words of our board member who had resigned after *Stevedore*. We had signed petitions for senior citizens' pensions. We had actively participated in the war effort. We had protested the sale of scrap iron to Japan and concerned ourselves with the war in Spain. I had made speeches. We had created the Washington State Theatre and had done a Recreational and Cultural Survey of the State of Washington. At Burton's trial, the survey was the sole charge against him.

Canwell stated on the stand that he "had information" that Burton had siphoned money from the Cultural Survey project to the Communist party. The newspapers carried the headline, "James Siphoned State Funds to Reds." At the time, a helpful if somewhat dim prosecutor asked, "But didn't James turn over $10,000 back to the state from that project?" He was squelched, and the papers did not carry that story. In point of fact, none of those funds could possibly have been used for any purpose other than that for which they were intended, for every penny expended had to go through the secretary of state's office on vouchers. And it was all accounted for.

The Legislature that had provided funds for the survey, not trusting an actor to do an adequate accounting job, had appointed a legislator, with a salary and an expense sheet, to watch over the operation. He had to come in to Seattle from out of town to do the job. At one point he complained to Secretary of State Belle Reeves, "I'm supposed to be watching James, but *he's* watching *me*. You should see the way he combs my expense sheet. I'm damned tired of it!" Yet that man's accounting, and the vouchers supporting the accounting, were never brought forward as evidence.

Before our trials began, some uneasiness began to appear in the prosecuting circles. Prosecuting Attorney Sharett asserted that this was "a proper avenue of inquiry for the Un-American Activities Committee under the legislative resolution creating that Committee. Many serious questions of law will doubtless be raised as to the right to prosecute a person for contempt of a legislative committee." In Judge Clay Allen's court, on October 4, Defense Attorney John Caughlan argued, "There is not any authority in the United States that gives any government body the right to inquire into what even a non-citizen thinks—either religious or political. These defendants are all lifetime American citizens."

Judge Allen took a week to search the law and his conscience, and found nothing to illuminate the Bill of Rights: "It is the court's view that committees created by the legislature cannot be expected to observe the same exactitude and accuracy in conducting their operations as would be expected of a court of law."

Our hopes rose at this hint that a court of law would act with "exactitude and accuracy." Perhaps we were right in accepting this ordeal, for had not Thomas Jefferson laid down guidelines: "It behooves every citizen who values liberty of conscience for himself to resist invasions of it in the case of others; or their case may, by a change of circumstances, become his own. It behooves him, too, in his own case, to give no example of concession, betraying the common right of independent opinion, by answering questions of faith, which the laws have left between God and himself."

The trials began in October 1948. Dr. Herbert J. Phillips, from the Philosophy Department of the university, was the first to come to trial and was acquitted because of what the jury stated it considered "the elements of high-handedness of the Canwell Committee" and "the improper service of the subpoena by an interested party." Mr. Stith, the subpoena-server and one of the investigators on the committee, was indeed interested in the extent of his $6,000-a-year job, and the jury believed he had a "very deep feeling" against Dr. Phillips.

Next on the docket was the case of Dr. Ralph Gundlach, in the Psychology Department at the university. The prosecutor had taken pains to detach the affidavit of services from his subpoena, so that the jury would not be able to consider that as a reason for bringing in an acquittal. Dr. Gundlach's case ended in a conviction.

As case after case came up for trial, the avenues for defense became more limited, until finally the judge's sole instruction to the jury as to grounds for conviction was "willful refusal to answer proper and material questions." The provisions for safety guaranteed by the Constitution and the Bill of Rights became, as Abraham Lincoln once said, "as thin as the homeopathic soup that was made by boiling the shadow of a pigeon that had been starved to death."

Any attempt to question the legality and procedures of the committee was dismissed by the judge—"The virtue of this Committee has been established."

One young lady, who worked at the Playhouse and had been in Al Ottenheimer's classes, was dismissed from the stand before she could testify, because, as the prosecutor said, "She doesn't know anything about Mr. Ottenheimer's subversive activities."

Again and again on the stand, Mr. Canwell would say he "had information" on this or that. Finally, in my first trial, we asked that this "information"—files, cards, letters, whatever it was—be subpoenaed so that the court could judge the validity of the material. If such information had existed, we could have been taking a daring chance in demanding it. We needn't have worried. Our action was dismissed as not material and Mr. Caughlan was put in contempt of court in the presence of the jury for his insistence that it be forthcoming, if indeed it existed.

Watching a jury being picked for a trial in which one is to be involved as a defendant is, to say the least, a learning experience. Watching the faces of the prospective jurors, hearing the questions asked by the lawyers and the judge, noting the answers, learning the jargon of the court, provides intensive education. The defense and prosecutors were allowed three challenges to the jury panel when it had been selected. In the recess, both sides scanned the panel to discover if these individuals could bring to the trial the same objectivity and willingness to listen to evidence that they had declared, under oath, they were prepared to do.

In my first trial, a gentleman answered "none" when asked if he knew any reason why he should not be on the jury. He had been out of town during the hearings, and outside of the fact that he had his own business to attend to, he could serve. He also mentioned that he represented the United Fruit Company. We seriously questioned the objectivity of this man because of his position with United Fruit. We felt that big business might not be sympathetic to our side of the issues. But as we scanned the panel, there seemed little choice. The other jurors all seemed to be in the same class. Thank God he made it to the trial. He hung the jury. He said he didn't know what this was all about, but he didn't like it. The high-handedness of the court proceedings disturbed him, and he would not bring in a guilty verdict on the basis of what he had seen and heard.

The jury had deliberated for twenty-nine hours, with the judge returning periodically to give instructions. The juries in the other cases had been out for as little as half an hour. It was all very heartening, but it meant that I had to be tried again.

At my second trial, in July, we became convinced that there had been some serious mishandling in the selection of the jury panels. My defense did a thorough job and discovered that the panels did not represent a cross-section of the community, as was the law, but had been weighted in favour of the more affluent sections of the city. Mr. Caughlan declared that "a series of grave crimes have been committed in the selection of the jury panels in King County" and demanded a full investigation by all King County Superior Court judges. "This panel has been co-opted and disturbed," he said. "The names appear to be in proper order, but someone has altered jury district designations behind the jurors' names. All of this constitutes a violation of almost every section of the criminal code."

We demanded a grand jury investigation. The prosecution said they saw no need for that, and our action was dismissed. Stunned by judicial complacence in the face of such a serious charge, Mr. Caughlan protested, "I'm not quite sure Your Honour understands." The press reported that Judge D. A. McDonald's smile was indulgent: "I didn't come to town on a load of hay," he said, and carried on.

The trial proceeded in the pattern of the cases that had preceded it. Any attempt to bring in witnesses or testimony about my life and many years of work in the community was ignored or suppressed by objections from the prosecution and sustained by the judge, who sometimes rapped a tattoo on his desk to remind them to get into action.

The prosecution had brought in a woman attorney for this trial, perhaps in an attempt to glamourize the proceedings—a woman trying a woman. She was no better and no worse than the men. No photographs were permitted in the courtroom during the trials, so the newspapers were reduced to trying for posed shots after court had recessed for the day. One man asked me if I would get back up on the stand so he could photograph the lady lawyer questioning me. I declined, as I thought we could do without that touch of glamour in any publicity for Canwell.

The verdict was guilty as charged.

The day this decision came from the court, our neighbour, a retired naval officer, called me and asked what had happened. When I told him, he gasped, "My God, I don't know what's happening to this country!" I must confess I had the same thoughts myself.

Finally, on the morning of July 19, 1949, I stood in the courtroom facing Judge McDonald as he prepared to pass sentence on me: "Mrs.

James, a jury of this county has convicted you of the crime of wilful refusal to answer a proper and material question before a legislative committee. What, if anything, have you to say why judgement should not be pronounced upon you?"

Earlier that morning, as my attorney drove me to court to be sentenced, he asked me what I was going to say when I was asked that question.

"I'm not going to tell you."

"You know they could charge you with contempt."

I was touched, but amused. "After two trials, with what I've already endured, have I anything more to fear?"

It is court procedure at the conclusion of a trial to allow the prosecution and defense time for what is called a "summing up." I had asked my attorney to let me have a little of that time to talk to the jury, to let me get past all the legalisms that had so far obstructed my defense. He refused, afraid that I might say something to spoil my case. But the time to answer the judge's question was to be all mine. As the old-timers would have said, I was gunning for bear that morning. After two trials in this court, the April one ending in a hung jury after twenty-nine hours' deliberation, and the July one that ended in my conviction, I spoke from the depths of my being:

> Your Honour, I am at this moment in a strange and terrible position, not for any crime committed by me, for in fact, myself and my attorney were the only innocent principals in this action. I am about to be sentenced for a crime of which I have been convicted by a criminally selected jury. Irrefutable evidence of this crime was presented to this court. My action in this cause was denied and no action whatever has been taken on this matter of criminally packing juries in these courts.
>
> I accuse the court of denying me my proper defense, refusing permission for my witnesses to appear for me. Even my own daughter was refused an opportunity to appear in my defense on some flimsy legal pretext. The prosecutor has been given every opportunity for his witnesses, even including the testimony from one George Hewitt, who is now under

> indictment in his office for perjury. I accuse the prosecutor of defacing and destroying evidence—evidence so important in this action that in the first of these trials it won acquittal. Never once in the course of these trials have we been able to wring from these gentlemen that such evidence existed until the deputy prosecutor, John Vogel, was put on the stand, where under oath he impudently and brashly admitted that he himself had been guilty of this crime of removing, defacing, or destroying evidence. Now, finally—and this is so terrible I find it difficult to phrase the words—I accuse this court, you, Your Honour, of being biased and prejudiced against me, of giving every assistance within the power of your high office to the prosecution, and of being more concerned with obtaining a guilty verdict than with serving the ends of justice in this court.
>
> I feel in making this statement I am acting not only in my best interests but in the interests of every citizen who may find himself involved in the Superior Courts of King County.

When I finished speaking, the court was silent. The steno-typist asked my daughter for a copy of my statement, as he had failed to get it down.

The judge answered:

> I regret very much that you feel that way toward me. I never had any enmity against you or your counsel. There is no question at the time this Canwell Committee was launched that you were quite within your rights to oppose it. In fact, I might say that a great many members of the Bar, and indeed many judges, doubted the constitutionality of this, in fact, some of the Supreme Court judges.
>
> But of course, I am by my oath required to follow what the Supreme Court says, and before this hearing, the case which has generally been construed—which I believe was decided in April … March 18, 1948—the case of the State ex. rel. Robinson v. Fluent held … it is true by a divided court, but I am bound by what the majority say …

> The concurrent resolution of the 1947 legislature which created the interim committee on Un-American Activities was an authorized act of the legislative body, and it is effective for the purpose for which it was adopted. By that resolution, the legislature provided, as it had the inherent power to provide, for the payment of expenses of the members of the committee.
>
> That has been taken by my colleagues and the Bar generally to have foreclosed the position you took. I want to say this for you. You have been consistent. Your real defense was that this committee was unconstitutional. Your counsel, I felt, realizing that the jury under my instructions could not very well have returned any other verdict than they did, attempted to show—which undoubtedly was true—that you suffered very great financial reverses by the actions of this committee. I have been accused of following a program—I believe that was the word—a procedure of other judges.
>
> This is to your credit. You stood by your guns. You didn't commit any perjury. And maybe I am a little chivalrous, but I am not going to sentence you to jail. I don't regard you as a criminal in the ordinary sense, but I do think the jury had to find you guilty as they did. It will be the sentence of this court that you pay a fine of $125, and thirty days in the county jail, which will be suspended.

So there I stood, in an American courtroom, convicted of the crime of being consistent. After reading accounts of trials on similar issues held in later years, I realize that I got off very lightly. Our trials in 1949 seemed to be a sensible expression of our court system when compared to the circus of the Chicago trials in 1969.

Five of the six of us were convicted, with fines and jail sentences of thirty days for the men, a suspended sentence and a fine for me.

During the trials, Burton suffered a slight stroke. It was nightmarish, happening on top of our other tribulations, but Burton retained his spirit and his sense of humour, probably as much for my sake as for his own. He'd been working in the garden, just before the attack came. He was dressed in his favourite gardening garb, old dungarees tied around the waist with a bit of rope, and a much-loved, tattered sweater that had been washed almost to pieces, which he kept rescuing whenever I tossed it into the gunnysack for the Goodwill Industries.

When I came into the bedroom after calling for an ambulance, the doctor was preparing to give Burton an injection and had his scissors out to cut the sweater. Burton raised his head and protested, "Don't you cut that! That's a good sweater." I didn't know whether to laugh or cry.

It was after the stroke that Burton was sentenced. When his doctor heard that he was to be jailed, he said, "My God, man. You can't go to jail. It would be fatal!"

The sheriff told the prosecutor, "You're not going to put James in my jail. We'll put him in the hospital and hire deputies to watch him."

The court ordered a thorough physical examination. Burton was in the clinic for two days, at a cost of fifty dollars a day, which for some reason we did not have to pay—we seemed to have to pay for everything else. The doctor's prognosis was that a jail sentence might be fatal, which could result in most unfavourable publicity. The court decided not to jail him but to put him on probation for a year. This came as a severe blow, for it then became necessary for Burton to report in person to a parole officer every thirty days. It was degrading, and inconvenient, but life had to go on somehow.

That year of 1948–49 had been an incredible one. We had experienced the hearings, the long drawn-out trials, then the Court of Appeals, the State Supreme Court, and finally the United States Supreme Court, with divided opinions, all upholding the convictions. For weeks and months, we had lived literally on sheer nerves, with moments when we wavered on the brink of abject misery. Then, a gradual awareness began to take over, and our lives gained some sort of equilibrium again. This awareness grew from our conviction that it was necessary and right that we should face this obscenity, not solely for ourselves but for the America that had given us life, liberty, and possible opportunities for the pursuit of happiness. We succeeded in holding firm to our convictions, but at an agonizing cost.

The judge's statement that I "had suffered serious financial loss" was quite correct. The theatre is particularly vulnerable to attack. It is a very public occupation, for it must successfully bid for public support to survive. Our incomes and those of our staff were dependent on the sale of tickets to our plays, income from the school, and periodic rentals.

We had no assistance grants or subsidies. It was inevitable that with the hearings and lengthy trials, some of those who supported the work of the theatre would react unfavourably. Surprisingly enough, we and the theatre managed to survive—for a while, at any rate.

We produced our plays for the adult and children's audiences and maintained the work of our schools. But in the summer of 1949, the most formidable blow of all fell. Burton was away, teaching in Banff, Alberta, for the summer when two men came to our theatre. They said they were from the Building and Grounds Department of the university and asked if they could look at the interior of the Playhouse. When they seemed to be going into every nook and cranny, I asked what their interest was.

"The University is thinking of buying this place for the Drama Department," they said. Then they complimented me on the excellent condition of the building.

We were operating on a lease from Mr. Fitz, the owner. He had never mentioned any possible sale and had been most sympathetic during the turmoil of the Canwell business. I asked the men if Mr. Fitz had offered the theatre for sale. "He's a little reluctant, but we can condemn it if he proves too difficult."

An ordinance that enabled educational institutions to condemn property for their purposes had been enacted a year or so previously. This ordinance had been tested in the courts and upheld when property on Magnolia Bluff had been condemned and sold to a nearby high school. With a very good cash offer for the property, and the prospect of condemnation hanging over him, Mr. Fitz agreed to sell.

Our lease ran until December 31, 1950. On December 30, the final curtain came down on Shaw's *Pygmalion*, the last production in the Seattle Repertory Playhouse under our direction.

In January 1951, we moved our personal belongings to be stored in the building we had rented some years before for the Washington State Theatre. Our files, scripts, press books, and some pictures were sent to the University of Washington archives. A carload of flats, curtains, trunks of costumes and wigs went to the Banff School of Fine Arts in Alberta. The University paid us $3,500 for the installations and other property that we owned in the building. We paid all bills due, and with this money closed our theatre owing nobody anything. After twenty-eight years, our life in the theatre in Seattle was over.

There were some victories from the ashes. Canwell never did achieve his heart's desire. He was defeated in two primaries in his attempt to become United States Senator; his committee was defunct and two or three of its members were beaten in the next election, including the legislator who had sponsored the bill through the 1948 legislature.

Much later, in 1955, I was even able to find some wry amusement stemming from the incident. At the conclusion of the trials and hearings, all records of the proceedings—including, I assume, the "information" that Canwell repeatedly referred to in the course of the trials, material we had tried so hard to have subpoenaed for review by the court and for which Mr. Caughlan, for his efforts in that direction, had received a contempt of court charge—were supposedly placed in three safes in a locked room at the Legislative Buildings. The Legislature decided, in 1955, to turn this material over to the Federal Bureau of Investigation. Speaker of the House John L. O'Brien, Lieutenant-Governor E. T. Anderson, and an FBI agent unlocked the door of the room and had to drill open the safes—somebody had lost the combinations.

They found some dusty paper, Communist literature, and a history of the Soviet Union for beginners, but no records of either hearings or trials. Apparently the elaborate efforts to protect these records were a huge joke. Canwell, when questioned, said that he had burned the records at his home to keep them from falling into the hands of the Democrats and refused to say what he had done with the microfilm that had been made of this "controversial" material. The speaker of the House wanted Canwell placed in contempt of the Legislature for refusing to answer proper and material questions. If indicted, this might have resulted in a charge of gross misdemeanour that could have netted him a $1,000 fine and a year in jail. O'Brian said those records and documents "constituted property of the State and not of Albert F. Canwell, and the State didn't spend nearly $158,000 for Canwell's benefit." State Attorney General Don Eastvold and other Republican confrères saved Canwell the ignominy of an investigation.

Perhaps Canwell's ultimate fate was a victory with negative overtones, but we had other, more positive, victories. We became aware of the goodness of our neighbours, friends, and even total strangers:

the people who had put up the property bond for our bail, the man, totally unknown to me, who paused a moment before me on the street and raised his hat, another man who came to the house one Sunday morning and apologetically handed me a twenty-dollar bill. "My wife and I think you might be needing money." (We did, for the six cases for the three of us from the Playhouse cost nearly $12,000) When I offered a receipt, he shook his head. "I'd lose my job if anybody knew I gave you money." Guilt by association.

The man in the tavern. It was late Saturday afternoon, and my daughter and I were in the courtroom waiting for my hung jury. I wanted a cup of tea. All the restaurants in the neighbourhood were closed, so we went across the street to a tavern for a glass of sherry. We sat at the counter, and finally my daughter said, "Mother, finish that. The man is filling your glass every time you take a sip." When I came to pay for it, he said, "It's on the house, lady."

One day during the trials, I was standing waiting for a streetcar. An elderly lady standing near me asked if I would read the number on an approaching car for her. Then she peered more closely at me and asked, "Are you Mrs. James?"

"Yes, I am."

"Well, I want to shake your hand. I am a member of the Daughters of the American Revolution, and you are fighting for the very things my ancestors fought for." Then, as she mounted the steps of the streetcar, she turned back and smiled at me. "I wish you luck. It's a long battle, isn't it?"

All those blessed people. And the Playhouse Board members, actors, technicians, members of the ethnic groups, Black and White and other colours, over fourteen hundred of them. Neither Canwell nor the prosecutor was able to enlist even one of them as a "friendly witness" for the hearings or the trials, and it wasn't because they didn't try. Many of the group, particularly if they were immediately involved with us in any way, were pressured by their families and hounded by the FBI at their businesses or on their jobs.

The feeling of intense loyalty to the theatre was clearly revealed in the story of a young actress, told me by her mother. She was a doctor's daughter, and one evening passed a Canwell investigator as she was leaving her father's office. He asked where she was going in such a hurry.

"To a rehearsal," she answered. "At the Playhouse."

"The Playhouse? Isn't that place shut down?"

She turned on him savagely. "No! Did you think that you and that committee could shut us down? Think again!"

As she stormed out of the office, the investigator shook his head. "I don't understand it. They're all like that."

Sir Tyrone Guthrie, in his autobiography, notes the cohesive solidarity that can develop in a permanent acting company and is absent in the more casual and brief contacts in the profession. There may be personality gaps between individuals, but let the institution come under attack, and they unite to rend the attacker. We had developed a real ensemble, without which no theatre can ever achieve great distinction. We should have been permitted a longer life.

I wish I could report that all the activity recorded in this chapter was unique, or a lone incident, but you know it wasn't. It was simply a small flurry, one of many over the years, in the struggle of some to maintain the democratic process in the United States. John Adams, second president of the United States, had a personal animus toward democracy and once said, "Remember, democracy never lasts long. It soon wastes, exhausts, and murders itself. There never was a democracy yet that did not commit suicide."

It frightens me sometimes to see indications that Adams may have been right, that this great country really does have a self-destructive impulse. For example, a few years after our ordeal, we witnessed the advent of that noxious character Senator Joe McCarthy, who charged everyone, including Presidents Truman and Eisenhower, with being "soft on Communism." And at the time I wrote this, the media was labelling every protest march as Communist-led or inspired, a shabby attempt to avoid confronting real problems that answers nothing and has never solved anything.

But this memoir is the story of a theatre and the lives of the people who created it and worked in it. Our charming building, with some nice modernization by the university, still stands at the corner of 41st and University Way in Seattle and is being successfully used by the Drama Department of the university for a generation of students who have never heard of us, or of the hearings and the trials.

University Way has changed considerably. Where in our day there was a dreary cleaning establishment, a small grocery store, and gas station are now substantial office and bank buildings, and, next to the bank, a very nice continental restaurant.

One October day in 1969, I sat at a window of that restaurant, looking down and across at the theatre, and remembered that it was forty years before, almost to the day, that we opened the Playhouse with George Bernard Shaw's *Major Barbara*.

And the elm tree that made its first appearance in a teacup at a Sunday night supper so many years before still shades the building.

AS A FOOTNOTE TO this chapter, I suppose I should put down, at last, the answer to the question which so many of our friends have wanted to ask over the years but have been too shy or polite to ask: No, we were not then, nor had we ever been. Somehow, it didn't really make much difference, did it?

CHAPTER EIGHTEEN

I never really meant to write a book. If things had turned out differently, this would have been Burton's book. But there were "portents," as it says in Stephen Vincent Benét's *John Brown's Body*, which made that impossible. And so, these many years later, I have tried to sit down and sift through the memories and memorabilia of a lifetime, to get it all down on paper, however imperfectly, for those who remember any part of those times now gone, and for those who are yet to come.

Fists Upon A Star really had its beginnings in 1951, when Burton and a young newspaperman named Bob Johnson got together. During the trials, we were so hounded by the press that I refused to speak to any of them. One day, a man approached me from the gallery and said, "I'm a reporter from the *Post-Intelligencer*." I snapped, "I don't talk to reporters," and walked away.

One of my fellow defendants said, "Don't be so rough on him. He's a friend of ours."

I snorted. "What reporter is a friend of ours? They're all just after headlines."

"Not that one. He's one of our friends."

The young man was Bob Johnson, and he *did* turn out to be one of our friends. I'd never read any of his stories on the trials—just the headlines. All I could ever bear to read were the headlines, because it seemed that every night when we got home, the only thing in the paper would be "James Convicted," "Playhouse Implicated"—that sort of thing. The headlines never encouraged me to read further.

In his stories, Bob was trying to present our side. He told me later that he lost his job as a result of it. When I realized that he *was* a friend, I apologized to him, and he got very interested in us and the Playhouse. He used to come out to watch rehearsals, and eventually he and Burton started to write a book. For some reason, though we never had produced *John Brown's Body,* they chose an extract from it to use as their title. As things turned out, they hadn't time to do much more than start their book. But in tribute to them both, I kept the wish and the title, and have used them in this book.

During the time of the hearings and trials, when Burton was teaching summer classes at the Banff School of Fine Arts in Alberta, the head of the school said to him, "Burton, when this is over, come to Canada. Come to Banff. I'm planning bigger and better things for the school, and you can be helpful." To the eternal credit of the Banff School and its administrators, no action or censure was ever taken against him there after the hearings, or indeed after his trial and conviction, nor did they allow anyone else to harass him or take action against him while he was there, though I understand that the FBI made at least one attempt.

So we taught in Banff that summer, after the Playhouse ceased to exist. That was when Burton and Bob began to think about writing the story of all that had happened. Following our stint at the Banff School, we went to Saskatchewan to teach a two-week workshop in drama for the Saskatchewan Arts Board, the second such visit we had made. They were giving classes for community people, and the prospects for growth and development were very exciting. But even with prospects ahead, the strain and trouble had taken their toll.

During that summer, I could see that Burton was failing fast. We were frantic—our daughter, our friends, myself—but there seemed to be no way to stem the ebb tide. One day after we returned home, I went to Burton's doctor and pleaded, "What should we be doing that we're not doing?"

He looked away from me for a long time before he spoke. "I don't know," he said at last. And then, softly, "Did you ever hear of someone dying of a broken heart?"

My husband died on November 13, 1951. His grip on life and all he loved had been unloosed at last, but it had taken portents.

Someone remarked at the time that November 13, 1951, was the date of the opening of the first University of Washington production in our former theatre.

CHAPTER NINETEEN

In one of the early drafts of this book, I gave titles to each of the chapters. I titled the first one, without too much imagination I'm afraid, "Beginnings." All beginnings, of course, come eventually to some sort of end.

My husband's bright beginnings came to an end with the loss of his theatre. His death in 1951 was really just the final extension of that end. But his ideas and his influence still go on, I know, through the thousands of students he worked with, the thousands of people who saw him perform, spoke to him, met him, were touched by him; and through his daughter and her children, and now their children, who carry in them some small part of what it was that made Burton James place his fists upon a star. It's something like the ever-widening ripples that spread across the water when you skip a stone. Action and reaction and after-effects that can't be seen from the beginning point but are there all the same.

When Burton and I taught at Banff, he used to love to drive up into the mountains to a most beautiful lake. He said often that it was the most perfect place he'd ever seen. It was so still there, peaceful and lovely, and he called it heaven. "If I had my way," he'd say, stretched out under the trees, watching the changing shadows on the incredibly blue water, "I'd just stay right here for eternity." I scattered his ashes there when I returned to Canada for good, the summer after his death.

And when I think of Burton now, I think of him by that lake, with wildflowers blooming, and ripples spreading from the shore.

My life went on. I was blessed by new friends, who made a place for me in their lives, and by a happy quirk of fate that enabled me to keep working in the theatre long past the age when I might reasonably have expected to have been put out to pasture. I have had many good and happy years in Canada, first with the Saskatchewan Arts Board and then with Globe Theatre, building a climate for theatre in the province and in my adopted country.

When someone talks or writes of a life full of memories of experiences lived to the full in growing up and growing old, reviewing the past might seem to be a trifle tedious. But remembering so much of yesterday's work, and the struggles in which we were involved, those memories seem as contemporary as today's headlines. All the problems we saw emerging nearly fifty years ago have reached a climax today. Then, we thought that time and hard work would obviate the difficulties, but now time is of the essence. Will there be time before global disaster, from war or pollution, overtakes us, or will the future be silence? We don't know. The trouble with life today is that the future is not what it used to be—the future is now, and it doesn't seem to be working.

Rusty Schweickart, the astronaut, speaking in Saskatoon in the spring of 1971 during Earth Awareness week, said: "Unless we solve the problems of this planet, that we viewed from space and which we were able to blot out with our thumb held at arm's length, it will be whirling through space as dead as the moon … and there isn't much time. Earth has the same limitations as a space ship, and no back-up systems as we had. If we blow it here, there's no other place to go."

I mentioned in my "Beginnings" chapter the inheritances and environmental pressures that guided me into the pattern that became a way of life. My inheritance gave me excellent health and lots of energy, and my environment gave me standards that have served me all my life—courage when courage was needed, and a determination to carry through with any project, no matter how difficult or frustrating, to complete what was begun.

Looking back from the vantage point of more than eighty years, I would have to say there's been more good than bad. My marriage could well have been described with that phrase from the fairy tales, "and they lived happily ever after." We had an essential ingredient for a happy marriage—shared attention toward objective shared concerns. My work with my husband, and all the wonderful people who worked with us, was a memorable learning experience for me—and for them too, I gather. I meet them now, years afterward, or receive letters from them, and they all talk about those happy Playhouse days—what we thought, our philosophy, how we worked—all of the things I have tried to touch upon in the preceding chapters of this book. We had many victories, some discouragements and defeats, but never once did all of us succumb to them at the same time. We always had the spiritual and physical stamina to stand up, lend a hand, and go on.

I remember the wonderful Black people who worked with us in the Federal Theatre on WPA, where I came to know the dedication they brought to something they thought important and rewarding, and we grew to understand and love each other. The project was set up to answer an emergency of the devastating Depression. If only an enlightened government had seen fit to develop a National Arts Project with representation in the Cabinet, what a different story the theatre, which holds "a mirror up to nature," might reflect today!

In this rapidly changing world, the theatre is changing too, and I must confess that some of the changes appall me. Sir Tyrone Guthrie once said that theatre should lift, but he hoped not uplift, the audience. I think it should do both. Too often, it does neither—one merely looks on without involvement. When theatre both lifts and uplifts, it fulfils its historic objective, which is to reveal some divine intention and help man to better understand his relationship with God or the forces which govern his life.

It still happens. In June 1969, I was both lifted and uplifted by the inaugural theatre production of the National Arts Centre in Ottawa—a play called *The Ecstasy of Rita Joe* by a brilliant Canadian playwright, George Ryga. The play's theme is the tragic struggle of the Indian, particularly the Indian woman, who too often faces disaster when she moves from the reservation to the perilous adjustments of the big city.

Through the years, Burton and I counted as our greatest victories the achievement of some individual who only dreamed he had potential for creative work until he found himself in a situation where he received encouragement and help. When we taught at Banff, one of our young students was a boy named George Ryga. My husband, who was keenly perceptive, said, "That kid has something." I would like to think that he knows now how right he was.

Playwrights today, frantically concerned with breaking forms apparently for breaking's sake, seem pushed into a desperate frenzy. In *The Ecstasy of Rita Joe,* Ryga has succeeded, for the content breaks the form, which is as it should be. I am compelled to say that I think this work will be recognized someday as one of Canada's first great plays.

But what about the other changes in "modern" theatre? There is a great deal of discussion, pro and con, about bawd and nudity in productions. There is, in my opinion, nothing wrong with bawd when it clarifies by word or action some necessary question in the play. Nor is there anything wrong with nudity, though personally I think it more appropriate at the swimming pool or on a beach—good taste and custom should govern that. But when either bawd or nudity is used to titillate the jaded sensibilities of the overdressed, overfed, and sometimes overdrunk members of an audience, or for profit, it is out of place and should be in some other establishment of the sort usually designated for such entertainment. Dressing actors in their skins seems to be a highly unnecessary, if economical, way of costuming a play, and generally offers nothing more, to my way of thinking, than a curious distraction to any content the play might have.

The theatre—live actors for a living audience—will go on, in spite of all the usual, or unusual, "slings and arrows." It has endured in the past, for from time immemorial it has been part of man's heritage. It will continue to show "the very age and body of the time his form and pressure." Some of it will be very good, some very bad, and a great deal mediocre, but time will sift the values.

When human achievements outdistance even the wildest imaginings of the science fiction writers, dislocations in philosophy, manners, and mores must follow, and inevitably the theatre reflects these dislocations. The artist sees the present as it is, and in consequence, prophetically, the future in the present. In my time, men have paced across the last frontiers and walked upon the moon. I would be much happier about our achievements if all men were walking "safe and dry shod on the shifting sands" of planet Earth as well. Be that as it may, the "players cannot keep counsel. They'll tell all"—ultimately.

So, I have written this memoir. Some may say I have written with bitterness in places. I can't deny it. What I have recorded are my memories of my life and it has contained joys, victories, struggles, and defeats. Some of my memories are bitter, and writing of them has been a painful and traumatic experience. It is impossible for me, still, to think of the untimely death of a good and honourable man without bitterness. Perhaps that is where the root of the bitterness lies, in that loss. But as Bernard Shaw said of his friend William Morris, "You can lose a man like that by your own death, but not by his."

There is a Tibetan proverb: "Not to be cheered by praise, not to be grieved by blame, but to know thoroughly one's own virtues or powers are the characteristics of an excellent man." We tried all our lives, Burton and I, not to be overly cheered nor grieved, but to achieve excellence in our lives and work.

The experiences of my life, even though they may not all have been ones that I would have chosen had I been given the opportunity, have all been *my* experiences, and I am grateful for what they taught me.

EPILOGUE

Rita Shelton Deverell

"They Looked Awfully Poor"

Seven decades have past since Florence Bean James arrived in Regina and her newly adopted Canada to work and live until her last breath. "Mrs. James," as she was most frequently addressed, was in her early sixties then: handsome, fashionable, urbane, a cigarette always in her hand. She'd just come from the United States, which was much richer in things, including sophistication, in 1952.

As we know from Florence's last chapters in *Fists Upon a Star,* she'd managed to leave Seattle not owing anyone any money. This was amazing, since her theatre had been forced into bankruptcy. Florence owed no one. And, in a spectacular act of denial, Seattle did not think it owed Florence and Burton James. There was no trace of the huge contributions they'd made to civilization in the Pacific Northwest. The slate was wiped clean. This epilogue is about Florence's contributions to Saskatchewan and Canadian society, her new balance sheet of debits and credits.

Canada had always seemed impoverished to Mrs. James. But not now.

> I used to come to Canada and they looked awfully poor to me when I'd come across the border. I used to be glad that

> my immigrant parents, grandparents, had come to the States and not to Canada. I thought that was an advantage.
>
> And I'd never earned any money really for theatre work until I came to Canada, or gotten any recognition for anything—except maybe a jail sentence—anywhere else ... [1]

When Florence immigrated, Saskatchewan did not yet have full electricity. Farming was the largest industry—family farms run by generations of individuals. Most of the small towns did not need or have hotels where a traveler might be put up overnight.

What Saskatchewan *had* though, which was a remarkable achievement, was an Arts Board. In a truly dramatic, historical irony, at the same time that the State of Washington legislature resolved to have an un-American activities committee, Saskatchewan's legislature voted in favour of an Arts Board. Tommy Douglas's Cooperative Commonwealth Federation, the first social democratic government in North America, had been elected in 1944. In 1948 the CCF proclaimed, as a priority, the Saskatchewan Arts Board to give "the people ... the opportunity to participate in music, drama, visual arts, handicrafts, and the other arts."

The Arts Board's Annual Report in 1952 further elaborates its mission. The Saskatchewan Arts Board's ambitious activities are "designed to help people enjoy a fuller, more satisfying community life." The arts were seen as creating community in a province without a decent auditorium in the capital city. With great foresight a small province supported the arts in a country that did not yet have a Canada Council. We Canadians had not acknowledged that federal subsidy to the arts was a good thing. Saskatchewan saw the light first and put its money on the line.

The James team had made their first appearance in the province in 1950, two years after the Arts Board's birth. The Board's 1951 Annual Report to the Honourable Woodrow Lloyd, Minister of Education, notes:

> A workshop, dealing with the problems of production and acting in small communities, was conducted by Mr. and Mrs. Burton James, of the Seattle Repertory Playhouse, in

> late August. Forty people were registered and many others joined this group from time to time.... From several sources requests have come in for a second such Workshop.... Plans are now being made for this to take place, again in August, at the Qu'Appelle Valley Centre, and for a longer interval.[2]

The 1952 Annual Report records:

> The Saskatchewan Arts Board sponsored Drama Workshop at the Qu'Appelle Valley Centre during August 1951, was again directed by Mr. and Mrs. Burton James, the distinguished community theatre directors from Seattle....
>
> The Board has plans made for a further and larger workshop next August, encouraged by the interest shown and the enthusiasm for this kind of activity....
>
> The Saskatchewan Arts Board expresses its sincere regret in reporting the unexpected death ... of Mr. Burton James. The rich contribution he made from his experience of theatre to the Drama Workshop is deeply appreciated.[3]

Thereafter, Florence James appears permanently, and alone, in Saskatchewan. She had lost everything, as Seattle friend Helen Taverniti observed, and yet she was "quite cheerful." Florence had lost her theatre, her life's work, her husband, her reputation, her central place in Seattle society. And yet she is cheerful. Why?

Perhaps because she has found her philosophic "home." The same 1953 Annual Report that names Mrs. James as a permanent hire asserts the Arts Board's imaginative worldview:

> In times which are full of tension it is difficult for any of us to decide on the best use of our energies but we can try to meet the challenge of building creative attitudes in our immediate environment. The most reliable security against destructive influences is the development of human creative effort. This can be stimulated wherever there are people—in our cities, our towns, our homes. It can only come from within the individual.[4]

Florence had certainly experienced times of tension and destructive influences. And she was the person the Arts Board turned to to develop human creative powers, to help that power grow out of the flat but fertile prairie ground.

> During August, the Saskatchewan Arts Board was able to procure the services of Mrs. Florence James to direct a third Drama Workshop ... conducted at the Qu'Appelle Valley Centre.
>
> Following upon the Drama Workshop, a number of interested people attended a brief provincial drama conference.... The conference recommended the appointment by the Board of a drama specialist who would be available throughout the year, with the aim of making the Workshop with year-round consultant services an integrated training programme.
>
> Consequently, Mrs. Florence James, who is already known here for her competence as a director and teacher of drama, was appointed to the staff.[5]

Florence is off and running. She's been given a chance to use her enormous intelligence, skill, competence, and creative effort to develop the creativity of others and to build community.

> Because of the requests which have been made for her services, Mrs. James has already visited many places in the past few months. Two play groups have been organized in the Tisdale-Carrot River area, workshops and rehearsals have been conducted at Yorkton, Prince Albert and North Battleford. Mrs. James also assisted with the program at a Co-op Women's Guild meeting of approximately 90 delegates, at the Qu'Appelle Valley Centre in October. Mrs. James also served as director-producer for the United Church pageant, "The Triumphs of Faith," presented in Regina in November.[6]

Thus the annual reports of the Saskatchewan Arts Board read for the next fifteen years. When Florence retires in 1968 the building at the Summer School of the Arts in Fort Qu'Appelle, where she coached so many and directed numerous plays, is re-named James Hall in her honour.

Mrs. James travels to a huge number of communities geographically and to different communities of interests and skills. She travels, as she would later say to me, "the length and breadth of this province," to hundreds of locations. All are inspired, all grow and create, and Florence perceptively begins her drama teaching at the level of skill that each group has. Anything and anybody she touches gains in confidence, purpose, style, awards, and rewards. Who knew they had that much in them?

The first year of Florence's permanent position we learn that she is venturing outside Saskatchewan and influencing Canada. Saskatchewan had hired a super-nova and a workhorse.

> The Saskatchewan Arts Board was asked to give assistance, through Mrs. James, to the Saskatchewan branch of the Dominion Drama Festival, especially in view of the fact that Saskatchewan will play host to the Festival in 1955, Saskatchewan's Golden Jubilee year. Mrs. James was able to persuade Mr. Patterson, general manager of the Stratford Shakespearean Festival, to contribute an article on this highly successful Canadian venture to a forthcoming issue of "Saskatchewan Community." Subsequently the Saskatchewan Arts Board was able to reciprocate the courtesy by agreeing to arrange auditions for Saskatchewan actors and actresses for the Stratford Festival's Artistic Director.[7]

As for the neighbouring prairie provinces, a small debate rages about whether Saskatchewan should lend its Drama Consultant's artistic hand to Manitoba and Alberta. The Arts Board's Drama Committee has a letter "from the Manitoba Drama League requesting Mrs. James' services for provincial adjudications there, May 25 and 26. It was agreed that if Mrs. James could fit it in, she could do it on the basis of expenses. Although the Saskatchewan Arts Board was designed primarily to serve Saskatchewan, we were concerned about the development of the arts elsewhere in Canada."[8]

"Concerned about the Arts in Canada"

Saskatchewan could be seen to be way ahead of Canada. Florence helped push and shape the centre of the universe—the central cities of Ottawa, Toronto, Montreal, and Stratford—from her outpost in Regina. There are parallels in her earlier work certainly. In Seattle she and Burton were way ahead of New York. They pushed and shaped United States theatre from their outpost in Seattle.

Perhaps what made the theatre scene in Saskatchewan different from the rest of Canada in the 1950s were three unique assets: the Arts Board, Florence James, and the notion that the arts had social, communal, and political purposes as well as cultural intent. The amateur/professional divide was not the important one for Florence, Burton, and their Seattle colleagues. The term they used to describe their work was "serious." The work was not approached lightly.

> *Marjorie Nelson Steinbrueck, former Seattle Repertory Playhouse actress:*
>
> The attitude of this theatre was very professional, even though everyone had a job during the day and they came at night to work. There was a discipline ... Florence and Burton—very much both ...
>
> I remember the fun of everybody working together and her having a wonderful and open laissez-faire attitude to letting things happen ... But always in the background she had a very sharp eye and a good staging sense ... Pop James was there to give the final touches ...
>
> They worked well together. There was really this amazing camaraderie ... and a sense that you could work hours and hours far into the night and people wouldn't care. There was a different kind of attitude than we have today to giving oneself to this dream of having a great theatre.
>
> So the theatre was not off the cuff. It was carefully organized ... The Jameses were, too, in their own way. The work was regulated extremely well. I always had a sense that somehow they could always make it work even though there was often very little money ...

> I would say of all of them, Mrs. James was the workhorse. Pop was much more flamboyant and liked to be looked up to in a way. Florence was far more businesslike. She didn't have any airs. Although she had a much more foreboding personality to me at the time because of her aloofness …
>
> This was our space. This was our part of the world and we owned it …. We felt at home in the community, the University District. The theatre was respected.[9]

This serious attitude, respect for the work and the people who did it, Florence brought to Saskatchewan. She gained the respect of the province's equally serious farmers, teachers, church and synagogue women's auxiliaries, and little theatres. In 1954 Florence characterizes the people she works with in her consultant's report:

> I would like to add how impressed I have been with the composition of these groups—the maturity of the people, the wide range of community interests represented, the ministers, lawyers, local carpenters, housewives, and shopkeepers working together to make their community a more interesting and exciting place to live.[10]

Florence shared some of the memories of her travels with me more than twenty years later. She didn't drive, but travelled by train, and was very proud of her ability to tough out the winters:

> One of the first things, I'd been teaching summer school and there was a young lady there from Carrot River …. And I think she was a minister's wife and she was interested in developing a drama program. I said to Norah [Norah McCollough, then secretary of the Arts Board], "Well I'm off to Carrot River tomorrow."
>
> She said, "Oh do you know what it's like up there? They're having a blizzard. You haven't got a fur coat." And I said, "listen, I wasn't hired 'weather permitting' …"

> I had to change I think at Melville to get another train to Carrot River and the trainmen had come in all covered … It was snowing …
>
> And a lady came along and I asked her where would the hotel be? She looked down. It was I think my first trip out, I learned to travel light. And said, "you've got two—Oh mercy come on"—and she picked up one of the bags and took me to the hotel.[11]

A retired Regina high school teacher, Marge Ziolkowski, was living in Carrot River at the time and remembers Mrs. James' trip. Florence did indeed arrive without a fur coat. She arrived in a cape. This was considered most dramatic and eccentric by the citizens of the town. The United Church minister's wife had requested the visit, and the drama workshop was held in the church. Mrs. James, while addressing the group, put her foot up on the pew. The citizens were shocked a second time.

But what is mainly remembered is neither the cape nor the leg on the pew. Mrs. Ziolkowski remembers that Florence took a group of people with no training, with little obvious talent, a stiff group of people, "and did not worry about what they could not do." Mrs. James had every confidence in the Carrot River hardware store owner, high school teacher, and church members. The new drama group was successful and confident after her coaching.

Meanwhile, in the rest of Canada, theatre was much more a gentleman's hobby for the well-off or for those with enough time away from paid jobs to pursue a labour-intensive pastime. Florence shared her "serious" ethic and that helped to drive Canadian theatre towards professionalism. Her distinction was not whether one was paid and therefore professional, or not paid and therefore amateur. Florence's distinction was serious versus froth:

> The standards of both plays and productions in the Dominion Drama Festival were this year much above last year's presentations at Hamilton, Ontario. So much so that many people questioned whether the … Festival was demanding too high a level of professionalism. But there is no virtue in

> something labeled amateur that reflects mere lack of skills and knowledge. Our work must count for something and the contribution being made in the Dominion by the Stratford Festival is having its effect. Canadian theatre, whether amateur or professional is on the march.[12]

When Florence met a lack of standards, or a frivolous attitude in her travels, she could be quite scathing. As her former son-in-law observed, "Florence did not suffer fools gladly."

> On November 21, I left for Marshall. Last August my workshop there came to an abrupt stop because of an early harvest. People in the group dropped out one by one as the fields ripened and they were needed on the land. While there last summer I had them working on good plays—three one-acts for a fall production and a three-act play for spring. When I arrived in Marshall I was horrified to see a very bad play that we had rejected added to the program at the insistence of a lady director in the community ... There is always it seems this lady to contend with in every community, very ambitious and not at all capable. I was quite at a loss what to do. I couldn't say, "Take it out," but when she saw the others at work she decided she hadn't had enough time to work on hers and withdrew it from the program, to everyone's satisfaction.[13]

"Our Work Must Count for Something"

In the 1950s Florence was received in Saskatchewan the way she had been throughout her working life. There were those who saw her as a dazzling theatre wizard who could solve all their staging problems. These fans knew nothing of the philosophies and theories of community building behind the skill.

On the other hand, there were those who understood and respected the philosophies and theoretical framework behind Florence's competence. One such was J. M. C. Meiklejohn who, in his memoir *Theatre Education in Canada After World War II*, describes the drama scene and his understanding of Florence and Burton's life situation:

...[I]n 1950, I was invited to be a speaker at the annual meeting of the Western Canada Theatre Conference in Regina. This organization was started at the beginning of the Second World War by the four western regions of the Dominion Drama Festival.... [T]he Conference decided to terminate itself in view of the revival of the DDF national festival.... I had arranged to fly on to attend the U.S. national children's theatre conference in Minneapolis and consequently was catching a plane from Regina, leaving at half past three in the morning. A party was arranged to see me onto the plane. This party consisted of:

–Mary Ellen Burgess, Physical Fitness and Recreation Division, Department of Extension, Saskatchewan
–Elsie Mackenzie, Department of Extension, University of Alberta and the Banff School of Fine Arts
–Jessie Richardson, perpetual chairperson of the British Columbia region of the Dominion Drama Festival
–Dick MacDonald, cultural relations for the province of Alberta...
–Donald Wetmore, drama adviser, Department of Education of Nova Scotia
–Burton and Flo James of the Seattle Repertory Theatre.

Burton was a professional actor and director and Florence a qualified speech coach ... They had been on the staff of the Banff School of Fine Arts and just been teaching at Dorothy Somerset's Summer School of the Theatre at UBC. Very shortly after this they became the victims of an extremely vicious attack by Senator McCarthy's Committee on Un-American Activities and were forced out of their theatre in Seattle. Burton died, his friends say of a broken heart, and Flo was found a job by Tommy Douglas in the Arts Board of Saskatchewan....

> I think that it is necessary to remember that in the spring of 1953 when I attended the DDF Final Festival in Victoria, the Stratford Festival was not yet open and the Canada Council was not to be established for four more years. This was the event that would completely alter the whole spectrum of the Arts in Canada.[14]

Florence was able to be a major catalyst for the artistic ferment in Saskatchewan and, through the Dominion Drama Festival, the rest of Canada. Burton James had observed during their trials that the tragedy of the McCarthy era was "not so much the lives it ruined, but the processes it arrested." He wrestled with how he and Florence could ever possibly resume their valuable work.

> *Burton James letter to David Stevens, National Theatre Congress.* This is an interim period and … soon we must go back to work … The alternatives are few. Then, too, time is running out. The fact that I am 63 and Mrs. James will be 60 this year does not help solve the problem, yet somehow all the rich experience of these past years must be put to some use. To re-establish our theatre in Seattle seems out of the question …
>
> There is the Canada scene and the Banff Foundation which is headed by Donald Cameron. Too, last summer Mrs. James and I headed a workshop for the Arts Council of Saskatchewan. We go again this summer and also to Banff … Cameron has planned to make Banff a year-round school … the opportunity for group and community work is offered, as well as the developing of a national Canadian theatre training school.
>
> The atmosphere in Canada is completely different from the States, and their attitude toward the arts, the artist, and the teacher—a combination of recognition and "we need you," leads us to believe that Banff may be the niche for us. I hope so, for it's a kind of pioneering and we like pioneering.[15]

Burton, who died seven months later, obviously did not get to benefit from the Canadian "we need you" attitude of the 1950s. What is breathtaking, though, about Florence's next steps is that in Canada she so successfully reinstituted, re-created, was a catalyst for, the artistic processes that had been arrested in the United States.

Florence simply moved their shared ideas and ideals across the border. She reflected on Burton's notion of a populist theatre:

> He had certain definite ideas that theatre tickets should be low enough so that people could afford them. Our highest price was $1.50 and we had some seats at the side of the building, the auditorium, for $1.25. Kids who came to the theatre paid no more than 25 cents.
>
> People should (be able to) afford the theatre and we were very generous with comps...We were very generous because if they had a desire to see a play—this grew out of my husband's attitude—they should have the opportunity to see it.[16]

Florence placed numerous individuals in civil service and arts positions in Saskatchewan where they could have the same kind of vigorous creative life she had had and was still having. The protégés could make a difference in their towns, cities, and beyond. She knew the theatre was a community-building activity. Florence made it possible for professional theatre to find a home in her new province and in Canada.

"Theatre Belongs to the People"

I met Mrs. James little more than ten years after the founding of the Canada Council, the development that changed everything. In 1971 I was hired by the recently born Globe Theatre to be one of five professional actors who would tour the province from Thanksgiving to Victoria Day, travelling to over two hundred communities in a yellow school bus.

Florence was an elderly white-haired woman sitting in the back of our windowless rehearsal room in the Saskatchewan Centre of the Arts. She was increasingly deaf and blind, and generally asleep, except when she snapped that she couldn't hear us. We should "speak up!" To say that I didn't know Florence's story back then is a thundering understatement. I didn't even know why she was sitting in on our rehearsals.

Five years later I was asked by Ken Kramer, one of the Globe's founding artistic directors, to take on the task of recording Florence's life on reel-to-reel audiotape. The two of us met in her small room in Regina's Canadian National Institute for the Blind residence. Hours talking with Florence then mushroomed into numerous taped conversations in Saskatchewan, Ontario, Vancouver, and Seattle with those who knew her life and work.

One of Florence's funnier anecdotes was about moving to Ottawa in the late 1960s after her retirement from the Arts Board. She told me that she had to come back to Regina where there was lots going on. Ottawa was dull. There was no National Arts Centre yet. It was a civil service town. Everyone went home at 4:00 p.m. Who would live in a place like that if they had a choice?

In Saskatchewan there were theatre performances and rehearsals to watch, tons of music, lectures, and many lively intellectuals with whom to have philosophic arguments. Florence and her Arts Board colleagues had caused Saskatchewan to be a place that Ottawa couldn't rival. With the coming of professional theatre to Saskatoon and the Globe with its extensive provincial tour from Regina, Florence was given, and could justifiably take, a lot of credit.

Florence traced the beginnings of the Globe Theatre to a chat she had with Bette Anderson, another Seattle Repertory Playhouse refugee, also in Canada. Anderson's career in the United States was smashed. For many members of the talented group around the Seattle Repertory Playhouse, there was no way to continue the work they did. Many tried to transplant and never found another ensemble. Others gave up on the arts. But Bette Anderson came to Canada where she, too, had a respected career as a drama educator. Anderson first re-located from Seattle to Vancouver. She worked as an actress and teacher. One of the plays she was in was directed by veteran theatre person Joy Coghill. Coghill reports that the Royal Canadian Mounted Police visited rehearsals. The Mounties wanted to know about Bette Anderson. She was applying for Canadian citizenship. There had been some trouble in the States. The FBI said they had a record on Anderson. Could she possibly make a good Canadian citizen?

Coghill gave Anderson a glowing recommendation. Anderson then moved on to Edmonton, and headed the drama program of the city Parks and Recreation Department. And in 1964 she told Florence James about one of her students from the 1950s, Kenneth Kramer. Ken and

Sue Kramer, said Anderson, wanted to start a fulltime, professional theatre for children in Western Canada. Florence's interest was piqued. One of her great contributions to the State of Washington had been sending high quality plays on tour to schools. Young people saw these shows regardless of geography, race, or economics. This seemed to be an opportunity to do precisely the same thing in Saskatchewan.

The Kramers, said Bette Anderson, were excellent people bursting with talent and energy. Ken had written Anderson from London, England, where he had gone to study at the London Academy of Dramatic Arts. Then he'd gotten an acting job with the touring theatre company of Brian Way, the London Theatre Centre.

Brian Way had the right idea, Kramer wrote to Anderson. Ken had met English-born Sue Richmond in Brian's company. They were getting married. They were coming back to Ken's home. They would start a Brian Way–style theatre. Could Anderson help? Their theatre would be called, in an effort to summon the powers of Shakespeare and the world, "The Globe." It would do the audience participation plays of director and playwright Brian Way and the classics of Shakespeare. The work was to be of the highest professional quality, in the round, close to its audience, and it would take children and their ideas very seriously.

Years earlier, Florence James had brought Brian Way to Saskatchewan. She had suggested that the distinguished creative dramatist, on a Canadian tour himself, be brought in to advise them. The Saskatchewan Arts Board had agreed to pay for Way's trip from Winnipeg to Regina. In an article in the *Regina Leader-Post,* May 16, 1959, Florence invited those interested in theatre for young audiences to meet with him:

> Brian Way, one of the founders of the Educational Drama Association, himself an active leader in child drama and director of London Children's Theatre Company, a professional company of adults acting for children, will be in Regina May 26 to June 5 to conduct afternoon and evening classes at Saskatchewan House.[17]

Florence loved to say that to succeed you needed both "talent and opportunity." The Kramers had talent, but, so far, had been denied opportunity. Other western cities had said "no" to their proposal. They started in Vancouver, where Coghill found them some work. But British Columbia was not interested in supporting an extensive theatre in education. The Kramers went on to Edmonton, where Anderson found classes for them to teach. Alberta was not interested in a serious traveling theatre for young people either.

Florence Bean James immediately saw the value of the work the Kramers wanted to do. Here were two artists with unusual gifts, boundless energy, a unique kind of training, and a vision. As Florence recalled:

> I talked to George Shaw who was then the secretary, or the boss … I told George about the Kramers. And he said there's no money in the budget for the Kramers.
>
> I said we could give them space—space in my office. We were out at the old Saskatchewan House and I had a large office. I said why don't we give them … the use of the telephone and a car and see what they can do to earn their own money. I think it would be marvelous to have them here. And they got started …
>
> One of the first things we did was to have them make a speech and Woodrow Lloyd came and he was very impressed with them and very helpful in getting them started. That was one thing about Woodrow Lloyd. For him the arts were not frills. He could see the educational advantage of these people coming.[18]

Talent without opportunity: Florence James said "yes" to Ken and Sue Kramer and their idea of a touring theatre for young audiences. Regina's Globe Theatre was born.

"We Were Very Impressed with Florence"

The interviews I recorded in the 1970s and 80s with Florence's colleagues, friends, and family made a huge impression on me. They also helped me to understand how the woman I met when she was elderly and somewhat frail had been a force of nature in people's lives, careers, and communities.

The people I spoke with had met Florence in the long prime time of her life and it was as if they got an electrical jolt that stayed with them. Florence James is remembered for her forceful personality, strong character, great intellectual, moral, and artistic courage, and the imprint she left on others.

> *Norah McCullough, former executive secretary, Saskatchewan Arts Board:*
> Florence was more than happy to come to us because … she got away from all this poison and friends had fallen away. Not only that, her trial had cost her an awful lot of money, something like $35,000. They were bankrupt.
>
> And it was sort of hopeless, opportunities in Seattle. Nobody was going to dare engage them.
>
> She was erased … It was kind of an honour wasn't it, to be convicted by that crowd of thugs?[19]

In Saskatchewan too, the *Recreational and Cultural Survey of the State of Washington,* conducted by the Jameses and their son-in-law, Jack Kinzel, surfaced as possibly subversive and was questioned by the Un-American Activities Committee. According to Norah McCullough, this study, which went to the people to ask them their needs and organized communities to solve their own problems, brought its controversial history with it. Education Minister Woodrow Lloyd was disturbed by the rumors he'd heard about the Jameses and *Recreation for All.*

> *Norah McCullough:*
> Woodrow drove me home and he said, "I want to ask you about Florence James and her husband. Do you think they were Communists?"
>
> I said, "I don't think so." And he said, "Well, it seems they were harassed in Seattle because of their leftwing tendencies and because of a proposal he made to the government at that time" … And he said, "Do you know what the proposal was?" And I said, "Yes, I've got a copy."
>
> So I trotted into my little house on Rose Street and found this and took it out to him. And he sat in the car and he

read over the thing. And he said, "Well, it sounds like the Saskatchewan Arts Board."

And I said, "Yes, exactly."[20]

What had been such a controversial idea in Seattle was a welcomed idea in Saskatchewan. Woodrow Lloyd approved. David Smith, the civil servant who designed the Saskatchewan Arts Board, understood the place of an arts board in their new society.

David Smith:
The Arts Board was one of the first things that was set up and most clearly expressed all of the things that were actually accomplished—most clearly expressed what we had in mind—a radically different kind of adult education than you find anywhere else...

I designed it ... Shumiatcher (Dr. Morris Shumiatcher, lawyer, 1917–2004) and I wrote the act.

Deverell: Tell me why an Arts Board?

Smith: Adult education in a socialist society ... is highly participatory, that's the new word ... In other words we were a democratic one in which the citizens make the decisions and determine the policies and determine the program.

It also is a society that values human ingenuity and capacity and creativity ... The purpose of it is full realization or development of these capacities ... and of course ... notions about equality.

Well an Arts Board, one of the things that people do... is to sing and write and sculpt and model and do all these kinds of artistic activities, so an Arts Board indeed is a way of mobilizing the citizen capacities and creativity wherever it may happen to be."[21]

Another initiative for which Florence had been criticized in Seattle was the creation of theatre for and with all kinds of people, including many ethnic groups. It was, of course, the Negro Repertory that caused the most comment. Norah McCullough remembers how Saskatchewan welcomed Florence's particular approach to dealing with the unique creativity of each human being.

> *Norah McCullough:*
> We didn't know what she would do, but we told her that the courses ran for two weeks. And that didn't faze her in the least.
>
> She had a reading and she picked her cast ... She said, "I can put on a production in two weeks" and she did. And we were very impressed. Very impressed. And also ... the quality of her teaching.
>
> She was a follower you see of the Russian, that was another strike against her ... She'd been to Russia and she was a follower of the Russian school of dramatic training where you try to live the part of the person.
>
> *Deverell:* Stanislavski?
>
> *McCullough:* Yes, that's right, method acting. And she was very strong for that. She didn't worry about people's accents and also something she didn't worry about was their physical appearance too much. She felt that a person who was intelligent, who could understand the play, could pull it off.
>
> And we had some quite corny people take part in these things and they worked awfully hard, quite willingly, the long drilling with people coming up on the stage and fussing with each other and moving off. All this kind of thing was done. I thought it was very impressive.[22]

Indeed Florence could and did work with all types of people, some "quite corny." She'd even been known to cast individuals against their will. Her grandson told of Florence virtually abducting an actor she needed. She'd been preparing to rehearse *Jack and the Beanstalk* in Seattle. A problem loomed though: no giant. "One day Grandma was standing at the bus stop." So was an exceedingly tall gentleman. He was bodily catapulted into the theatre, into rehearsals, and to opening night—without any opportunity for refusal—by the small lady with the grey hair.

Bill Harding, one of Saskatchewan's most distinguished civil servants when Florence immigrated, suffered a similar fate to the tall man at the bus stop. Mrs. James needed a Quince for *A Midsummer Night's Dream*. Harding would have to take time away from re-organizing the province into counties, the creation of Medicare, etc. He never shared Florence's theatrical enthusiasms, but she bullied him into serving his time in Shakespeare.

Observers of the Jameses' theatre over time were not gripped by the spectacle. They were not gripped by the staging. What mesmerized them was the intellectual focus of the acting and the clarity and meaning of the text. Audiences and theatre people alike were attracted by the strength, not the entertainment, of the work.

> *Louise Hastert Pennock, former Seattle Repertory Playhouse actress:*
> So some of the things they did there had a great influence—not only on my desire to get into the theatre, but on my personal life in setting me to think. I remember those plays so vividly …
>
> I will never forget those plays.[23]

"Florence James Bullied Us"

When Florence Bean James came to Saskatchewan in the 1950s she was totally capable of delivering highly polished theatre work according to formal and informal accounts. She created performances that made a lasting and profound impression. And she was at the height of her career.

It is therefore not surprising that in 1957 Florence was elected to the Board of Directors of the Canadian Theatre Centre. This group essentially took on the task of raising standards and kick-starting Canadian professional theatre. The board was a star-studded roster of "who's who," the founders of most of the developments in theatre that we are proud of sixty years later.

> *December 17, 1957, Regina Leader-Post*
> Mrs. Florence B. James, Drama Consultant of the Saskatchewan Arts Board, has just been elected to the Board of Directors of the Canadian Theatre Centre. The … Centre

> will speak for professional and educational theatre in Canada and will eventually join the International Theatre Institute representing Canada …
>
> The Chairman of the Canadian Theatre Centre is Mr. Mavor Moore of Toronto and the Board of Directors include Mr. Jean-Louis Roux, Montreal, vice chairman, Miss Dorothy Somerset of Vancouver, secretary, and Mr. Tom Patterson of Stratford, treasurer. Mr. Dennis Sweeting of Toronto is executive secretary.[24]

Helen Taverniti, former Playhouse musician and composer, said it is ironic to think of Florence "so dishonoured in Seattle and so honoured in Canada." Florence, in fact, gets the highest honour in 1976 from the Canadian Conference of the Arts:

> The *Diplôme d'honneur* is presented annually to a Canadian who has made a sustained contribution to the cultural life of the country … More than 70 of the visionaries and creators of Canada's rich cultural identity, including Glenn Gould, Maureen Forrester, Oscar Peterson, and Roch Carrier, have been recognized since the award's inception in 1954. The award is in the form of a silver talisman designed by the late Bill Reid.[25]

Upon her death, Mavor Moore, the revered arts journalist, producer, and one of Florence's fellow Canadian Theatre Centre board members, had this to say in the *Globe and Mail*:

> *Theatre pioneer was a welcome U.S. invader*
> "The world will not be saved on the political, military or economic level but on the level of education and art."
> Saskatchewan Theatre Pioneer
> Florence James (1892–1988)
>
> In Regina tomorrow they will be holding a memorial event for Florence Bean James. She died Jan. 18 at the age of 95. Although she was already past 60 when she arrived in Saskatchewan from

> Seattle, the news of her death merited a full-page obituary in *The Regina Leader-Post.* But outside of the theatre community, and outside of the West, it appears to have gone unnoticed—perhaps because we've paid very little attention to the phenomenon she personified: the benign American invasion of Canada that accompanied the McCarthy years in the United States.
>
> Florence James was one of the most remarkable of a small group of remarkable women who bullied the performing arts in this country into professionalism, not because she believed in art for art's sake but because she believed the arts have a job to do. She once quoted to me James Baldwin's remark, "Life is more important than art, that's what makes art so important." Born in Idaho and trained in Boston and New York as actor, director and playwright, she reversed the trend and came to Canada to fulfill her ambition. Her ambition was to make human beings, not money.
>
> ...She was godmother to the now nationally important Globe Theatre, and to generations of young people who learned to share her social conscience and her love of theatre as its crucible. ...
>
> There will be those today who see the Florence Jameses as political infiltrators bent on subverting our youth, just as the burghers of Seattle did ... They miss the point that she and others like her grasped: that if you want to build human beings, you start with their humanity, not with their color, sex, class, consumer status or political persuasion. You build a society in which humanity can grow ... Then you keep working at it, through education and art, until you die.[26]

"What Else Needs to Be Done?"

And yet, a scan of the contemporary scene suggests that we still can reach out in our time, in different ways, towards what Florence James and the Saskatchewan Arts Board accomplished from 1950 to 1980. The mere existence of professional arts, supported by the government—Florence would never have seen that as the highest pinnacle of achievement.

Professional arts, rather, are an option that an enlightened society owes those with the talent and inclination the opportunity to pursue.

All other citizens are owed the opportunity to participate and enjoy. Full access to the arts to build a more satisfying community life is what wise governments, Florence would say, owe to all:

> In times which are full of tension it is difficult for any of us to decide on the best use of our energies but we can try to meet the challenge of building creative attitudes in our immediate environment.[27]

From Florence's philosophic vantage point there are four areas in particular where we still have work to do. In these areas we are frequently less adventuresome in our arts programming now than we were from Florence's arrival in Saskatchewan in the 1950s through to the flourishing of professionalism in the 1970s and 80s. First, she had a philosophy of casting beyond race, accent, or other traditional barriers for which many still strive in Canada:

> There's no distinction. When talent emerges, whether it's black or white or any other colour, it's there. It's completely integrated.
>
> When talent emerges it doesn't make any difference what colour it is. This is the strangest thing—that somehow or other in my generation and your generation that you had to learn that there isn't any distinction.[28]

Second, the extensive theatre tours, especially to young people "throughout the length and breadth" of the province, have almost disappeared. Can a rich society no longer afford them? Third, there are fewer plays created and produced by, for, and about Saskatchewan and its issues. And, finally, the arts now are less participatory, less inclusive, and less available to all sorts and conditions of women, men, and children.

It is hard to keep up with Florence Bean James. Her former son-in-law Jack Kinzel, a longtime Saskatchewan civil servant, reflected on her character.

> *Jack Kinzel:*
> Florence was ... one of the strongest people I know in terms of the will to live, the will to go on, the will to achieve, and

> she was able to relate to the times she was living in and to say, "OK, what else needs to be done?"[29]

There are many things in the world more important than art, more important than theatre, said Florence. There is life. We can look around us with her and say, "What else needs to be done?"

Fists Upon a Star concludes with Florence observing that their theatre building in Seattle is still used "by young people who have never heard of us and our trials." They have heard now, although this, too, has taken a long time.

Ten years after Florence's death, in 1998, the State of Washington started to come to terms with its past. The Harry Bridges Chair in Labour Studies was endowed at the University of Washington, named for the deposed union leader who lost everything as a result of the cold war. Also in 1998, the president of the University of Washington apologized to the descendents of the fired tenured professors, fifty years after the events, and admitted the wrongdoings of the past. *All Powers Necessary and Convenient*, a courtroom play recounting the Canwell hearings by University of Washington drama professor Mark Jenkins, was first staged in 1998 and published by the University of Washington Press in 2000.

Describing the history of the theatre sixty years after Burton and Florence lost their life's work, the University of Washington Drama School's website acknowledges their enormous contributions.

> The School of Drama's Playhouse is the nation's oldest historic theatre building continually in use. Originally a warehouse, the building was re-designed into a theatre space in 1930 by Florence and Burton James, co-founders of the Seattle Repertory Playhouse company.
>
> The Playhouse participated in many of the political and cultural transformations of the twentieth century. A history of the United States could be told by the story of this red-brick theatre.
>
> The Seattle Repertory Playhouse was considered a "civic" theatre that "kept in direct contact with all the activities and needs of a people." ... New dramas by Northwest play-

wrights were regularly produced ... It had the largest theatre education program in the United States, ultimately touring plays by Shakespeare to over 70,000 high school students throughout the state.

The Playhouse continues to play a critical role in training top-notch theatre artists at the School of Drama.[30]

Since 2009 there has been a plaque in the lobby of the renovated Playhouse acknowledging the work of Al Ottenheimer and Florence and Burton James. Photographs and mementoes of their work are on permanent display. The students now know the history of the theatre building in which they learn their craft and who its original creators were.

Florence James:
Remembering was a very traumatic experience. But somehow we survived. We survived.

And one of the marvelous things—was this ensemble that we had. Every one of those people suffered in one way or another, either by being interviewed by FBI agents or by their parents who wanted them to get away from the Playhouse and forget the whole thing and hope to goodness they wouldn't be caught up in it.

Not one ever appeared as a witness against us. Tyrone Guthrie in his book makes a point: He said if you have an ensemble in the theatre nothing else matters. He said if you haven't … it doesn't matter what your subsidy is or your glamour, you have to have an ensemble—and they stuck.

I'll tell you something else, Rita, I always got from my father. Two things that I'll never forget: Pay your bills, don't run bills.

And the other thing is: Stand up for what you believe. And it was never any effort for me when I felt that I was right to stand up for what I thought and express myself. And instead of killing me it made me tougher.[31]

Florence Bean James made Saskatchewan stronger, the arts in Saskatchewan and all of Canada tougher. And the many, many individuals and communities who were touched by her standards, her ensemble, her creative drive, can still reach forward to do what else needs to be done.

NOTES

Abbreviations:
FBJ= Florence Bean James
SAB= Saskatchewan Arts Board
SRP= Seattle Repertory Playhouse

1 Florence Bean James in conversation with the author, Regina, 1976–77.
2 1951 *Annual Report of the Saskatchewan Arts Board to the Legislature*, p. 11.
3 1952 *Annual Report of the SAB*, p. 12.
4 1953 *Annual Report of the SAB*, preamble.
5 1953 *Annual Report of the SAB*, p. 4.
6 1953 *Annual Report of the SAB*, p. 4.
7 1953 *Annual Report of the SAB*, pp. 11–12.
8 Drama Committee Report, SAB, FBJ, Oct.–Nov. 1955.
9 Marjorie Nelson Steinbrueck, former Seattle Repertory Playhouse actress, in conversation with author, Seattle, 1988.
10 Drama Committee Report, SAB, FBJ, January 15, 1954.
11 FBJ in conversation with author, Regina, 1976–77.
12 Report on Drama Consultant Services, FBJ, March 1–June 1, 1955, p. 2.
13 Report on Drama Consultant Services, FBJ, October–November, 1955.
14 J. M. C. Meiklejohn, *Theatre Education in Canada after World War II: A Memoir*, Denis W. Johnston, ed. *Theatre Research in Canada/Recherches Théatrales au Canada* 12, no. 2 (1991). Online at http://journals.hil.unb.ca/index.php/tric/article/view/7263/8322 . Full memoir, National Archives of Canada.
15 Letter from Burton James to David Stevens, National Theatre Congress, April 14, 1951.
16 FBJ in conversation with author, Regina, 1976–77.
17 *Regina Leader-Post*, May 16, 1959, provided by FBJ.
18 FBJ in conversation with author, Regina, 1976–77.
19 Norah McCullough, former executive secretary, SAB, in conversation with author, Guelph, Ontario, 1988.
20 Norah McCullough, former executive secretary, SAB, in conversation with author, Guelph, Ontario, 1988.
21 David Smith, former head of Adult Education Department, Saskatchewan, in conversation with author, Barrie, Ontario, 1988.

22 Norah McCullough, former executive secretary, SAB, in conversation with author, Guelph, Ontario, 1988.
23 Louise Hastert Pennock, former SRP actress, in conversation with author, Seattle, 1988.
24 *Regina Leader-Post*, Dec. 17, 1957, provided by FBJ.
25 Canadian Conference of the Arts website, 2009.
26 Mavor Moore, *The Globe and Mail*, Feb. 13, 1988.
27 1953 *Annual Report of the SAB*, preamble.
28 FBJ in conversation with author, Regina, 1976–77.
29 Jack Kinzel, former SRP actor, FBJ's former son-in-law, Saskatchewan civil servant, in conversation with author, Regina, 1988.
30 University of Washington Theatre Department website, 2013.
31 FBJ in conversation with author, Regina, 1976–77.

APPENDIX 1

Seattle Repertory Playhouse productions, 1928–29 to 1947–48

As compiled in an annotated typescript by Florence James, lightly edited

Seattle Repertory Playhouse Repertoire

FIRST SEASON 1928–29

Juno and the Paycock .... O'Casey
The Jest .... Benelli
The Romantic Young Lady .... Sierra
The Wild Duck .... Ibsen
Rip Van Winkle .... Jefferson
In His Image .... Ethel
The Ticket-of-Leave Man .... Taylor

SECOND SEASON 1929–30

The Guardsman .... Molnár
The Master Builder .... Ibsen
The Romantic Young Lady .... Sierra
Little Women .... Alcott–De Forest
A Bill of Divorcement .... Dane
L'Envoi .... Ottenheimer
Six Characters in Search of an Author .... Pirandello
The Chaste Mistress .... King

THIRD SEASON 1930–31

Major Barbara .... Shaw
Leading Man .... Kimball
A Christmas Carol .... Dickens–Ashley
Peer Gynt .... Ibsen
Our American Cousin .... Taylor
The Living Corpse .... Tolstoy

FOURTH SEASON 1931–32

Aren't We All? .... Lonsdale
Romeo and Juliet .... Shakespeare
Uncle Tom's Cabin .... Stowe–Aiken
Green Fire .... Hughes
Faust .... Goethe
The Cherry Orchard .... Chekhov
The Wild Duck .... Ibsen
Peer Gynt .... Ibsen
A Doll's House .... Ibsen

FIFTH SEASON 1932–33

Liliom .... Molnár
Mad, Bad and Dangerous to Know .... King
The Comedy of Errors .... Shakespeare
Prunella .... Housman & Barker
In Abraham's Bosom .... Green
Funny Man .... Ottenheimer
The Sunken Bell .... Hauptmann
The Living Corpse .... Tolstoy
The Vikings at Helgeland .... Ibsen

SIXTH SEASON 1933–34

Love and Geography .... Björnson
Richard III .... Shakespeare
Treasure Island .... Stevenson

No More Frontier .... Jennings
Kolokala .... (A Revue)
Volpone .... Jonson
Hay Fever .... Coward
The Master Builder .... Ibsen

SEVENTH SEASON 1934–35

The Tavern .... Cohan
Little Ol' Boy .... Bein
The Blue Bird .... Maeterlinck
Home Chat .... Coward
A Midsummer Night's Dream .... Shakespeare
Squaring the Circle .... Katayev
Private Lives .... Coward
Six Characters in Search of an Author .... Pirandello
Brief Candle .... Powel

EIGHTH SEASON 1935–36

The Hairy Ape .... O'Neill
After Such Pleasures .... Parker
Tom Sawyer .... Twain–Kester
Waiting for Lefty .... Odets
Peer Gynt .... Ibsen
Twelfth Night .... Shakespeare
The Dark Tower .... Woollcott & Kaufman
Noah .... Obey
Stevedore .... Peters & Sklar
Swing, Gates, Swing .... (A Revue)

NINTH SEASON 1936–37

Yellow Jack .... De Kruif–Howard
The Affairs of Anatol .... Schnitzler
The Comedy of Errors .... Shakespeare
Bury the Dead .... Shaw
No More Frontier .... Jennings

Ethan Frome .... Wharton–Davis
As Husbands Go .... Crothers
Autumn Crocus .... Anthony
The Seagull .... Chekhov

TENTH SEASON 1937–38

Boy Meets Girl .... Spewack
The Taming of the Shrew .... Shakespeare
Fly Away Home .... Bennett–White
Anne of Green Gables .... Montgomery–Chadwick
Excursion .... Wolfson
George and Margaret .... Savory
Hymn to the Rising Sun .... Green
She Stoops to Conquer .... Goldsmith
Julius Caesar .... Shakespeare

ELEVENTH SEASON 1938–39

Yes, My Darling Daughter .... Reed
French Without Tears .... Rattigan
Jack and the Beanstalk .... Chorpenning
On Stage (one-acts):
1. Red Head Baker .... Maltz
2. The Happy Journey .... Wilder
3. A Marriage Proposal .... Chekhov
4. The Rising of the Moon .... Gregory
Judgement Day .... Rice
Julius Caesar .... Shakespeare
Andrew Takes a Wife .... Cotton
American Made .... King
The Children's Hour .... Hellman
Our Town .... Wilder
An Enemy of the People .... Ibsen

TWELFTH SEASON 1939–40

Our Town .... Wilder
A Christmas Carol .... Dickens–Donaghey, Gyger
Of Mice and Men .... Steinbeck
The Indian Captive .... Chorpenning
Storm over Patsy .... Bridie
Susan and God .... Crothers
The Barber of Seville .... Rossini
My Heart's in the Highlands .... Saroyan
Die Fledermaus .... Strauss

THIRTEENTH SEASON 1940–41

Tony Draws a Horse .... Storm
Die Fledermaus .... Strauss
The Gentle People .... Shaw
Little Black Sambo .... Chorpenning
Peer Gynt .... Ibsen
Family Portrait .... Coffee–Cowen
Lady Precious Stream .... Hsiung
A Slight Case of Murder .... Runyon–Lindsay
Bertha, the Sewing Machine Girl .... Kremer

FOURTEENTH SEASON 1941–42

The Man Who Came to Dinner .... Hart–Kaufman
Flight to the West .... Rice
The Time of Your Life .... Saroyan
Rumpelstiltskin .... Chorpenning
The Male Animal .... Thurber–Nugent
The Rivals .... Sheridan
Suspect .... Percy–Denham
Thumbs Up! .... (A Revue)
No Mother to Guide Her .... Mortimer

FIFTEENTH SEASON 1942–43

The Walrus and the Carpenter .... Langley
Thumbs Up! .... (A Revue)
Heart of a City .... Storm
Heidi .... Spyri–Miller
My Dear Children .... Turney–Horwin
Jason .... Raphaelson
Papa Is All .... Greene
The Fatal Wedding .... Kremer

SIXTEENTH SEASON 1943–44

The Guardsman .... Molnár
Radio Rescue .... Chorpenning
The Romantic Young Lady .... Sierra
Aladdin and the Wonderful Lamp .... Norris
Counterattack .... Stevenson(s)
Mr. Dooley, Jr. .... Franken–Lewin
Grumpy .... Hodges–Percyval
The Emperor's New Clothes .... Chorpenning
Village Green .... Allensworth
Uncle Rube .... Townsend

SEVENTEENTH SEASON 1944–45

Boy Meets Girl .... Spewack
Here Comes Tomorrow .... (A Revue)
Little Women .... Alcott–Spencer
Spring Again .... Leighton–Bloch
Kings in Nomania .... Wilde
Uncle Harry .... Job
Decision .... Chodorov
Bobino .... Kauffmann
Suds in Your Eye .... Lasswell–Kirkland

EIGHTEENTH SEASON 1945–46

Calico Cargo .... Ottenheimer
Tom Sawyer's Treasure Hunt .... Twain–Chorpenning
The Christmas Nightingale .... Groff–Kelly
Chicken Every Sunday .... Epstein(s)–Taylor
Over 21 .... Gordon
Once upon a Clothesline .... Harris
But Not Goodbye .... Seaten
Home of the Brave .... Laurent
Bertha, The Sewing-Machine Girl .... Kremer

NINETEENTH SEASON 1946–47

San Juan Story .... Ottenheimer–Gyger
The Ghost of Mr. Penny .... Musil
Cinderella .... Chorpenning
The Merry Wives of Windsor .... Shakespeare
Once upon a Clothesline .... Harris
The Man Who Came to Dinner .... Hart–Kaufman
Mary Poppins .... Travers–Spencer
A Sound of Hunting .... Brown
Our Town .... Wilder

TWENTIETH SEASON 1947–48

A Highland Fling .... Curtis
Heidi .... Spyri–Miller
Twelfth Night .... Shakespeare
Grandmother Slyboots .... Chorpenning
Parlor Story .... McCleery
Circus Day .... Harris
Heavenly Express .... Bein
The Bees and the Flowers .... Kohner–Mannheimer

[*handwritten from this point*]

Power .... Fed. Theatre
Uncle Vanya .... Chekhov
The Fifth Column .... Hemingway
Showdown .... Russian
Rocket to the Moon .... Odets
Ryther Child Center
Professor Mamlock
Herman's No Angel .... Lovitt & Fiske
The First Year
The Sin Flood .... Berger
Forty Niners .... Hanshew

APPENDIX 2

Telegram from James Cagney to Florence, October 26, 1976.

From the personal papers of Florence James, courtesy of Jean Freeman.

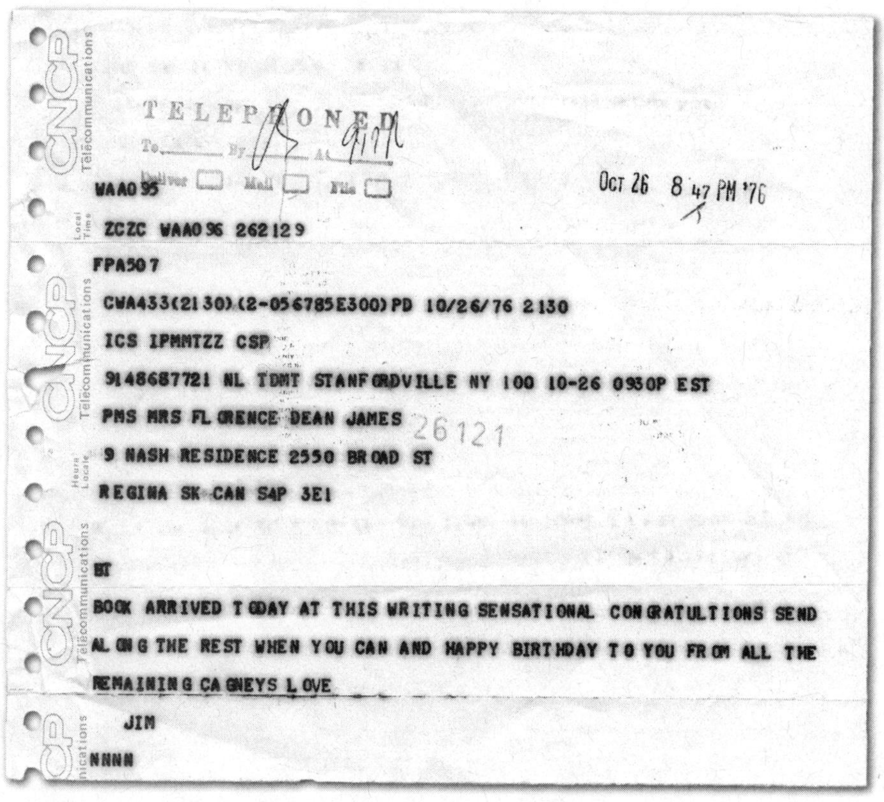

TELEPHONED

WAA095 OCT 26 8 47 PM '76

ZCZC WAA096 262129

FPA507

CWA433(2130)(2-056785E300)PD 10/26/76 2130

ICS IPMNTZZ CSP

9148687721 NL TDMT STANFORDVILLE NY 100 10-26 0930P EST

PMS MRS FLORENCE DEAN JAMES

9 NASH RESIDENCE 2550 BROAD ST

REGINA SK CAN S4P 3E1

BT

BOOK ARRIVED TODAY AT THIS WRITING SENSATIONAL CONGRATULTIONS SEND ALONG THE REST WHEN YOU CAN AND HAPPY BIRTHDAY TO YOU FROM ALL THE REMAINING CAGNEYS LOVE

JIM

NNNN

APPENDIX 3

Florence James' 1977 Christmas letter.

From the personal papers of Florence James, courtesy of Jean Freeman.

#9 - 2550 Broad St.,
Regina, Sask., Can.,
Christmas, 1977.

Dear friends:

My best greetings to all of you, across the miles, and across the years! Friendship is wonderful at all times, but especially so at this season, when we must look forward, but can't help looking back as well.

1977 was a year of highs and lows ... ups and downs ... I don't quite know how to categorize it. For those of you who haven't heard from me since last Christmas, you may not be aware of the tragedy which occurred soon after the holiday, when my only daughter, Marijo, died of an unexpected heart attack. My only solace was that it happened very suddenly, and she did not suffer a long and agonizing illness. She taught her regular classes in Sociology at the University, came home from work, sat down in her arm chair, and died peacefully there of a heart attack. It was a great shock to me to outlive her, but one finds the strength from somewhere to go on, and so I have tried. The loving messages from so many of you helped greatly to ease the pain of loss, and I thank you again.

My friend Jean and I had finally finished the umpteenth rewrite on my book, "Fists Upon A Star", and we sent the manuscript off again, with at least medium hopes, if not high ones. Just last week, another rejection slip from Washington University Press! Disappointing, but not unexpected, I must admit. So now, there's another publisher to try, and if that's unsuccessful, I think I may have the book published myself, though it's a very expensive undertaking. But, with any luck at all, you may yet see the thing in print in 1978.

I mustn't forget to do a little grandmotherly boasting too, while I have the opportunity. My grandson Jim and granddaughters Kathy and Debbie are all in Vancouver, doing us all proud in their studies and at their work. And my great-granddaughter Kyla (Jim's daughter) is now 5, at school, and able to ride a bicycle!

Among the other blessings of this year, I count the fact that I am still in very good health, except for my failing vision. I celebrated my 85th birthday in October, and still go in half days to Globe Theatre, to do what I can to be of assistance. Another good thing has been the rediscovery of old friends such as Megan Terry, now a successful playwright, and James Cagney, who has said he would try to write an introduction for my book. And of course, I'm grateful for the discovery of new friends like Chet Skreen of the Seattle Times who wrote those fine articles on the Playhouse, and the young people in Washington and Virginia who are collecting information on the old Federal Theatre Project, in which many of us were involved. Most of all, I am thankful for the friends who have been in touch all along, so concerned and so supportive and helpful ... Al and Mies Ottenheimer, Anci Koppel, Jim Romeyn, Sue and Ken Kramer and the other dear people at the Globe, Jack Kinzel, and my dear Jean. Friends, old and new, are the high point of every year for me, I guess, and all the more so in 1977 with its many trials and tribulations.

May I wish you the very merriest of holidays, and the brightest New Year, with at least the promise of Peace on Earth, Good Will to All Men.

Fond memories, Ever ...

Florence

Florence B. James

#9 - 2550 Broad St.,
Regina, Sask., Can.,
Christmas, 1977.

Dear friends:

My best greetings to all of you, across the miles, and across the years: Friendship is wonderful at all times, but especially so at this season, when we must look forward, but can't help looking back as well.

1977 was a year of highs and lows … ups and downs … I don't quite know how to categorize it. For those of you who haven't heard from me since last Christmas, you may not be aware of the tragedy which occurred soon after the holiday, when my only daughter, Marijo, died of an unexpected heart attack. My only solace was that it happened very suddenly, and she did not suffer a long and agonizing illness. She taught her regular classes in Sociology at the University, came home from work, sat down in her arm chair, and died peacefully there of a heart attack. It was a great shock to me to outlive her, but one finds the strength from somewhere to go on, and so I have tried. The loving messages from so many of you helped greatly to ease the pain of loss, and I thank you again.

My friend Jean and I had finally finished the umpteenth rewrite on my book, "Fists Upon A Star", and we sent the manuscript off again, with at least medium hopes, if not high ones. Just last week, another rejection slip from Washington University Press! Disappointing, but not unexpected, I must admit. So now, there's another publisher to try, and if that's unsuccessful, I think I may have the book published myself, though it's a very expensive undertaking. But, with any luck at all, you may yet see the thing in print in 1978.

I mustn't forget to do a little grandmotherly boasting too, while I have the opportunity. My grandson Jim and granddaughters Kathy and Debbie are all in Vancouver, doing us all proud in their studies and at their work. And my great-granddaughter Kyla (Jim's daughter) is now 5, at school, and able to ride a bicycle!

Among the other blessings of this year, I count the fact that I am still in very good health, except for my failing vision. I celebrated my 85th birthday in October, and still go in half days to Globe Theatre, to do what I can to be of assistance. Another good thing has been the rediscovery of old friends such as Megan Terry, now a successful playwright, and James Cagney, who has said he would try to write an introduction for my book. And of course, I'm grateful for the discovery of new friends like Chet Skreen of the Seattle Times who wrote those fine articles on the Playhouse, and the young people in Washington and Virginia who are collecting information on the old Federal Theatre Project, in which many of us were involved. Most of all, I am thankful for the friends who have been in touch all along, so concerned and so supportive and helpful … Al and Mies Ottenheimer, Anci Koppel, Jim Romeyn, Sue and Ken Kramer and the other dear people at the Globe, Jack Kinzel, and my dear Jean. Friends, old and new, are the high point of every year for me, I guess, and all the more so in 1977 with its many trials and tribulations.

May I wish you the very merriest of holidays, and the brightest New Year, with at least the promise of Peace on Earth, Good Will to All Men.

Fond memories, Ever …

Florence B. James

INDEX

C

Q

R

S

X

Y

Z